MO2 40006 28875

SO-CUD-334

Supervising Student Employees in Academic Libraries

DATE DUE

Supervising Student Employees in Academic Libraries

David A. Baldwin

Z
682.4
S89
B34
1991

1991
LIBRARIES UNLIMITED, INC.
Englewood, Colorado

Copyright © 1991 Libraries Unlimited, Inc.
All Rights Reserved
Printed in the United States of America

No part of this publication may be reproduced, stored in a retrieval system, or transmitted, in any form or by any means, electronic, mechanical, photocopying, recording, or otherwise, without the prior written permission of the publisher.

LIBRARIES UNLIMITED, INC.
P.O. Box 3988
Englewood, CO 80155-3988

Library of Congress Cataloging-in-Publication Data

Baldwin, David A. (David Allen), 1946-
   Supervising student employees in academic libraries / David A. Baldwin.
     xvii, 194 p. 22x28 cm.
     Includes bibliographical references and index.
     ISBN 0-87287-869-4
     1. Student library assistants.   2. Libraries, University and college--Administration.   3. Library personnel management.
   I. Title.
   Z682.4.S89B34   1991
   023'.3--dc20   91-19000
                                                        CIP

Record 934 of 1511

TITLE: Supervising student employees in academic libraries
AUTHOR: Baldwin, David A.
ISBN: 0872878694
PUBLISHER: Libraries Unlimited
DATE: 1991
EDITION: -
PRICE: 27.50
STANDING ORDER: -
PO #: B&T
CALL #: -
ACCOUNT: -
ORDERED BY: Erickson
NOTES: -
DATE ORDERD: Feb 29 92
DATE RECD: Mar 10 92

Filling Buffer...

Type entry or use @ commands   @-? for Help

To my wife, Donna

Contents

List of Tables, Figures, and Tests xv

Preface xvii

1 — The Student Employee — A Perspective 1
   Academic Libraries Today 1
   Responding to Change 1
      Students As Part of the Work Force 2
   The Roles of Student Employees 2
      Student Employees in Public Services 2
      Student Employees in Technical Services 3
   History of Student Employment 3
      Student Employment in the 1930s 3
      Student Employment As Potential Librarians 4
      Student Employment in Recent Years 4
   Size of the Student Work Force 5
      Student Workers and the Permanent Staff 5
      Work-Study Versus Nonwork-Study Student Employees 8
   Why Do Students Work? 8
      Work As a Unique Activity 9
      Library Expectations 9
   Who Supervises Student Employees? 10
      What Does a Supervisor Do? 10
      Why Is Good Supervision Important? 11
      The Rewards of Student Employee Supervision 11
   Looking Ahead 12
   Notes 12
   Bibliography 13

2 — The Student Employee Supervisor 15
   The Role of the Student Employee Supervisor 15
   Definition of Supervisor 15
      Getting Things Done through Others 16
   Who Are the Student Employee Supervisors? 16
      Identifying Prospective Student Employee Supervisors 17
      The Best Worker May Not Be the Best Supervisor 17

2—The Student Employee Supervisor—*Continued*
Personal Qualities of Good Student Employee Supervisors...................17
  Types of Persons Who Should Not Be Supervisors...................18
  Student Employee Supervisor Attitudes...................18
Moving from a Staff to a Supervisory Position...................19
  Differences between Worker and Supervisor...................20
  Transition from Worker to Supervisor...................20
  Seven Transition Stages...................21
Problems Faced by New Student Employee Supervisors...................21
  Expectations for Student Employee Supervisors...................22
  Common Mistakes New Supervisors Make...................23
  What Employees Don't Like about Their Supervisors...................23
  Why Student Employee Supervisors Fail...................25
Preparing to Become a Student Employee Supervisor...................25
The Student Employee Supervisor...................26
Notes...................26
Bibliography...................27

3—Basics for Supervisors...................29
Becoming a Supervisor...................29
Leadership...................29
  Your Leadership Potential...................30
Authority...................32
Accountability...................33
  Assessing Your Degree of Accountability...................33
Managing Change...................34
Managing Time...................35
  Identifying Timewasters...................35
  Time Management Guidelines...................36
Dealing with Stress...................37
Determining Your Potential...................38
  Tips on Getting Noticed and Promoted...................38
  Learn from Your Mistakes...................39
  Types of Behavior to Avoid...................40
  Getting Along with Your Supervisor...................41
  Writing Better Reports...................41
Keep Learning...................42
Notes...................42
Bibliography...................42

4—Organizing for Student Employment 46
  Organizing Function of Management 46
  Organizing a System for Student Employee Positions 46
    Job Design 47
    Job Analysis 47
  Purposes of Job Descriptions 48
    Features of a Good Job Description 48
    Uses of Job Descriptions 49
  Guidelines for Preparing Job Descriptions 49
    Job Descriptions for the Library 50
  Student Employee Job Descriptions 50
    Group I Student Positions 50
    Group II Student Positions 50
    Group III Student Positions 53
  Differentiated Pay 56
  Student Employee Allotments 58
  Work-Study Eligibility 60
  Job Matching 61
    Student Employment Application Form 61
  Organizing Student Employees 63
  Bibliography 63

5—Hiring Student Employees 66
  Hiring and Firing 66
  Referral of Student Workers 66
  Recruiting Student Workers 67
  Screening Prospective Student Workers 67
    Preparing for the Interview 68
    Interview Types 68
    Conducting the Interview 69
  Legal Implications of Employment Decisions 71
    The Supervisor's Responsibility 72
    Nondiscriminatory Interviewing 73
  Reference Checks 73
  Communicating the Hiring Decision 74
  Interview Situations 75
  Bibliography 75

6—Understanding Federal Student Financial Aid 78
  Federal Aid for Student Employment 78
  Federal Student Aid Programs 78

6 — Understanding Federal Student Financial Aid — *Continued*

Financial Need. 79
    Cost of Attendance in Determining Financial Need. 79
    Family Contribution in Determining Financial Need. 79
    Independent Student Definition in Determining Financial Need. 80
    Citizenship Requirements for Financial Aid. 81
Eligibility Requirements. 81
Pell Grants. 83
Stafford Loan Program. 83
PLUS and SLS Programs. 83
Campus-Based Student Financial Aid Programs. 84
Supplemental Educational Opportunity Grants (SEOG). 84
The College Work-Study Program (CWS). 84
    Work-Study Employment Conditions and Limitations. 85
    Paying Work-Study Student Employees. 86
    Work-Study Employment During Nonenrollment Periods. 86
Perkins Loan Program. 86
State Student Incentive Grant (SSIG) Program. 87
Robert C. Byrd Honors Scholarship Program. 87
Counseling the Student on Financial Aid. 87
What You Can Do. 88
Notes. 89
Bibliography. 89

7 — Orientation and Training of Student Employees. 91
Training Is Everything. 91
Why Provide Orientation?. 91
    First Impressions. 91
    The New Student Employee. 92
    Orientation of Student Employees. 92
Training and Development Are Not the Same. 94
    Role of the Student Employee Supervisor in Training. 95
    Two Types of Training. 95
    Should the Supervisor Do All the Training?. 95
What Do You Train For?. 95
Four-Step Method for Training. 96
    Step 1. Preparation of the Learner. 96
    Step 2. Presentation of the Operation. 96
    Step 3. Performance Tryout. 97
    Step 4. Follow-up. 97
Extending the Training. 98
Common Training Errors. 98
Tips to Improve Training. 98
Active Versus Passive Learning. 99

Implementing Your Training Program 100
Developmental Training 100
    Training Present Employees to Improve Performance 101
    Training to Prepare Student Employees for Higher-Level Work 101
    Developmental Training Methods 101
Supervisor's Training Checklist 102
Orientation, Training, and Development 102
Bibliography 103

8 — Supervision Techniques for Student Employee Supervisors 105
Managing and Being Managed 105
Hierarchical Library Organization 105
Team Management 106
    Humanistic Management by Teamwork (HMBT) 106
    Participative Management 107
Five Functions of Management 107
Authority 108
    Exerting Authority 109
    Delegating Authority 110
Responsibility 110
Making Decisions 111
    Making Good Decisions 111
    No One Is Perfect — Bad Decisions 112
    If Your Decisions Are Challenged 113
Communication 113
    Communicating with Individuals 113
    Communicating with Groups 113
    Encouraging Employees to Communicate with You 114
    Communicating with Student Employees 114
Group Effort 114
Giving Directions 115
    Guidelines for Giving Directions 115
    Getting Cooperation 116
Motivation 116
    Coaching 117
    The Coaching Process 117
Counseling 118
    Counseling Sessions You Call 118
    Counseling Sessions the Employee Requests 119
    Not All Counseling Is Negative 120
Supervisory Principles 120
Notes 120
Bibliography 120

9—Resolving Problems with Student Employees 126
Student Employee Problems 126
The Student Employee Who Complains 126
The Unmotivated Student Employee 127
The Student Employee with Low Morale 128
The Disloyal Student Employee 128
The Student Employee Who Violates Library Rules 129
The Student Worker with Absenteeism Problems 130
Time, Telephone, and Dress Policies 131
The Student Who Is Dishonest 131
The Student Employee Who Violates University Rules 132
The Student Employee with Personality Problems 132
The Student Employee with Personal Problems 134
Dealing with Rumors in the Work Place 134
The Student Employee Who Procrastinates 134
The Student Worker Who Resists Change 135
Dealing with Stress 135
Dealing with Insubordination 136
Dealing with Older Student Employees 136
Resolving Problems 136
Notes 136
Bibliography 137

10—Performance Appraisal 139
How Am I Doing? 139
"Praises and Raises" 139
Job Evaluation Versus Performance Appraisal 140
Purposes of Performance Appraisal in Industry 140
Purposes of Performance Appraisal in Libraries 140
How Formal Should the Performance Appraisal Be? 141
Peer Evaluation 141
More Than the Supervisor's Opinion 142
Questions to Be Answered in an Appraisal 142
How Often Should Student Employee Appraisals Be Done? 142
Sequence of Activities in Performance Appraisal 142
Set Performance Standards 143
Communicate Standards 143
Observing Employees As They Work 143
Collect Data 143
Employees' Self-Appraisal Process 144
Utilizing the Information Gathered 144
Evaluating the Employee 145

Appraisal and Response...145
    Preparing for an Appraisal Meeting............................145
    Conducting an Appraisal Meeting..............................146
    Discussing Poor Performance..................................147
    The "Sandwich" Technique....................................147
    Allowing the Employee to Save Face...........................148
    Handling Charges of Favoritism...............................148
    Appraisal Errors...148
    Validity and Reliability.....................................149
    Making Nondiscriminatory Appraisals..........................149
    Confidentiality of Appraisals................................150
Good Evaluations Do Not Always Result in Advancement...............150
Good Evaluations Do Not Always Result in More Money................150
Appraisal Formats...150
    Comparative Appraisal Formats................................151
    Absolute Appraisal Formats...................................152
    Outcome-Based Appraisal Formats..............................152
What Happens to the Appraisal Forms?..............................152
After the Appraisal...153
Do Not Wait for the Annual Review.................................153
Positive Approach to Performance Appraisal........................153
Notes...154
Bibliography..154

11—Employee and Employer Rights and Responsibilities............157
Employee and Employer Rights......................................157
Legal Rights..157
    The Right to a Safe Work Environment.........................157
    The Right to a Nondiscriminatory Workplace...................158
    The Right to a Workplace Free of Harassment..................159
    Termination Rights...159
    Privacy Rights...160
    Union Participation Rights...................................161
Rights Granted by the Employing Institution.......................162
    The Right to an Appeal and Grievance Process.................163
    The Right to Equitable Compensation..........................164
Employee Responsibilities...165
Ethics for Supervisors..165
    Library Ethics...166
    Managerial Ethics..167
Rights and Responsibilities.......................................168
Notes...169
Bibliography..169

12 — Progressive Discipline and Termination Procedures 172
   Discipline and Discharge 172
   Termination of Employment 172
   Reasons for Termination 174
   Limiting the Number of Problem Employees 176
   Progressive Discipline 176
      Steps to Take before Discharging Any Employee 177
   How to Discharge Employees 178
      The Discharge Interview 178
      Mistakes Made in Discharges 179
   The Psychological Impacts of Termination 180
   Bibliography 180

13 — Questions Asked by New Supervisors 182
   Bibliography 184
      The Future of Libraries 184
      Library Administration and Management 186

Index 189

List of Tables, Figures, and Tests

Tables

Staffing in ARL Libraries, 1988-89   6-7

Pay Rate Structures for Student Employees   57

Sample Pay Rates   57

Number of Hours That Can Be Worked in Twenty Pay Periods   59

Eligibility Requirements for Federal Student Financial Aid Programs   82

Purposes of the Performance Appraisal Process   140

Figures

Job Description: Group I Position   51

Job Description: Group II Position   52

Job Description: Group III, Level II Position   54

Job Description: Group III, Level III Position   55

Work-Study Eligibility Form   60

Student Employment Application   62

Tests

Test of Leadership Potential   31

Supervisory Responsibility Survey   33

Preface

This handbook is one of a kind. There are a number of excellent library administration books in print as well as whole libraries of business management and employee supervision books. The library administration titles give little notice to the fact that academic libraries employ thousands of students and the supervision literature virtually ignores university students as an employee group. Most authors have failed to recognize that in today's academic libraries, student employees are a critical part of the work force and that few of their supervisors have adequate supervisory training or experience.

The student work force and its supervisors have been taken for granted for a long time. They are, after all, only student workers and anyone can supervise them, or so the conventional wisdom holds. Library administrators are only now beginning to realize how important this group has become to the library and that student employee salaries comprise a significant portion of the operating budget.

Library personnel are, for the most part, persons who enjoy working in an academic environment with young people and with others who are interested in bringing information and people together. Many student employee supervisors began their library careers as student workers, who, as they became experienced workers, were given more responsibility, including supervising fellow students. Later, as regular staff members, they became supervisors of student employees, and then, often, supervisors of other staff. How were these skills developed? Do the library staffers you know come to the job with supervisory training and experience? Are they given on-the-job training? Are they given any training at all? How systematic is the training given to all supervisors, let alone supervisors of student employees? Most have become good supervisors through trial and error.

This book is designed to provide a foundation in the principles of supervision and to serve as a handbook for the day-to-day problems which arise in supervising student employees in academic libraries. Throughout, the emphasis of this book is on humane treatment of employees. This handbook will confirm much of what you already know and will also, I hope, provide you with new information.

The first three chapters describe the role of student employees in the academic library, the role of the student employee supervisor, and basic principles of supervision. The next describes how to organize for student employment and includes information on student job descriptions and why they are needed. Chapter 5 deals with the hiring of student employees. Because federal student financial aid is an important part of student employment, information is provided on the various federal aid programs in chapter 6. The next two chapters discuss orientation, training, and supervision techniques. Chapter 9 provides suggestions for resolving the most common problems encountered by supervisors. Performance appraisal is covered in chapter 10 and employee and employer rights in chapter 11. Chapter 12 deals with corrective discipline and termination procedures. The final chapter provides answers to questions commonly asked by new student employee supervisors.

If you supervise student employees or aspire to such a position in your library, this handbook is written for you. Your comments and suggestions on the content would be much appreciated by the author.

The Student Employee – A Perspective

Everyone goes to the forest: some go for a walk to be inspired, and others go to cut down the trees.

— Vladimir Horowitz

ACADEMIC LIBRARIES TODAY

More changes have occurred in academic libraries in the past thirty years than in all of previous history. Those changes have been brought about in large part by the dramatic technological advances made in recent years. Libraries have evolved from virtually self-sufficient producers of bibliographic databases to organizations having nearly unlimited access to bibliographic data through networks. Student employees play an important role in the changes taking place in today's libraries.

RESPONDING TO CHANGE

All staff positions, including those filled by students, have been greatly affected by automation. Librarians are required to focus their efforts on improving access to information through database development and management and on interpreting that information for users. They must also devote time to library and university committee work and to professional activities. Many librarians have to meet requirements for tenure and promotion, including publishing.

Clerical, technical, and professional staff now perform high-level technical and public service duties that previously have been librarian responsibilities. As a result, student employees are also being asked to assume more complex technical and service responsibilities. Student employees play an important role in the ability of today's academic library to respond to technological change.

Job responsibilities of staff at all levels are affected by online systems and increasing user demand. Technical services staffers are required to perform complex acquisitions, cataloging, and processing tasks as well as mastering terminal and system operations. Improved access has resulted in increased demands for assistance not only in finding but also in interpreting information. Reference and information desks must be staffed by knowledgeable personnel to assist library users in effectively using the library's systems and resources. Interlibrary loan staff must respond to greater numbers of requests, and staffers in the circulation department are often required to be skilled in the use of an automated circulation system.

Only with librarians, staff, and student employees working together can libraries respond effectively to the information explosion, the technological challenge, and the research and information needs of faculty, staff, students on campus, and users from the community. Success hinges on the effective use of a large segment of the library's staff resources—student employees.

Students As Part of the Work Force

Student employees form a very large and important part of any college or university library work force. Student employees make up approximately 22 percent of university libraries' staffing and 27 percent of all staff in college libraries (see table 1.1 on p. 6). In academic libraries, the number of student employees often exceeds the number of regular staff. It follows that academic libraries need to place a high priority on the effective management of student employment.

THE ROLES OF STUDENT EMPLOYEES

Visit any library at a college or university and you will find students working at circulation, information, reference, special collections, documents, or periodicals desks. Students can be observed assisting patrons, shelving materials, or working as security staff. Stop by the director or dean's office and you may be greeted by a student employee. In the nonpublic areas, you will find student assistants engaged in a wide variety of technical and clerical tasks. If you happen by in the late hours of the evening or night, you might be hard put to find a staff member on duty except perhaps in circulation or reference areas.

Do the student assistants run this library? No, but the library would not function efficiently without them. Student employees are a crucial part of the staffing of today's academic library. Do students do only the work that staff will not do? No, student assistants now perform very technical and demanding work as well as providing for the coverage needed for long hours of access to collections and services. Libraries depend on student employees to perform all manner of job duties formerly reserved for "regular" staff employees.

Student Employees in Public Services

Student workers are most heavily utilized in public services. The charging, discharging, and file maintenance tasks for circulation are most often performed by student employees, with the most experienced given additional supervisory or training responsibilities. Reshelving and stack maintenance are often accomplished almost entirely by student workers. Student employees are involved in the management of periodicals and newspaper collections, as well as in assisting users. Microform files and equipment maintenance and patron assistance are typical student worker duties.

In reference departments, student assistants usually handle all of the filing of loose-leaf services, microforms, etc., and the more senior student workers are relied upon to provide ready reference either at information desks or with librarians and staff at the reference desk. In branch libraries and government publications units, student employees are usually involved in all public and technical service activities. Often student workers oversee operations during late night and weekend hours. Academic libraries without the benefit of campus security patrols in their buildings often rely on student workers to make regular rounds in the stacks and study areas. These student assistants are identified as library security staff and are charged with enforcing policies relating to food, drink, and quiet. Usually they summon campus or local police to deal with illegal activities.

Student Employees in Technical Services

Technical service operations depend on student employees to perform many tasks. Acquisitions departments use students for preorder searching for monographs and serials. Automated acquisitions systems are quickly learned by students who perform many of the same functions as permanent staffers. Routine receiving activities and serials check-in are usually assigned to student workers. Many bindery and preparation operations are handled by student workers. Cataloging departments utilize student assistants in many of the more routine cataloging activities, such as catalog maintenance for automated and manual files. Student assistants with language abilities can be indispensable to cataloging departments.

Clerical tasks in all departments have become the responsibility of student employees in most libraries. The dean or director's office staff is supplemented with student hours, as are library personnel, facilities, and fiscal services offices. There are very few clerical or manual tasks that cannot be assigned to student assistants. Former student employees remember, with varying degrees of fondness, their experiences in dismantling and building shelves, shelfreading, shifting books, and moving whole library collections.

Student employees bring to their library jobs a wide range of talents and skills, which, if properly identified and matched with jobs, can provide meaningful employment for the students, valuable contributions to the operation of the library, and lifelong friendships among students and staff. The reliance of American academic libraries on student employees can be traced back to the early 1800s.

HISTORY OF STUDENT EMPLOYMENT

In a report of the Librarian's Conference in 1853, G. B. Utley noted that some university librarians had only student assistants and others didn't have any help at all.[1] During the late 1800s, American universities experienced rapid growth, adding new programs in many scientific and technological fields, among others, and adding greatly to the need for research facilities by faculty and students. Library collections, services, and staffs expanded to meet the demand. Brown University Librarian Harry Lyman Koopman reported that in 1893 the staff consisted of himself, an assistant librarian, and one student helper. By 1930, the staff number had grown to twenty-five and the number of student assistants to seventeen.[2]

Student Employment in the 1930s

Mary Elizabeth Downey, in a paper delivered at ALA Midwinter in 1932, commented on the conflicting attitudes of librarians on student employees.[3] She said so far as the attitude of college librarians is concerned, our problem naturally resolves itself into two sides: on the one hand are those who do not see how the library can be run without the aid of student assistants, and who feel that a greater amount of work can be done satisfactorily with them. This type of librarian gets a real kick out of seeing a boy come to college not knowing how to use his hands and legs, to say nothing of his head, to see him develop into a well-rounded adult, and from the feeling that his work in the library is somewhat responsible for the transformation. On the other hand are college librarians who do not know how to organize and manage such help, who do not have teaching ability, and so strenuously object to being bothered with student assistants. They feel that teaching and supervising the work of students has no part in their work as librarian and that none of it should be delegated to those not having come through a library school.

Ms. Downey, in addition to providing a long list of duties which may be performed by students, also reported that suitable work for students may include "emptying waste baskets; sweeping, dusting, and mopping floors; washing woodwork, shelves and windows; and even painting woodwork and floors in unsightly quarters to make them more sanitary and attractive. Sometimes men students, who cannot do clerical things well, are suited to this very necessary work." For their work, Ms. Downey suggested a rate of twenty-five to thirty cents an hour for freshmen, thirty to thirty-five cents for sophomores, thirty-five to forty cents for juniors, and forty to forty-five cents for seniors.

Student Employees As Potential Librarians

In addition to being the source of cheap labor and expediters of library processes and procedures, student employees were sometimes viewed as potential librarians. Wilson and Tauber in 1956 noted: "Through his activities in the library the student assistant sometimes discovers his interest in librarianship as a profession, and his training can be directed by the librarian to that end."[4] The same is true today. More than 30 percent of professional librarians were at one time student employees in libraries.[5] Many academic libraries provide encouragement and guidance to promising student employees who are interested in pursuing librarianship as a career. Special programs are in place in some academic libraries and library schools to encourage minority students to become librarians.

Student Employment in Recent Years

In recognition of student capabilities, librarians in recent years have treated student employees as co-workers, almost like colleagues. Keith M. Cottam, based on his work at Brigham Young University, suggested in 1970:

It is doubtful that any library, as a major resource for teaching and learning can reach a maximum level of service without full utilization of the capabilities, opinions, talents, and background of capable, part-time student employees as well as of its full-time staff. Librarians are in the business of education and in developing people for the future of the profession ... [and] should apply the widest possible latitude to their utilization of student assistants if they aspire successfully to accomplish their goals.[6]

The debate continues today about the cost effectiveness and efficiency of student employees in academic libraries and what kinds of responsibilities should be assigned to them. The title of Andrew Melnyk's 1976 article, "Student Aides in Our Library (Blessings and Headaches)," reflects that attitude.[7] Emilie C. White suggested that:

> At the very least, students constitute a labor reserve for the monotonous and repetitious tasks that are necessary for successful library operation. Their willingness to perform largely time-consuming, routine chores in the midst of their own intellectual accomplishments has contributed significantly to the professional posture of academic librarianship.[8]

Student employees today are not required to mop floors or paint woodwork in the library for thirty cents an hour. Academic libraries employ a large number of their institutions' students to augment their permanent staff positions in order to accomplish their missions.

SIZE OF THE STUDENT WORK FORCE

Students are employed on American college and university campuses for all types of jobs. The largest employers of students on most campuses are food services and libraries.

Student workers comprise a significant portion of academic libraries' staffing. An examination of Association of Research Libraries (ARL) statistics for 1988-89[9] shows that in the 107 university member libraries there are 7,771 full-time equivalent (FTE) student employees (see table 1.1). Using an average of seventeen hours per week or .425 FTE for each student, there are an estimated 18,285 student employees in ARL academic libraries. Generally, smaller college and university libraries have a larger proportion of students.

In ARL libraries, librarians comprise nearly 27 percent of all staff. Professional, technical, and clerical personnel make up 51 percent, and students account for 22 percent. At Brigham Young University, student employees comprise 59.7 percent of all staff (200 of 335). The University of California at Berkeley reports that about 42 percent of their staffs are students. The highest number of student FTE's was reported at the University of California at Berkeley (258) and the lowest at the University of Laval (Canada) with 7 student FTE's. At a rate of .425 FTE for each employee, the mean number of students employed in ARL libraries is estimated at 146.

Student Workers and the Permanent Staff

Student assistants are extremely important to the successful operation of college and university libraries. Student employees have much in common with permanent staff. Working closely with permanent full-time and part-time staff, students perform many of the same tasks and often work without staff supervision on nights and weekends. Students are expected to abide by the policies of the library and follow its procedures. Student assistants often participate in departmental staff meetings and have the opportunity to make suggestions for improvements.

Table 1.1. Staffing in ARL Libraries, 1988-89

ARL LIBRARY	PROF. STAFF (FTE)	% OF TOTAL STAFF	NONPROF. STAFF (FTE)	% OF TOTAL STAFF	STUDENT ASSTS. (FTE)	% OF TOTAL STAFF	TOTAL STAFF (FTE)
Alabama	59	33.1%	72	40.4%	47	26.4%	178
Alberta	86	21.7%	274	69.2%	36	9.1%	396
Arizona	101	25.9%	186	47.7%	103	26.4%	390
Arizona State	100	25.8%	219	56.4%	69	17.8%	388
Boston	69	25.2%	146	53.3%	59	21.5%	274
Brigham Young	89	26.6%	46	13.7%	200	59.7%	335
British Columbia	100	24.6%	259	63.6%	48	11.8%	407
Brown	86	31.0%	113	40.8%	78	28.2%	277
CA—Berkeley	173	22.0%	287	36.4%	328	41.6%	788
CA—Davis	76	22.7%	200	59.7%	59	17.6%	335
CA—Irvine	62	24.8%	122	48.8%	66	26.4%	250
CA—Los Angeles	155	22.6%	311	45.3%	220	32.1%	686
CA—Riverside	34	19.2%	94	53.1%	49	27.7%	177
CA—San Diego	94	25.8%	187	51.4%	83	22.8%	364
CA—Santa Barbara	62	24.8%	145	58.0%	43	17.2%	250
Case Western Reserve	64	36.6%	83	47.4%	28	16.0%	175
Chicago	78	21.1%	227	61.4%	65	17.6%	370
Cincinnati	74	24.5%	127	42.1%	101	33.4%	302
Colorado	55	24.7%	109	48.9%	59	26.5%	223
Colorado State	41	28.7%	78	54.5%	24	16.8%	143
Columbia	166	25.8%	337	52.3%	141	21.9%	644
Connecticut	70	30.4%	102	44.3%	58	25.2%	230
Cornell	166	30.1%	291	52.8%	94	17.1%	551
Dartmouth	46	26.3%	101	57.7%	28	16.0%	175
Delaware	58	25.8%	119	52.9%	48	21.3%	225
Duke	96	30.8%	164	52.6%	52	16.7%	312
Emory	67	25.4%	148	56.1%	49	18.6%	264
Florida	120	27.2%	208	47.2%	113	25.6%	441
Florida State	62	24.9%	123	49.4%	64	25.7%	249
Georgetown	75	25.4%	149	50.5%	71	24.1%	295
Georgia	79	22.5%	192	54.7%	80	22.8%	351
Georgia Tech	47	41.6%	47	41.6%	19	16.8%	113
Guelph	31	19.5%	115	72.3%	13	8.2%	159
Harvard	344	31.4%	614	56.1%	137	12.5%	1095
Hawaii	66	28.4%	100	43.1%	66	28.4%	232
Houston	51	26.6%	90	46.9%	51	26.6%	192
Howard	83	29.3%	131	46.3%	69	24.4%	283
Illinois, Chicago	77	25.8%	177	59.4%	44	14.8%	298
Illinois, Urbana	149	28.0%	266	50.0%	117	22.0%	532
Indiana	125	26.3%	202	42.5%	148	31.2%	475
Iowa	88	32.2%	116	42.5%	69	25.3%	273
Iowa State	46	20.7%	116	52.3%	60	27.0%	222
Johns Hopkins	97	28.6%	197	58.1%	45	13.3%	339
Kansas	97	29.1%	129	38.7%	107	32.1%	333
Kent State	56	23.5%	97	40.8%	85	35.7%	238
Kentucky	68	27.2%	123	49.2%	59	23.6%	250
Laval	70	26.2%	192	71.9%	5	1.9%	267
Louisiana State	62	24.6%	116	46.0%	74	29.4%	252
McGill	80	24.5%	203	62.3%	43	13.2%	326
McMaster	41	20.2%	141	69.5%	21	10.3%	203
Manitoba	58	25.4%	144	63.2%	26	11.4%	228
Maryland	95	27.5%	149	43.2%	101	29.3%	345
Massachusetts	54	26.7%	104	51.5%	44	21.8%	202
MIT	82	33.5%	135	55.1%	28	11.4%	245
Miami	71	28.5%	130	52.2%	48	19.3%	249
Michigan	136	23.3%	293	50.3%	154	26.4%	583
Michigan State	83	25.2%	124	37.7%	122	37.1%	329
Minnesota	123	25.4%	199	41.1%	162	33.5%	484
Missouri	56	23.8%	128	54.5%	51	21.7%	235
Nebraska	53	24.8%	112	52.3%	49	22.9%	214
New Mexico	74	22.0%	169	50.1%	94	27.9%	337
New York	104	25.5%	218	53.4%	86	21.1%	408
North Carolina	117	28.9%	205	50.6%	83	20.5%	405
North Carolina State	48	22.1%	121	55.8%	48	22.1%	217
Northwestern	110	32.2%	141	41.2%	91	26.6%	342
Notre Dame	41	21.5%	126	66.0%	24	12.6%	191
Ohio State	122	25.8%	211	44.6%	140	29.6%	473
Oklahoma	43	23.2%	81	43.8%	61	33.0%	185
Oklahoma State	49	27.7%	74	41.8%	54	30.5%	177

ARL LIBRARY	PROF. STAFF (FTE)	% OF TOTAL STAFF	NONPROF. STAFF (FTE)	% OF TOTAL STAFF	STUDENT ASSTS. (FTE)	% OF TOTAL STAFF	TOTAL STAFF (FTE)
Oregon	51	23.5%	92	42.4%	74	34.1%	217
Pennsylvania	108	29.0%	167	44.9%	97	26.1%	372
Pennsylvania State	107	22.7%	291	61.7%	74	15.7%	472
Pittsburgh	94	26.3%	173	48.3%	91	25.4%	358
Princeton	111	28.0%	235	59.3%	50	12.6%	396
Purdue	61	22.9%	146	54.9%	59	22.2%	266
Queen's	48	21.1%	151	66.5%	28	12.3%	227
Rice	44	30.3%	76	52.4%	25	17.2%	145
Rochester	74	30.3%	105	43.0%	65	26.6%	244
Rutgers	115	22.2%	268	51.6%	136	26.2%	519
Saskatchewan	38	21.2%	129	72.1%	12	6.7%	179
South Carolina	61	30.8%	103	52.0%	34	17.2%	198
Southern California	111	31.7%	145	41.4%	94	26.9%	350
Southern Illinois	50	20.4%	96	39.2%	99	40.4%	245
Stanford	167	28.0%	338	56.7%	91	15.3%	596
SUNY — Albany	48	27.6%	86	49.4%	40	23.0%	174
SUNY — Buffalo	94	32.5%	115	39.8%	80	27.7%	289
SUNY — Stony Brook	52	23.6%	120	54.5%	48	21.8%	220
Syracuse	69	25.8%	144	53.9%	54	20.2%	267
Temple	68	30.1%	110	48.7%	48	21.2%	226
Tennessee	64	24.7%	147	56.8%	48	18.5%	259
Texas	141	23.2%	383	63.0%	84	13.8%	608
Texas A&M	71	23.0%	151	48.9%	87	28.2%	309
Toronto	162	23.1%	466	66.5%	73	10.4%	701
Tulane	53	28.3%	105	56.1%	29	15.5%	187
Utah	49	21.3%	113	49.1%	68	29.6%	230
Vanderbilt	83	27.4%	150	49.5%	70	23.1%	303
Virginia	99	26.8%	195	52.7%	76	20.5%	370
VPI & SU	51	25.0%	106	52.0%	47	23.0%	204
Washington	123	25.3%	238	49.0%	125	25.7%	486
Washington State	45	21.3%	115	54.5%	51	24.2%	211
Washington U — St. L.	79	30.6%	132	51.2%	47	18.2%	258
Waterloo	48	23.3%	145	70.4%	13	6.3%	206
Wayne State	75	31.5%	102	42.9%	61	25.6%	238
Western Ontario	54	18.8%	191	66.6%	42	14.6%	287
Wisconsin	150	28.4%	221	41.9%	157	29.7%	528
Yale	195	27.7%	426	60.5%	83	11.8%	704
York	52	20.8%	148	59.2%	50	20.0%	250
UNIV. LIB TOTALS	9025	26.0%	17879	51.6%	7771	22.4%	34675
UNIV. LIB MEDIAN	74	26.5%	144	51.6%	61	21.9%	279
UNIV. LIB HIGH	344	26.7%	614	47.7%	328	25.5%	1286
UNIV. LIB LOW	31	37.8%	46	56.1%	5	6.1%	82
TOT UNIV LIBS	9025	26.0%	17879	51.6%	7771	22.4%	34675
NONUNIVERSITY ARL LIBRARIES							
Boston Public	239	36.5%	380	58.1%	35	5.4%	654
Canada Inst. SciTech	73	32.7%	139	62.3%	11	4.9%	223
Ctr for Research Libs	26	36.1%	32	44.4%	14	19.4%	72
Library of Congress	2597	56.1%	2035	43.9%	N/A	0.0%	4632
Linda Hall Library	20	33.3%	40	66.7%	U/A	0.0%	60
Natl. Agricultural	124	58.2%	79	37.1%	10	4.7%	213
Natl. Lib. of Canada	207	41.1%	297	58.9%	U/A	0.0%	504
Natl. Lib. of Med.	163	57.4%	101	35.6%	20	7.0%	284
Newberry	53	53.5%	46	46.5%	N/A	0.0%	99
New York Public	U/A	0.0%	U/A	0.0%	103	100.0%	103
New York State Lib	88	40.9%	127	59.1%	N/A	0.0%	215
Smithsonian Inst.	53	43.1%	70	56.9%	N/A	0.0%	123
NONU LIB TOTALS	3643	50.7%	3346	46.6%	193	2.7%	7182
GRAND TOTALS	12668	30.3%	21225	50.7%	7964	19.0%	41857

SOURCE: ARL Statistics, 1988-89, 12-32.

Student workers differ from permanent staff in their work schedules, job duties, benefits, funding sources, and their planned impermanence. Some universities prohibit student employees from working more than twenty hours per week, in part because of the desire to provide employment for more students and in part because it is felt that full-time students should devote their primary attention to academic pursuits. Their work schedules must be arranged around classes which change each semester. Students applying for work are often selected primarily because they can work the desired hours in a department's schedule.

Job duties for students are dependent on the department's needs and on available staff, but are typically the lowest level in the department. Student workers do not earn vacation or sick leave and are not eligible for the benefits provided to regular staff. The funding sources for student assistants are normally either the College Work-Study Program or a separate library student employment budget. Employers know when students are hired that they are temporary employees: some freshmen students may stay with the library throughout their undergraduate careers but, more often than not, they do not.

Not all permanent staff are model employees and the same is true of student employees. Nearly all of the problems associated with regular staff are also found in the student employee work force. Not all student assistants are productive employees: some lack the commitment expected or are simply unable to work and also keep up their grades. Student employees are not immune to any of the potential problems in the workplace. We will discuss how to deal with problems in a later chapter.

Work-Study Versus Nonwork-Study Student Employees

We should also dispel, once and for all, the myth that nonwork-study students are better employees than work-study students and therefore deserve better pay. It is true that fewer upperclassmen qualify for work-study awards because grants, loans, or scholarships reduce their financial need. Often students begin as work-study qualified students, become invaluable to the department, and then have their work-study awards reduced or eliminated. Those students are either lost to the library or must be paid from other funds.

Many nonwork-study students are more experienced than beginning work-study students and are viewed as better employees. In some libraries, nonwork-study students are permitted to work more hours than work-study students who must stay within their award amounts. Some supervisors prefer not to be bothered with tracking work-study students' awards, but they definitely do not want to lose needed help near the end of the year because awards have been exhausted. The most significant difference, however, between the work-study and the nonwork-study student employee is the account from which wages are paid.

A salary scale which pays work-study and nonwork-study employees at different hourly rates should be avoided if at all possible. We will discuss pay rates in the chapter on organizing for student employment.

WHY DO STUDENTS WORK?

Most people work, first, for the money to pay for the necessities and pleasures of life, and, second, for the satisfaction work can provide—being with other people or gaining satisfaction from accomplishment. The college student's first priority is to gain an education and a degree which will lead to a "real" job, a career. The money earned by student workers is generally used for food, shelter, and college expenses, as well as for supporting families. Until their paychecks become sufficient to cover basic living expenses, job satisfaction and collegiality in the workplace will not be the primary reason students work. That is not to say, however, that supervisors should not strive to provide for job satisfaction, but only that job satisfaction is not the reason students seek employment in the library.

How many people are truly happy with their jobs? A study published in 1974 showed that nearly 90 percent of all employees were satisfied, if not happy with their work.[10] Studies show that blue-collar workers are more dissatisfied with their work than white-collar workers and young people are more dissatisfied than older workers. Job satisfaction tends to increase with age.

Different people gain satisfaction from different things. Some factory workers place the most importance on wages, while others feel that comfortable working conditions, good hours, or good transportation are most important. Generally speaking, the more education a person has, the greater the value placed on challenging and interesting work. Satisfaction in the workplace is also a function of how many hours a person works. A student working half-time or less is most concerned with money but still wants to be challenged by the work. Concerns about working conditions are more important to full-time staff members than to student employees who normally work half-time or less.

Work As a Unique Activity

Work is a unique activity in that one is required to conform to certain rules and procedures, one has to report to a supervisor, and one's performance becomes a matter of written record. Students may be working in this type of formal situation for the first time and adjustments may have to be made. Recognition of this by supervisors will help new student employees. In addition, incoming freshmen will most likely be experiencing a whole new sensation of freedom and lack of structure in their lives. When students arrive on campus, there is, suddenly and for the first time, no one to tell them when to go to class, when to go to work, or when to study. The real challenge for eighteen-year-old freshmen is not the course work, but the management of the hours of the day and week. They must attend classes, study and do homework, maintain a work schedule, and remember to eat and sleep, all the while resisting a myriad of temptations to do everything else. Library employment can provide an anchor for students, a place where people care about them, and a constant amid the whirlwind of other activities. Recognition of the place of work in their students' lives is part of the information supervisors must possess in order to effectively supervise student employees.

Library Expectations

Are libraries just providing a way for students to get spending money? No, libraries require that essential work be accomplished by students and, in the process, provide positive work experiences for many students for whom this is often their first job. True, there is no time to study on the job, but the supervisor must be humane, remembering what it was like to be a college student. Employers must require that student assistants perform essential work, but, at the same time, realize why students seek employment on campus in the first place. Allowances must be made to permit students to accomplish their first objective—the degree. We will discuss the seemingly perpetual problem of student employee requests for time off or rescheduled work time in the chapter on student employee problem resolution.

Supervisors have a right to expect that student employees will perform their assigned duties, practice good work habits, and contribute to the library's mission. Student employees are expected to maintain a schedule, come to work on time, and adhere to the library's policy on reporting absences. These expectations constitute a two-way street however. The employees have a right to expect fair treatment and consideration of their special needs in return for their contributions to the library. The rights of the employee and the employer are detailed in chapter eleven.

The student employees' primary contact with the library organization is the student employees' supervisor. Much of what student employees learn and think about the library will be a direct result of their relationship with the supervisor.

WHO SUPERVISES STUDENT EMPLOYEES?

In academic library organizations it is most efficient to assign student employee supervision responsibilities to a staff member in the appropriate department. The department head often delegates student employee supervision to a person who does not have responsibility for "regular" staff supervision. In many cases, there are two or more student employee supervisors in a single department. For example, in acquisitions, there may be separate units for searching, receiving, gifts, and serials, and each may have a group of student assistants reporting to a separate supervisor.

Job descriptions for many staff positions include the supervision of student assistants. Attrition in these staff positions, especially at the lower levels, sets the stage for a relatively high number of new supervisors each year, many without prior supervisory experience. Assuming there are ten student assistants reporting to each supervisor, ARL libraries should have approximately 1,830 staff members with student supervisory responsibilities.[11] Generally, however, student supervisors work with fewer than ten students each.

What Does a Supervisor Do?

A supervisor plays many roles, some well defined, some not. Supervision is by definition a people-oriented activity. One study found that supervisors spend two-thirds of their time relating with other people. One of the roles of supervisors is that of a connecting bridge between management and operations. The supervisor has the responsibility of communicating and interpreting library policy and procedures to student employees, making recommendations, and communicating employee concerns to management. Supervisors serve as role models to workers by interpreting and carrying out those activities which help the library achieve its goals. A study performed in industry showed that supervisors spend much more time with those they supervise (55 percent) than with those with the same or higher level positions in the organization.

In addition to the bridging role of supervisors, they perform all of the managerial functions: planning, organizing, staffing, leading and motivating, and controlling. Planning includes determining the goals and objectives of the unit and the strategies for achieving them, and includes such activities as examining alternate uses of staff, thinking, gathering data, and evaluating procedures. Organizing involves creating a structure for accomplishing unit objectives: the supervisor identifies the tasks to be performed, groups those tasks into jobs, and establishes relationships between people and jobs. Staffing is the process of selecting, training, evaluating, and rewarding employees. By leading and motivating, the supervisor directs the work of student employees so their tasks are performed correctly and efficiently. The final managerial function of supervisors is controlling — the process by which actual performance is compared to planned performance. Controlling involves monitoring the work being accomplished and taking corrective action if necessary.

Managerial functions are not discrete or independent activities. The objectives set in planning are used in controlling. Organizing, staffing, and leading and motivating activities are continuous. Although most supervisors of student workers don't think about the names of these functions, all supervisors perform the whole range of managerial functions. Supervisors of student employees plan and organize the work to be done by students, hire, train, evaluate, and reward workers, and monitor the results, and since supervisors of student employees have their own job responsibilities in addition to supervision, they lead and motivate by example.

Why Is Good Supervision Important?

Since most library staff members were at one time student employees or at least college students, it is assumed that student employee supervision is not difficult. There could be no real problems, because — after all — they are only students. You hire them, you train them, and if they do not like it, they quit. Why worry? They are students who will inevitably quit anyway because college isn't supposed to be forever.

This assumption is simply not valid today. Libraries are so dependent on the work done by student employees that it is critical that students perform their work effectively and efficiently. Training and supervision must be taken seriously as only through careful selection can libraries maximize their investment in students while giving them meaningful work experiences. The need for proper training and support by student employee supervisors also makes good sense because pay rates for students are such that they must be expected to produce and the need for training new employees reduced to a minimum.

Are student employees worth the hassle? Absolutely! Are good supervisory techniques and skills needed to make the experience worthwhile? You bet! Should students expect to develop and practice good work habits through library employment? Yes! Should libraries expect their supervisors of student employees to practice sound supervision and management principles while giving students valuable work experiences? Yes, absolutely!

The Rewards of Student Employee Supervision

The effort exerted in student employee supervision is not without its rewards. Library staff members, whether they supervise or not, value their associations with students over the years. Supervisors see students mature and become self-confident and take pride in students' accomplishments long after their departure from the library. The student supervisory experience translates well to staff supervision, permitting staff members to advance to higher level positions. How many librarians and professional, technical, and clerical staff members do you know who were library student employees? Many of those people will tell you that the primary reason they are in their present positions is because of positive student work experiences. The student employee position in a library is often the experience which starts people on the track to library careers. Good supervision gives students the correct message — library careers are worthwhile options.

Student employee supervision is a skill which can be acquired, providing the supervisor has the desire to learn, the ability to get along with people, and the knowledge of their jobs. It is an important responsibility which can be very rewarding. A poor supervisor will most certainly be remembered, but a good one will be thought of fondly for providing a meaningful work experience. If successful supervision is your goal, the information in this handbook can be adapted to your own situation.

LOOKING AHEAD

You are, or have decided that you would like to be, a student employee supervisor. Remember that while not everyone has the aptitude for supervision and that, while it is true that the skills come more naturally to some people than to others, many of the skills can be learned. Supervision is a difficult yet rewarding job which can be performed well by those who are willing to work at it. If you are willing to learn, this book is designed for you. In the course of the next twelve chapters, we will review the basic principles of supervision and relate them specifically to student employees in libraries. Suggestions and advice are offered throughout to help you improve your knowledge and skills in supervision and to help you apply what you know to your student supervisory responsibilities. The following chapter describes the student supervisory role in libraries.

NOTES

[1]Elizabeth W. Stone, *American Library Development, 1600-1899* (New York: H. W. Wilson Company, 1977), 115-16.

[2]Harry Lyman Koopman, "The Student Assistant and Library Training," *Libraries* 35 (March 1930): 87.

[3]Mary Elizabeth Downey, "Work of Student Assistants in College Libraries," *Library Journal* 57 (1 May 1932): 417-20.

[4]Louis Round Wilson and Maurice F. Tauber, *The University Library*, 2d ed. (New York: Columbia University Press, 1956), 57.

[5]ALA Office for Library Personnel Resources Advisory Committee, *Each One Teach One: Recruiting for Quality* (OLPR Program, Dallas ALA Conference, 1989).

[6]Keith M. Cottam, "Student Employees in Academic Libraries," *College & Research Libraries* 31, no. 4 (July 1970): 248.

[7]Andrew Melnyk, "Student Aides in Our Library (Blessings and Headaches)," *Illinois Libraries* 58 (February 1976): 141-44.

[8]Emilie C. White, "Student Assistants in Academic Libraries: From Reluctance to Reliance," *The Journal of Academic Librarianship* 11, no. 2 (May 1985): 97.

[9]Association of Research Libraries, *ARL Statistics 1988-89* (Washington, DC: ARL, 1990), 12-32.

[10]*Job Satisfaction: Is There a Trend?* Manpower Administration Research Monograph no. 3 (Washington, DC: U.S. Dept. of Labor, 1974), 4.

[11]Association of Research Libraries, 11-32.

BIBLIOGRAPHY

Association of Research Libraries. *ARL Statistics, 1988-89*. Washington, DC: Association of Research Libraries, 1990.

Boyer, Ernest L. *College: The Undergraduate Experience in America*. New York: Harper and Row, 1988.

Brown, Helen M. "Conditions Contributing to the Efficient Service of Student Assistants in a Selected Group of College Libraries." *College and Research Libraries* 5 (December 1943): 44-52.

Camp, Mildred. "Student Assistants and the College Library." *Library Journal* 59 (1 December 1934): 923-25.

Cottam, Keith M. "Student Employees in Academic Libraries." *College and Research Libraries* 31 (July 1970): 246-48.

Downey, Mary Elizabeth. "Work of Student Assistants in College Libraries." *Library Journal* 57 (1 May 1932): 417-20.

Downs, Robert B. "The Role of the Academic Librarian: 1876-1976." *College and Research Libraries* 37 (November 1976): 491-502.

Evans, Charles W. "The Evolution of Paraprofessional Library Employees." *Advances in Librarianship* 9 (1979): 64-102.

Heron, Alexander R. *Why Men Work*. Stanford, CA: Stanford University Press, 1948.

Holley, Edward G. *The Land-Grant Movement and the Development of Academic Libraries*. College Station, TX: Texas A & M University Libraries, 1977.

Hunt, H. Allen, and Timothy L. Hunt. *Clerical Employment and Technological Change*. Kalamazoo, MI: W. E. Upjohn Institute for Employment Research, 1986.

Job Satisfaction: Is There a Trend? Manpower Administration Research Monograph no. 3. Washington, DC: U.S. Dept. of Labor, 1974.

Koopman, Harry Lyman. "The Student Assistant and Library Training." *Libraries* 35 (March 1930): 87-89.

Lyle, Guy R. *The Administration of the College Library*. 4th ed. New York: H. W. Wilson, 1974.

McHale, Cecil J. "An Experiment in Hiring Student Part-Time Assistants." *Libraries* 36 (October 1931): 379-82.

Melnyk, Andrew. "Student Aides in Our Library (Blessings and Headaches)." *Illinois Libraries* 58 (February 1976): 141-44.

Shiflett, Orvin Lee. *The Origins of American Academic Librarianship*. Norwood, NJ: Ablex, 1981.

Shores, Louis. *Origins of the American College Library, 1638-1800*. New York: Barnes & Noble, 1935.

Shores, Louis. "Staff Spirit among Student Assistants." *Libraries* 34 (July 1929): 346-48.

Smith, Jessie J. "Training of Student Assistants in Small College Libraries." *Library Journal* 54 (1 April 1930): 306-9.

Stone, Elizabeth W. *American Library Development, 1600-1899*. New York: H. W. Wilson, 1977.

Student Assistants in ARL Libraries, SPEC Kit 91. Washington, DC: Association of Research Libraries, 1983.

White, Emilie C. "Student Assistants in Academic Libraries: From Reluctance to Reliance." *The Journal of Academic Librarianship* 11, no. 2 (May 1985): 93-97.

Wilson, Louis Round, and Maurice F. Tauber. *The University Library*. 2d ed. New York: Columbia University Press, 1956.

Worthy, John. "A Graduate Assistant at the University of Florida." *Library Association Record* 67 (November 1965): 395-96.

The Student Employee Supervisor

Deep swimmers and high climbers seldom die in their beds.
—Proverb

THE ROLE OF STUDENT EMPLOYEE SUPERVISOR

The student employee supervisor occupies a unique and important position in the academic library. The job description likely includes the line, "supervises student employees," and in fact, the supervisor of student employees has responsibility for hiring, training, scheduling, assigning duties, disciplining, evaluating, counseling, and, above all, assuring that student workers contribute to the accomplishment of the unit's or department's objectives and the objectives of the library.

Supervisors of student workers have much in common with supervisors in industry. The basic principles of supervision apply equally to the academic library situation. The supervision of student employees, while it has much in common with general supervision, is different in very important ways. The type of employees supervised is quite different from industry. Nearly all of the student employees are postsecondary students who typically work half-time or less, seldom work all year, are not considered regular or permanent employees, and usually aspire to a career different from the work they are asked to do in the library. Recognizing these differences, let us examine the student employee supervisor's role.

DEFINITION OF SUPERVISOR

By definition, "anyone at the first level of management who has the responsibility for getting the 'hands-on-the-work' employees to carry out the plans and policies of higher level management is a supervisor."[1] The Taft-Hartley Act of 1947 defines a supervisor as

> any individual having authority, in the interest of the employer, to hire, transfer, suspend, lay off, recall, promote, discharge, assign, reward, or discipline other employees, or responsibility to direct them, or to adjust their grievances, or effectively to recommend such action, if in connection with the foregoing the exercise of such authority is not of a merely routine or clerical nature, but requires the use of independent judgement.[2]

The word supervisor derives from a Latin term which means "look over." Early on, the supervisor was the person in charge of a group of workers, a foreman, or "fore man," at the lead of a group and setting the pace for the rest. A supervisor today is a leader, one who watches over the work, and a person with technical or professional skills.

Getting Things Done through Others

The most common definition of management is "getting things done through other people." The emphasis is placed on "through other people." The primary task of any employee is "getting things done" and, as a staff member, "getting things done" is the most important part of your job. Since there is more work than any one person can accomplish, it is necessary to utilize additional employees to do the work. As a student employee supervisor, you must not only accomplish your own work, but you must also get things done through student workers.

Doing a job and getting someone else to do it are entirely different. Simply telling someone to do something correctly very seldom works. The employee must be motivated to do it correctly, as well as have the prerequisite knowledge and skills. If the work is not done properly, it is the supervisor's responsibility to teach the needed skills or knowledge and to apply those supervisory techniques which will allow the student worker to do things well.

Every student employee has different needs, skills, attitudes, and motivations. The student employee supervisor needs to deal with each employee differently while dealing with all employees fairly. There is no universal technique that will work with every student employee. What works today with one student may have no effect tomorrow and what works on one may have a completely negative effect on another student worker. The purpose of this handbook is to help you get student workers to accomplish work.

WHO ARE THE STUDENT EMPLOYEE SUPERVISORS?

In most organizations, supervisors rise from the ranks and are usually employees with seniority who have worked at different jobs in the organization. Supervisors normally have more education or training than those they supervise.

The student employee supervisor either advances within the library to a position with student employee supervisory responsibilities or is hired into a position which has student supervision as a part of the job. The most experienced employees are often not student employee supervisors, but supervisors of other regular staff. Student supervision is a valuable training ground for staff supervisors.

As a rule, most student employee supervisors are not senior members of a unit or department. Typically, the student employee supervisors report to senior staff in the department or to the unit or department head, usually a librarian. In libraries with clerical, technical, and professional staff classifications, student employee supervisors will be found in all classifications, with the majority at the technical level. Some students are supervised by librarians and occasionally by senior student employees.

Identifying Prospective Student Employee Supervisors

Student employee supervisors may be chosen on the basis of seniority, proficiency, favoritism, demonstrated leadership, experience, or educational background. It is not unusual (and is often desirable) to select someone on the staff for a supervisory position. Making the transition to a student employee supervisory position requires a great deal of effort on the part of the employee as well as psychological, social, and educational support from management.

Persons who will become good supervisors of student employees can be identified quite easily from among existing staff: they are very skilled at their jobs, have good communication skills, get along well with co-workers and management, and have a positive attitude. All of the attributes of a good staff member are needed to become a good supervisor. Above all, prospective supervisors must like their work, students, and themselves.

The Best Worker May Not Be the Best Supervisor

The best worker, however, is not necessarily the best student employee supervisor. The skills required of an effective student employee supervisor are different from those required of a skilled worker. Selecting the best worker to be a student employee supervisor is a common and dangerous practice. Good workers often accept supervisory positions because of money, prestige, or status without realizing that the skills required of a good worker are not the same as those required of good supervisors. They may perform poorly because they do not have or do not develop the necessary supervisory skills. If they do not enjoy the work, some quit, while others may receive poor evaluations, possibly leading to termination. Others may stay in student employee supervisory positions they dislike because they do not want to lose face.

People should go into supervisory positions because they *want* the challenge and satisfaction to be gained. If these are not your reasons for seeking student employee supervisory responsibility, no amount of pay, prestige, or status will compensate for the stress and other problems associated with work you dislike.

In selecting someone to be a student employee supervisory position, an administrator must look for someone who has good communication skills, likes people, has the aptitude for the work, and has energy and enthusiasm.

PERSONAL QUALITIES OF GOOD STUDENT EMPLOYEE SUPERVISORS

What are the personal qualities of good student employee supervisors?

1. Energy and good health. Supervision is a demanding activity and requires that individuals not only be able to handle a variety of activities but also be physically and emotionally up to the task.

2. Leadership potential. Supervision requires the ability to motivate people to work for you and with you to accomplish the objectives of your unit.

3. Ability to get along with people. One of the most important qualities management looks for in a student employee supervisor is the ability to get along with others. Getting others to carry out their responsibilities depends greatly on their feelings toward their supervisor.

4. Job know-how and technical competence. The supervisor must know the job thoroughly in order to train students and to solve problems. Student employee supervisors usually have their own additional job duties and responsibilities and must be proficient in those duties as well.

5. Initiative. The student employee supervisor needs to be able to recognize when adjustments or changes must be made in the work flow to improve procedures. Initiative is required to be able to take action when problems or potential problems are discovered.

6. Dedication and dependability. The example set by the supervisor will be followed by the employees and workers who sense that their supervisor is not dedicated to the job or employer, will display the same attitude. For example, a supervisor who is regularly absent will find employees will also be absent often.

7. Positive attitude toward management. Workers will mirror the feelings of the supervisor in this regard also.

These qualities are desirable in any employee, but are even more important in student employee supervisors. If supervisors don't exhibit all of these positive attributes, training and staff development should be provided to enhance all of these characteristics.

Types of Persons Who Should Not Be Supervisors

There are definitely types of persons to avoid when filling student employee supervisor positions. When selecting a person from your staff, managers should avoid the negative employee, the rigid employee, the unproductive employee, and the disgruntled employee. The negative employee's attitude will be contagious among student employees. The rigid employee will be unable to effectively deal with the special needs of student employees. The unproductive employee will find it difficult to get others to work hard and the employee who is unhappy with the work, the supervisor, the organization, or life in general will not be able to effectively deal with student employees, who may mirror any of those feelings.

Student Employee Supervisor Attitudes

Attitude is extremely important to good supervision. Student employee supervisors have the proper attitude if they agree with the following statements:[3]

1. Supervisors must manage with a high degree of integrity and lead by example.

2. Supervisors must keep their word to employees.

3. Supervisors must earn the respect, trust, and confidence of employees.

4. Supervisors must strive to help employees develop to their full potential.

5. Supervisors must give credit to employees who do a good job.

6. Supervisors must accept higher level management decisions and directives and explain and support them to employees.

7. Supervisors must not discuss personal feelings about management or other employees with employees.

8. Supervisors must be responsible for the performance of their employees.

9. Supervisors must be objective in judging the actions of employees.

10. Supervisors must decide matters involving employees on the bases of facts and circumstances, not on personal sympathies.

11. Supervisors must accept the responsibility for rehabilitating rather than punishing employees whenever possible.

12. Supervisors must be prepared to support employees in cases where employees are in the right and to help them understand when they are not.

13. Supervisors should attempt to allow employees to have as much control over their own work as possible.

14. Supervisors must work to maintain a climate in the workplace which allows employees to express their own feelings and concerns openly without fear of reprisal.

MOVING FROM A STAFF TO A SUPERVISORY POSITION

The transition from worker to supervisor is a difficult move for any staff member. The new student employee supervisor must realize that "doing" and "supervising" require entirely different skills. The supervisor has, in effect, a contractual arrangement with student workers. You, as the student employee supervisor, have a right to expect certain things from them and they have the right to expect certain things in return. You represent management to the students and your student employees to management. This delicate balance of responsibilities must be achieved if supervision is to be successful. Without question, supervision is one of the most difficult responsibilities anyone can assume.

Differences between Worker and Supervisor

Because most new supervisors of student employees are selected from among present staff members in the department, it is important to remember that the move represents a significant change for everyone involved. Here are five major differences between being a subordinate and being a supervisor:

1. Need to manage other person's time. Supervisors must set schedules that others must meet as well as managing their own time.

2. Satisfaction becomes more abstract. A supervisor's satisfaction is often indirect: it comes from taking pride in helping others succeed, rather than from completing a job alone.

3. Shift in job evaluation. Performance is judged not only by one's boss but also by one's subordinates as well—both top down and bottom up.

4. Problems are long-term. A supervisor must deal with problems that may persist for weeks, months, or even years.

5. People are key resources. Because a supervisor must get things done through others, people are the supervisor's most important resource. Learning the capabilities of each person is essential to making good use of this resource.

Transition from Worker to Supervisor

The step from employee to supervisor is a large and important one for both the individual and the organization. Much time and thought goes into selecting the right person for the job. The same careful attention is seldom given to helping this person develop into a productive member of management. All too often, new supervisors are left to "sink or swim" in their new positions. There are many changes which accompany a promotion from subordinate to supervisor.

1. Perspective. Most employees are concerned primarily with doing a good job and planning how to get ahead. Supervisors, however, must keep the big picture in mind, considering the impact of their decisions on the department and the library.

2. Goals. A supervisor's primary concern is with meeting the organization's goals. This contrasts with the employee's focus on meeting personal goals, such as becoming more skilled at a specific job.

3. Responsibilities. A supervisor must supervise and speak for a group of people in addition to completing technical and administrative tasks. A supervisor must also accept responsibility for decisions instead of criticizing others.

4. Satisfaction. Because a supervisor does less of the actual work personally, satisfaction comes from watching others succeed.

5. Job skills. Becoming technically competent is important, but supervisors must also become proficient at communicating, delegating, planning, managing time, directing, motivating, and training others. Many of these are new skills which must be developed.

6. Relationships. If one is promoted to a supervisory position, new relationships with former peers, other supervisors, and possibly, a new boss must be developed. People quickly change how they act toward the new supervisor, whether or not the supervisor changes behavior toward them.

Seven Transition Stages

The new supervisor does not make an overnight transformation from thinking and behaving like a subordinate to thinking and behaving like a boss. Normally, the supervisor passes through several predictable stages. While people seldom move neatly from one stage to the next, they generally experience all seven stages.

1. Immobilization. The person feels overwhelmed by the changes. This may be typified by: "This job is a lot bigger than I thought. Everyone is making demands. How can I possibly do everything?"

2. Denial of change. This phase allows the individual involved time to regroup and fully comprehend the change. "This job is not so different from your other job. Let's see, first I'll take care of this and then I'll begin to work on that."

3. Depression. Awareness sets in regarding the magnitude of the changes that must be made in one's habits, customs, relationships, etc. "Why did I ever leave my other job? I wish I could afford to quit. I hate my job!"

4. Acceptance of reality. Feelings of optimism return and the person is ready to let go of the past. "Maybe this isn't so bad. Forget about that old job. I'm doing fine."

5. Testing. This is a time of trying out new behaviors and ways of coping with the new situation. "If I meet with staff every Thursday and try this schedule, I think I can manage."

6. Search for meanings. The person's concern shifts to trying to understand both how and why things are different now. "Now I feel comfortable in this job. It is different but not really that bad."

7. Internalization. In this final stage, the person incorporates the new meanings into behavior. "I like my job and I'm good at what I do."

PROBLEMS FACED BY NEW STUDENT EMPLOYEE SUPERVISORS

Probably the biggest problem facing new student employee supervisors is their lack of preparation for the job. Employees are often selected for promotion to a management position because of their performance as a specialist. Those skills and abilities are often quite different than those needed by a supervisor. As a result, the new supervisor must develop new skills.

Organizations normally expect new supervisors to step into the job and function right away. This expectation exists even though most organizations offer little help or support to them. Often, formal supervisory training is not provided to the new supervisor until after six to twelve months on the job: the "sink or swim" philosophy is prevalent.

Also, the new student employee supervisor often lacks an immediate peer group. Former peers no longer regard the new supervisor as one of them while other supervisors are hesitant to consider this person a part of their group until the new supervisor has demonstrated the ability to think and act like management. The new supervisor belongs to neither group at a time when support from both is badly needed.

The new supervisor of student employees must be willing to learn, change, adapt, and ask for help when needed. A person must have realistic expectations about supervision. Newcomers can expect expertise from a previous job to be helpful in some, but not all, situations. They can expect to make mistakes, an unavoidable part of learning any new job. New supervisors must recognize that it takes a lot of hard work to gain the loyalty and support of other people. New behaviors are needed and learning takes time. Practicing supervisors also must recognize that it takes time for the new supervisor to become effective and they must give their help and support. The process of becoming a good supervisor is an ongoing process, and one never stops learning.

Expectations for Student Employee Supervisors

Supervising people is undoubtedly the most difficult and complex activity of managers. Supervisors are the direct link between the managerial structure and the operational structure of an organization. To employees, the supervisor represents "the organization" and the workers' feelings about the organization, management, and their jobs are directly affected by their relationship with their immediate supervisors. Management's assessment of a unit's and of a supervisor's effectiveness is based on the productivity of the employees. Supervisors are in a unique position because their ability to accomplish work through others has a direct impact on the organization's accomplishing its mission.

Many people in technical and staff positions fail to recognize or appreciate the demands placed on student employee supervisors. Medical research has shown that supervisory positions carry with them tremendous stress. While it is true that some people work better under stress and that channeling stress into productive activity can be satisfying, stress nonetheless contributes to heart attacks, ulcers, and clinical depression. Successful supervision requires considerable training and skill development.

In the past, the role of supervisor was far less complex, partially because supervisors of the past had far more personal authority. The controls and penalties imposed on employees for not following a supervisor's directives were much more immediate and severe. The student employee supervisor today may still use indirect force to get cooperation, but the supervisor is more often frustrated by policies, rules, and regulations imposed by management. In some organizations, even though the supervisor has the power to discipline student employees, it is not unusual for these decisions to be overruled by management, causing even further frustrating supervisors.

Student employee supervisors are called upon to represent the interests of both the employees and management. If they represent only employees' views, they will find themselves at odds with management, whereas if they represented only management, their effectiveness will diminish considerably. Successful student employee supervisors must continually work to balance both organizational and individual needs. Is it any wonder that today's student employee supervisors feel confused, frustrated, and torn between two groups?

Libraries expect that student employee supervisors will recruit, hire, and train student employees in addition to performing other duties requiring technical expertise. Many are given the responsibility without training. The practice of hiring a new student employee supervisor to begin work after the previous incumbent has left further exacerbates the problem. The new student employee supervisor, whether new to the library or promoted to new responsibilities, and the supervisor's manager both have to recognize that the development of supervisory skills takes time and effort.

Common Mistakes New Supervisors Make

We have all seen mistakes supervisors can make. This is a list of the most common:

1. Overcontrolling. The new supervisor (or the experienced supervisor, for that matter) may believe that it is necessary to show everyone who is boss.

2. Undercontrolling. One who refuses to make decisions in an attempt to make everyone happy is headed for trouble.

3. One-way communication. The supervisor may be guilty of just giving orders without listening, or just listening and providing no leadership.

4. Half-way delegation. Some supervisors are good at delegating responsibility without the authority to act. This too leads to problems for all concerned.

These are only some of the mistakes which can be made by new supervisors. Mistakes will be made, but it is part of the responsibility of practicing supervisors to help new supervisors develop an effective management style.

What Employees Don't Like about Their Supervisors

One way to learn how to be a good supervisor is to think about all of your supervisors and what you would have changed if you could. By considering the traits, actions, and skills of supervisors you have known, you know what to avoid in your own supervisory style. The following are some of the things employees don't like about their supervisors:

Supervisor Traits

1. Too much sensitivity. Employees should not have to tiptoe around their supervisors for fear the supervisor is in a bad mood. Nor should they fear a boss who takes everything personally.

2. Indecisive. Indecisive supervisors can survive in an organization but will not win the support of employees.

3. Opinionated. Supervisors who will not listen to any kind of reasoning but always have their minds made up will find that employees will soon stop making suggestions.

4. Autocratic. Supervisors must understand if they do not allow their employees to participate in decisions, a lot of good talent is wasted.

5. Vulgar language. Crude language impresses no one and is to be avoided at all costs.

6. Unstable personality. Employees should not have to guess which supervisor came to work that day. Unpredictable changes in the supervisor's personality cause problems.

7. Dishonesty. Supervisors need to recognize the importance of honesty in the workplace and make it easy for employees to be honest.

Supervisor Actions

1. Shows favoritism. Even if other employees are treated fairly, they resent another employee being given favorable treatment. This can lead to discrimination charges, even though, in most cases, prejudice is not involved.

2. Does not listen. Good supervisors are anxious to hear what employees think about the job and try to get employees to talk. Nothing is more frustrating than to talk to a supervisor who does not listen.

3. Unable to accept bad news. Supervisors must be willing to listen to bad news and not punish the bearer. It won't take long for employees to realize that a supervisor wants to hear only good news; problems which need attention will then be ignored.

4. Ridicules employees. A supervisor who ridicules or makes sarcastic remarks to employees may not even realize it. Ridiculing an employee in front of peers is unforgiveable. Supervisors must be tactful and aware of how their words affect employees.

5. Makes uninformed decisions. Employees respect supervisors who make decisions based on information (and who explain the bases of those decisions).

6. Does not trust employees. The supervisor must trust employees and the employees must be able to trust their supervisor.

7. Makes impossible promises. Employees know when the supervisor makes promises which can not be kept. The supervisor's credibility is destroyed if this happens often.

8. Breaks reasonable promises. Employees also know when the supervisor's promises can be kept and are not. Supervisors must keep to their word or be able to explain why a promise is not kept.

Supervisor Skills

1. Poor time management. A supervisor with poor time management skills will waste their employees' time as well as their own.

2. Disorganization. Employees want a supervisor who is organized and can get things done.

3. Failure to exert authority. Employees respect supervisors who know how to use their authority and is a leader.

4. Poor planning. The supervisor who fails to plan in advance wastes employees' time. Poorly planned meetings, for example, are terrible time wasters.

5. Poor communication. Supervisors must develop good communication skills.

Why Student Employee Supervisors Fail

Supervisory styles cover the full spectrum, from laissez-faire to authoritarian. The supervisor who lacks self-confidence or feels uncomfortable in the supervisory role tends to let the unit run itself. The dictatorial or authoritarian supervisor tends to over-supervise. Good supervisors are rarely found at either extreme, but are most often in the middle of the spectrum.

When a student employee supervisor does not succeed the manager must look at the specific situation to determine the exact reasons. It is possible that the failure can be traced to lack of support from the boss, or lack of training or encouragement. Most failures, however, can be attributed to one of the following six supervisory pitfalls:

1. Poor personal relations with student employees, management, or other supervisors.

2. Lack of initiative or emotional stability on the part of the supervisor.

3. Unwillingness or inability to understand the management point of view.

4. Failure to spend the necessary effort or time to improve skills.

5. Lack of skill in planning and organizing the work of student employees.

6. Unwillingness or inability to adjust to changing conditions.

PREPARING TO BECOME A STUDENT EMPLOYEE SUPERVISOR

Many people begin their careers in libraries in public service or technical service positions without supervisory responsibilities. The aspiring student employee supervisor would do well to begin with the first function of management—planning.

1. Develop a career plan based on a realistic appraisal of your interests, aptitudes, and abilities.

2. Take advantage of a career development program, if available.

3. Talk to student employee supervisors to learn more about what they do.

4. Talk to your supervisor to learn about opportunities for supervisory responsibilities.

5. Participate in supervisory and management training courses offered by the university.

6. Complete your college education. Many supervisory positions require a bachelor's degree. In addition, being a student will help you relate to those you will be supervising.

7. Remember that advancement depends on successful performance. Although successful performance of your job will neither guarantee advancement nor guarantee that you will be a successful supervisor, good supervisors advance from the ranks of good workers, not bad ones.

THE STUDENT EMPLOYEE SUPERVISOR

The importance of the role of the student employee supervisor is underestimated in many libraries for a number of reasons. Librarians often do not receive the level of training in management in library school that is required to manage large organizations and usually develop their skills through postgraduate workshops and through on the job experience. Many supervisors have no formal training whatsoever. It is therefore not expected of staff who supervise students. Students are clearly on the bottom rung of the library staffing ladder.

By understanding the importance of student employee supervision and developing supervisory skills, the student employee supervisor can make a valuable contribution to the operation of the library and help students gain life-long job skills. Yours is a critical role in the organization.

NOTES

[1]Lester R. Bittel, *What Every Supervisor Should Know* (New York: McGraw-Hill, 1980), 3.

[2]Labor Management Relations Act, 1947 (PL101, 23 June 1947), *United States Statutes at Large* 61, pt. 1 (Washington, DC: GPO, 1948), 138.

[3]Adapted from Louis V. Imundo, *The Effective Supervisor's Handbook* (New York: AMACOM, 1980), 12-14.

BIBLIOGRAPHY

Abboud, Michael J., and Homer L. Richardson. "What Do Supervisors Want from Their Jobs?" *Personnel Journal* (July 1972): 308-12.

Bailey, Martha J. "Requirements for Middle Managerial Positions." *Special Libraries* 69 (September 1978): 323-31.

Baker, H. K., and S. R. Holmberg. "Stepping Up to Supervision: Being Popular Isn't Enough." *Supervisory Management* 27 (January 1982): 12-18.

Bedeian, Arthur G. *Management*. Chicago: Dryden Press, 1986.

Benson, Carl A. "New Supervisors: From the Top of the Heap to the Bottom of the Heap." *Personnel Journal* (April 1978): 176.

Bittel, Lester, R. *What Every Supervisor Should Know*. New York: McGraw-Hill, 1980.

Bridges, William. *Transitions: Making Sense of Life's Changes*. Reading, MA: Addison-Wesley, 1980.

Carroll, Stephen J., and Dennis Gillen. "Are the Classical Management Functions Useful in Describing Managerial Work?" *Academy of Management Review* 12, no. 1 (January 1987): 38-51.

Certo, Samuel. *Principles of Modern Management*. 3d ed. Dubuque, IA: Wm. C. Brown, 1985.

Daughtrey, Anne Scott, and Betty Roper Ricks. *Contemporary Supervision: Managing People and Technology*. New York: McGraw-Hill, 1988.

Donnelly, James H., James L. Gibson, and John M. Ivancevich. *Fundamentals of Management*. 6th ed. Plano, TX: Business Publications, 1987.

Flamholtz, Eric G., and Yvonne Randle. *The Inner Game of Management: How to Make the Transition to a Managerial Role*. New York: AMACOM, 1987.

Fulmer, William E. "The Making of a Supervisor." *Personnel Journal* (March 1977): 140-43, 151.

Gellerman, Saul W. "Supervision: Substance and Style." *Harvard Business Review* 54 (March-April 1976): 89-99.

Hampton, David R. *Management*. 3d ed. New York: McGraw-Hill, 1986.

Ianconnetti, Joan, and Patrick O'Hare. *First-Time Manager*. New York: Macmillan, 1985.

Imundo, Louis V. *The Effective Supervisor's Handbook*. New York: AMACOM, 1980.

Library Administration and Management Association, Middle Management Discussion Group. *You'll Manage: Becoming a Boss*. Chicago: LAMA, 1980.

Lynch, Beverly P. "The Role of Middle Managers in Libraries." *Advances in Librarianship* 6 (1976): 253-77.

Martell, Charles. "Automation, Quality of Work Life, and Middle Managers." Paper prepared for ALA, LAMA, Systems and Services Section, Management Practices Committee. ALA Conference, New York, 1986.

Mintzberg, Henry. "The Manager's Job: Folklore and Fact." *Harvard Business Review* 53 (July-August 1975): 49-61.

Sullivan, Maureen. *Librarians as Supervisors. Workbook for ACRL Continuing Education Course CE 101*. Chicago: ALA, 1982.

Van Fleet, James K. *The 22 Biggest Mistakes Managers Make and How to Correct Them*. West Nyack, NY: Parker Publishing, 1973.

Weiss, W. H. *Supervisor's Standard Reference Handbook*. 2d ed. Englewood Cliffs, NJ: Prentice-Hall, 1988.

Basics for Supervisors

Fewer sleeping pills would be sold if more people went to bed at night content with what they are doing to others.

—John W. Gardner

BECOMING A SUPERVISOR

This chapter includes discussions of basic supervisory qualities and skills required of good supervisors, the process of becoming a supervisor, and suggestions on how supervisors can be successful. Leadership is one of the most important skills or qualities a successful supervisor can develop.

LEADERSHIP

Leadership is the basic requirement for good supervision. There are many definitions of leadership as evidenced by the number of books on the subject, however, simply put, leadership is the ability to get others to follow you and do the things you want them to do. It is a trait which may be developed with hard work or which may come naturally, but all successful leaders possess the following qualities:

1. Belief in their ability to lead

2. Sense of mission

3. Willingness to put the organization's well-being above their own egos

4. Honesty

5. Courage

6. Sincerity

7. Dependability

8. Job knowledge

9. Common sense

10. Sound judgement

11. Energy

12. Willingness to work hard

There are three basic kinds of leadership:

1. Autocratic leadership is a style in which the leader makes the decisions and demands that workers follow instructions without question.

2. Democratic leadership involves those supervised: the leader consults with workers and lets them help set policy.

3. Free-rein or participative leadership occurs when the leader exercises minimum control, allowing workers to exercise their own judgement and sense of responsibility in accomplishing the necessary work.

Different kinds of leadership can be successful with different employees. An autocratic style works best when the student employee supervisor has both real authority and a personality which can exert strong control. It works best in assembly-line-type situations. Participatory and democratic leadership work best in situations where the supervisor's authority is less defined, the procedures are subject to change with the situation, and the employees are able to or required to use creativity and initiative.

The leadership style practiced by student employee supervisors is dependent largely on the situation. Usually, participative (or free-rein) leadership is most effective with student employees who are typically cooperative, self-reliant, and desirous of exercising their own judgement. It is up to the supervisor to communicate to employees the idea that they are to "do as I do, which is the same as what I say." Leaders are responsible for setting good examples for employees to adopt and follow.

The style of leadership, however, is less important than the leaders themselves. All organizations seek the qualities of leadership in employees for their supervisors and managers. Good leadership is essential for good supervisors of student employees in academic libraries.

Your Leadership Potential

The following test is designed to help you measure your leadership potential.[1]

Test of Leadership Potential

Directions: Record the number that indicates where you fall, from 1 to 10, on the scale. Interpretation of the results follows the scale.

I can develop the talent and confidence to be an excellent speaker in front of groups.	10......5......1	I could never develop confidence to speak in front of groups.
I have the capacity to build and maintain productive relationships with workers under my supervision.	10......5......1	I'm a loner. I do not want the responsibility of building relationships with others.
I intend to take full advantage of all opportunities to develop my leadership qualities.	10......5......1	I do not intend to seek a leadership role or to develop my leadership skills.
I can develop the skill of motivating others. I would provide an outstanding example.	10......5......1	I could never develop the skill of motivating others. I would be a poor example to follow.
I can be patient and understanding with others.	10......5......1	I have no patience with others and could not develop it.
I could learn to be good at disciplining those under me—even to the point of terminating a worker after repeated violations.	10......5......1	It would tear me up to discipline a worker under my supervision: I'm much too kind and sensitive.
I can make tough decisions.	10......5......1	I do not want decision-making responsibilities.
It would not bother me to isolate myself and maintain a strong discipline line between workers and myself.	10......5......1	I have a great need to be liked; I want to be one of the gang.
I would make an outstanding member of a "management" team.	10......5......1	I hate staff meetings and would be a weak or hostile team member.
In time, I would be a superior leader— better than anyone I have known.	10......5......1	My leadership potential is so low it is not worth developing.

TOTAL SCORE _____

Interpretation of your score: The total number of possible points is 100. If you circled any number less than 5, you should reexamine your career objectives. Perhaps supervision is not an activity you should seek until you can honestly circle a 5 or higher on every question.

If your score is:

100 - Are you sure this is an honest appraisal?

90-99 - You will enjoy supervision.

80-89 - You have great supervisory potential.

70-79 - You should be a good supervisor.

60-69 - Are you sure supervision is your goal?

50-59 - Supervision will not be easy for you!

0-49 - Supervisory responsibilities will make you miserable!

To be effective, supervisors must have authority with which to carry out their responsibilities.

AUTHORITY

Authority is the right to exercise power legitimately. Authority and responsibility are handed down from the top, beginning with the highest levels to the university president, to the vice presidents, to the dean/director of the library, and so on. Authority and responsibility are delegated to student employee supervisors by their immediate supervisors, by virtue of having given them supervisory responsibility. As the authorities and responsibilities come down the line, they become more specific. For instance, while the dean or director has the authority to manage the personnel budget and a large staff, it is the supervisor's responsibility to manage a specific group of student employees with specific jobs and work to perform.

Authority and responsibility go hand in hand but are quite different. Authority is the power you need to carry out your responsibilities as student employee supervisor, whereas responsibility is the cumulation of those things for which you are held accountable by management.

Authority and power are not the same. Power does not require legitimacy. An armed robber, for instance, has power but no authority: the robber has no legitimate right to rob, but has a gun and the ability to make people follow instructions.

Authority carries with it the responsibility for using it wisely. The student employee supervisor has the authority and the attendant responsibility to manage. A student employee supervisor who, in the opinion of the employees, exceeds supervisory authority will find that employees will question or even resist that authority. Student employee supervisors must remember that their authority is retained only so long as its use is approved by the organization and accepted by the majority of employees supervised.

ACCOUNTABILITY

The student employee supervisor is accountable to the unit or department boss. For example, you may be responsible for the efficient and accurate charging and discharging of books. You delegate the responsibility for performing those activities to students who are accountable to you, but if the boss complains that there are too many books waiting to be discharged, you are accountable. You have the responsibility to investigate and correct the problem if possible. There may be any number of explanations, but you must solve the problem. In other words, you can delegate the responsibility, but you cannot delegate the accountability. The boss expects you to meet your responsibilities, which include the work actually performed by student employees.

Assessing Your Degree of Accountability

You can gain an idea of the degree to which you are responsible (or accountable) in your supervisory job by completing the Supervisory Responsibility Survey.[2]

Supervisory Responsibility Survey

DO YOU FEEL IT IS YOUR RESPONSIBILITY TO...

		YES	NO	DON'T KNOW
1.	Request that additional employees be hired as needed?	——	——	——
2.	Approve new student employees assigned to you?	——	——	——
3.	Tell employees about upgrading and pay ranges?	——	——	——
4.	Prepare employee work schedules?	——	——	——
5.	Assign specific duties to workers?	——	——	——
6.	Delegate authority?	——	——	——
7.	Discipline student employees?	——	——	——
8.	Discharge student employees?	——	——	——
9.	Specify the number and level of student employees to do a job?	——	——	——
10.	Determine the amount of work to be accomplished by each employee?	——	——	——
11.	Authorize overtime?	——	——	——
12.	Transfer student employees within your department?	——	——	——
13.	Lay off employees for lack of work?	——	——	——
14.	Grant leaves of absence?	——	——	——
15.	Explain to student employees how their pay is calculated?	——	——	——
16.	Start jobs in process?	——	——	——
17.	Stop jobs in process?	——	——	——
18.	Make suggestions for improvements in departmental procedures?	——	——	——
19.	Make recommendations on changes in departmental layout?	——	——	——
20.	Participate in setting up your departmental budget?	——	——	——

Interpretation: If you are able to say YES to all of the questions, you have supervisory responsibilities. If you also have the authority and accountability for all of these activities, your supervisory role is very clear. If you responded NO to more than five of the twenty questions, your supervisory role needs to be clarified with your boss. If you answered DON'T KNOW to any of the questions, you also need to speak to your boss about your responsibilities: if you don't know whether an activity is your responsibility, you certainly don't know whether you should be performing that activity. You cannot have authority or be accountable for any activity which is not clearly your responsibility.

Change occurs in all organizations whether supervisors plan for change or not. Change is brought about by changing technology, by library patron demands, by administrative policy, or by recognized need for improvement. An important part of an effective supervisor's job involves the ability to deal with and manage change.

MANAGING CHANGE

Change is any modification or alteration of the status quo. Student employees are, for the most part, amenable to change, while the regular staff, as a group, tend to be less so. Different employees have different responses to change, including rejection, resistance, tolerance, or acceptance. Outright rejection or acceptance is uncommon; most often there is resistance or tolerance which usually is the result of conscious thought. Employees base their decisions on their assessment of the effect of the change on them personally. Employees' resistance to change comes typically from the fear for their jobs, a general dislike of change, pressure from the group, lack of understanding, or plain shortsightedness.

If managed properly, employees will not only tolerate the change, but will also accept it. There are four steps for managing change which should be carried out sequentially:

1. Define the change. The supervisor must fully understand the change before introducing it to the workers.

2. Identify the situational factors. Will there be resistance? Who is likely to resist? How can that resistance be met? How much advance notice should be given?

3. Develop a change strategy in cooperation with employees. Explain the change, encourage participation in developing an implementation plan, provide support, and, if necessary, use persuasion to reduce resistance. If resistance is too great, the supervisor may have to exert whatever authority is available to overcome it.

4. Implement and monitor the change. Implement the strategy and examine the consequences.

The acceptance of change by employees depends to a great extent on their perceptions of their supervisor. If they feel they are involved in the decisions made in the department and believe that changes are made for good reasons, the chances that change will be accepted will be greatly improved.

MANAGING TIME

Many supervisors feel that they need more hours in each day in order to complete their work. If you often feel that, at the end of the day, you didn't really accomplish anything, it may not be the amount of work but the way you do it. The focus of time management is on working smarter, not harder. Supervisors are very busy and that is why time management is so important.

There are three basic types of supervisor time: boss-imposed, subordinate-imposed, and self-imposed. Boss-imposed time is that time your supervisor requires of you and includes assignments and tasks performed at the behest of the boss. Subordinate-imposed time is that time those persons you supervise require of you: this is time which is spent helping employees in their work. Self-imposed or personal time is that time which remains for you to use or manage as you need. This is the time equal to the number of hours an individual works minus boss-imposed and subordinate-imposed time.

The supervisor has little control over the amount of time the boss requires. You can, however, manage boss-imposed time by keeping a list of "to do" items arranged according to the boss's priorities and work to complete them on time.

The supervisor can and should examine the amount of subordinate-imposed time spent. Are your employees delegating work to you? Are you working twelve hours a day so they can work less? Supervisors need to learn techniques which will help them avoid having to solve all of the employees' problems.

Self-imposed time is that time which the supervisor has in which to accomplish the work which must be done. In effectively managing that time, the supervisor must first keep subordinate-imposed time to a minimum and then use time management techniques to make the best use of personal time.

Identifying Timewasters

In order to manage time, one must first know how it is presently spent. One way to accomplish that is to keep a time log to record exactly how time is spent in each and every activity. After keeping a log for a week or two, most supervisors are amazed at both how many activities are listed and how little is accomplished. The following are the most common timewasters:

1. Telephone interruptions

2. Drop-in visitors

3. Unscheduled meetings

4. Crises

5. Personal disorganization

6. Failure to set priorities

7. Failure to delegate

8. Trying to do too much at once

9. Unclear lines of authority and responsibility

10. Inability to say no

11. Physical fatigue

12. Poor communication

Time Management Guidelines

Time management is a personal challenge. If you are sincere in your desire to manage time, it can be done, but success depends on desire and a plan of action. The following suggestions are designed to help you attack the timewasters in your workday and to gain control of your time:

1. Use a daily planbook to keep track of what needs to be done each day and, if possible, schedule a quiet time each day when you can work without interruption.

2. Establish priorities and work on the most important first: focus first on doing the right things, then on doing things right.

3. Delegate work to subordinates.

4. Know yourself: if you are a morning person, work on your most important priorities in the morning, but if you work better in the afternoon, plan to do them then.

5. Learn to say "no" graciously: don't let others who don't manage their time waste yours.

6. Whatever you do, do it right the first time. This applies to tasks you perform yourself and to directions to others.

7. Get organized. Clean up your desk and files and throw out unnecessary papers.

8. Handle paper once. Avoid cluttering your desk with correspondence by acting on each piece of paper when you pick it up. If you can, write a response, give it to someone to handle, forward it, or file it and do so immediately.

9. Group tasks together. Handle your correspondence or make phone calls between 2 and 3 P.M., for example.

10. Break up large projects into smaller tasks and plan to do each task. For example, don't write a book, write chapters.

11. Make better use of bits of time. Don't start on a large project ten minutes before lunch. Do something you can complete.

12. Reduce interruptions. Schedule quiet time or turn your desk so your back is facing the door: visual interruptions can be just as wasteful as drop-in visitors.

13. Recognize that although you can do a better job of managing personal time, you can't reach perfection.

14. Don't overdo time management to the point that you lose your friends, alienate your co-workers, or get the nickname "time freak."

DEALING WITH STRESS

Stress is a feeling of anxiety, pressure, or tension which is experienced by everyone to some degree. Stress can be caused by everything from job-related incidents to everyday happenings. Stress is brought about by poor light, too much noise, or adverse temperature in the workplace. It can come from unclear job assignments, too much work or responsibility, or interpersonal conflict in the organizational environment. Most of us also bring stress to the workplace from home. Students are also subjected to stressful situations by their coursework.

Stressful situations affect people in different ways. Most persons work best under moderate degrees of stress: if there is too little stress, boredom results, but if there is too much stress, individuals are likely to suffer from lack of memory, indecision, depression, and poor judgement. Stress can be self-induced, but supervisors can help both their employees and themselves to deal with it by recognizing that diet, physical fitness, and mental relaxation are important. The following are suggested remedies for stress.

1. Walk away from the source of stress. A walk around the block can release pent-up tension.

2. Talk it out with a friend or mentor.

3. Release your anger by exercising or by expressing your anger in writing and then destroying it. (Don't forget the last step.)

4. Don't procrastinate: taking action can eliminate the stress.

5. Short naps can effectively reduce tension.

6. Avoid irritating and overly competitive people if you can. Stay away from persons who produce stress in others but seem to have no stress themselves.

7. Take advantage of staff development programs or continuing education sessions which teach stress reduction techniques.

8. Seek professional counseling.

DETERMINING YOUR POTENTIAL

Most people wonder at one time or another if they have the potential to get better jobs than they presently have. What is it that indicates whether or not individuals have the potential to rise in an organization? What can individuals do to demonstrate their interest in advancement? Answers to the following questions provide indicators of potential for growth:

1. Do you enjoy your work? If you get satisfaction from your work, you are probably self-motivated and will not be content to just do the minimum required. Self-motivation is one key to success.

2. Are you given encouragement by your supervisor? If you are told either verbally or through evaluations that you are doing a good job, you may have the potential to advance.

3. Do you enjoy solving problems? If so, you can demonstrate your potential by fully participating in departmental and library activities to the extent possible in your job. Persons who provide useful suggestions and ideas will get recognition.

4. Are you mature? Mature persons are usually practical in their viewpoints and demonstrate practical approaches to problems.

5. Are you stable? Stable persons can control their emotions and are able to handle stress effectively.

6. Do you read the professional literature? If you are interested in broader library issues and keep up with not only local but also national library issues, you can demonstrate an interest broader than just your job.

7. Do you join professional organizations? If you are interested in making a career in libraries at the staff or faculty level, you can demonstrate your interest by becoming a member of local, state, and national library organizations and actively participating in those organizations if possible.

Tips on Getting Noticed and Promoted

In today's libraries, the competition for more responsible and rewarding positions is great. Being in the right place at the right time for promotion is mostly luck and can't be counted on. If you want to advance, you have to do more than perform an excellent job. No matter how qualified you are for promotion, you must be *viewed* as qualified and ready for promotion. Your work must be recognized and your accomplishments known. Since few people are going to do this for you, the following are suggestions on how you can do it yourself.

1. Do an excellent job. There is no point in thinking about promotion if you do not perform your present job in an outstanding manner.

2. Act like a professional and dress appropriately.

3. Acquire more knowledge and education. Learn by reading, by listening and asking questions, by attending training sessions and workshops, or by attending classes.

4. Make it known to your supervisor that you want to get ahead but avoid giving the impression that you want to get ahead at the expense of others (including the supervisor).

5. Show your commitment to the organization. Complainers, moaners, and groaners don't get promoted often.

6. Prove that you are a team player. Participate as fully as possible in departmental and library activities.

7. Be willing to admit mistakes and to *say* you do not know when you do not know.

8. Prove that you have a sense of humor and are able to laugh at yourself.

9. Always exhibit honest and ethical behavior.

10. Don't become indispensable. If you are indispensable, you can't be replaced or promoted. If you are indispensable, it's a sign that you are not delegating properly, interacting with others, or training anyone to fill in during absences.

11. Participate in library committee activities.

12. Get yourself mentioned. If you do something newsworthy, let the editors of the library newsletter know about it.

13. Write for publication. If you have an area of expertise, write about it and get it published in library literature.

14. Converse with others at every opportunity. Offer your ideas and suggestions in committee meetings and get to know people outside your department.

Learn from Your Mistakes

Only a fool would assume that good supervisors make no mistakes, and, only a fool does not learn from them. Instead of simply dismissing a mistake by saying, "Everybody makes mistakes," why not take a few minutes to find out why the mistake was made? To learn from a mistake, you must analyze the situation to know what caused it. Ask yourself these questions:

1. What were you doing at the time?

2. What was the situation?

3. Were you under stress at the time?

4. Who else was involved?

5. Did you have incorrect or insufficient information?

6. Was the mistake the result of getting involved in the first place?

7. Was it the result of inattention, not placing enough importance on the situation?

8. Was your timing wrong? Should you have dealt with the situation earlier, later, or not at all?

9. Were other persons involved? While the mistake may not have been yours alone, accept your share of the responsibility. Should you be more careful when working with these persons in the future?

10. Was the mistake the result of insufficient follow-up?

Learning from mistakes will help you prevent making more of them. It is all part of gaining experience.

Types of Behavior to Avoid

It is as important to know what behaviors to avoid as it is to develop supervisory skills and knowledge. No matter how versed you are in supervision, good relationships with people must be developed. Any one of the following behaviors can prevent you from being the kind of supervisor you want to be:

1. Being distrustful: showing people that you don't trust them by questioning their motives or by not accepting their word.

2. Being untrustworthy: demonstrating that your word and actions cannot be trusted by others.

3. Being egotistical: talking about oneself too much.

4. Being selfish: saying and doing things that indicate that you have little regard for other people.

5. Being overly critical: finding fault with other people or criticizing them unnecessarily.

6. Being unwilling to accept blame: refusing to admit that you make mistakes.

7. Being defensive: making excuses or trying to justify your actions when you are wrong.

8. Being closed-minded: refusing to accept viewpoints which don't agree with yours.

Getting Along with Your Supervisor

In order to get along with your supervisor, place yourself in the shoes of those you supervise. How do you want your employees to view you? The following suggestions will help you get along better with your boss:

1. Provide support by keeping your supervisor fully informed. There should be very few "surprises."

2. Avoid wasting your supervisor's time. Don't go running to the boss for decisions that you should be making yourself.

3. Don't be a "yes" person all the time. If you don't agree with your supervisor, say so tactfully and be prepared to offer alternatives.

4. Avoid thinking you know more than your supervisor. Although you may indeed know more about certain aspects of the job, recognize that your boss is in that position for a reason.

5. Learn all you can from your supervisor if you wish to advance. That's how your boss became your boss.

6. Don't underestimate your supervisor's influence or ability to help you get ahead (or keep you where you are).

Writing Better Reports

One of the most common complaints of supervisors is having to write reports, yet writing good reports is extremely important. You can improve the quality of your reports by remembering the following:

1. Be concise: eliminate superfluous and redundant words.

2. Avoid jargon: the acronyms and phrases unique to your department or to the library may not be understood by someone outside of the field who may read the report. Spell out acronyms when you first introduce them.

3. Write the way you talk: avoid stilted language.

4. Always proofread your report: never allow a report to be distributed with misspelled words or typographical errors. This degrades you and those you work with.

5. Don't procrastinate: if you write a monthly report, do it monthly. No one wants to read a report that is six months old.

KEEP LEARNING

In this and the other three chapters on supervision I have attempted to provide basic supervisory techniques and information beneficial to supervisors of student assistants. Do not stop here, however: make a habit of reading supervisory literature and talking with co-workers who supervise students and staff. There is simply no way to adequately cover all you need to know to do your job. I only hope that the information contained in these chapters will be of use to you and that you will continue learning about supervision any way you can. The sources in the bibliographies should be helpful in learning more about supervision.

NOTES

[1]Adapted from Elwood E. Chapman, "A Self-Paced Exercise Guide," *Supervisor's Survival Kit*, 2d ed. (Chicago: Science Research Associates, 1980), 22.

[2]Adapted from Lester R. Bittel, *What Every Supervisor Should Know* (New York: McGraw-Hill, 1980).

BIBLIOGRAPHY

Adair, John. *Effective Time Management*. London: Pan Books, 1988.

Arroba, T., and K. James. *Pressure at Work: A Survival Guide*. Toronto: McGraw-Hill Ryerson, 1987.

Bedeian, Arthur G. *Management*. Chicago: Dryden Press, 1986.

Bittel, Lester R. *What Every Supervisor Should Know*. New York: McGraw-Hill, 1980.

Bold, Rudolph. "Librarian Burn-Out." *Library Journal* 107 (1 November 1982): 2048-51.

Bradley, Jana, and Larry Bradley. *Improving Written Communication in Libraries*. Chicago: ALA, 1988.

Brown, Nancy A., and Jerry Malone. "The Bases and Uses of Power in a University Library." *Library Administration and Management* 2 (June 1988): 141-44.

Bunge, Charles. "Stress in the Library." *Library Journal* 112 (15 September 1987): 47-51.

Certo, Samuel. *Principles of Modern Management*. 3d ed. Dubuque, IA: Wm. C. Brown, 1985.

Chapman, Elwood N. *Supervisor's Survival Kit*, 2d ed. Chicago: Science Research Associates, 1980.

Cherniss, Cary. *Staff Burnout: Job Stress in the Human Services*. Los Angeles: Sage, 1980.

Cherniss, Cary, E. Egnatios, and S. Wacker. "Job Stress and Career Development in New Public Professionals." *Professional Psychology* 7, no. 4 (1976): 428-36.

Creth, Sheila. *Time Management and Conducting Effective Meeting*. Chicago: ACRL, 1982.

Daughtrey, Anne Scott, and Betty Roper Ricks. *Contemporary Supervision: Managing People and Technology*. New York: McGraw-Hill, 1988.

Donnelly, James H., James L. Gibson, and John M. Ivancevich. *Fundamentals of Management*. 6th ed. Plano, TX: Business Publications, 1987.

Drucker, Peter F. *The Effective Executive*. New York: Harper and Row, 1985.

Edelwich, Jerry, with Archie Brodsky. *Burn-out: Stages of Disillusionment in the Helping Professions*. New York: Human Science Press, 1980.

Euster, Joanne R. *Changing Patterns in Internal Communication in Large Academic Libraries*. Occasional Paper no. 6. Washington, DC: ARL/OMS, 1981.

Fine, Sidney A., and Wretha W. Wiley. *An Introduction to Functional Job Analysis*. Kalamazoo, MI: W. E. Upjohn Institute for Employment Research, 1971.

Freudenberger, Herbert J. *Burn Out: The High Cost of High Achievement*. Garden City, NY: Anchor, 1980.

Freudenberger, Herbert J., and Gail North. *Women's Burnout*. Garden City, NY: Doubleday, 1985.

Fulmer, William E. "The Making of a Supervisor." *Personnel Journal* (March 1977): 140-43, 151.

Gellerman, Saul W. "Supervision: Substance and Style." *Harvard Business Review* 54 (March-April 1976): 89-99.

Ginzberg, Eli. *Understanding Human Resources*. Lanham, MD: University Press of America, 1985.

Gothberg, Helen M., and Donald E. Riggs. "Time Management in Academic Libraries." *College & Research Libraries* 49, no. 2 (March 1988): 131-40.

Grothe, Mardy, and Peter Wylie. *Problem Bosses: Who They Are and How to Deal with Them*. New York: Facts on File, 1987.

Hack, Mary, John W. Jones, and Tina Roose. "Occupational Burnout among Librarians." *Drexel Library Quarterly* 20 (Spring 1984): 46-72.

Hampton, David R. *Management*. 3d ed. New York: McGraw-Hill, 1986.

Herzberg, Frederick. *The Managerial Choice: To Be Efficient and to Be Human*. Homewood, IL: Dow Jones-Irwin, 1976.

Hollingsworth, A. T., and A. R. A. al-Jafary. "Why Supervisors Don't Delegate and Employees Won't Accept Responsibility." *Supervisory Management* 28 (April 1983): 12-17.

Killian, Ray A. *Managers Must Lead!* Rev. ed. New York: AMACOM, 1979.

Leach, Ronald G. "Finding Time You Never Knew You Had." *Journal of Academic Librarianship* 6, no. 1 (March 1980): 4-8.

Lynch, Beverly P., ed. *Management Strategies for Libraries: A Basic Reader*. New York: Neal-Schuman, 1985.

Maccoby, Michael. *The Leader*. New York: Random House, 1981.

Mackenzie, R. Alex. *The Time Trap*. Toronto: McGraw-Hill Ryerson, 1975.

McCabe, Gerard B. *The Smaller Academic Library: A Management Handbook*. Westport, CT: Greenwood Press, 1988.

McGregor, Douglas. *Leadership and Motivation: Essays*. Cambridge: MIT Press, 1983.

McKenney, James L., and Peter G. W. Keen. "How Managers' Minds Work." *Harvard Business Review* 52 (May-June 1974): 79-90.

McLean, Alan A. *Work Stress*. Reading, MA: Addison-Wesley, 1979.

Maslach, Christina. "Burned Out." *Human Behavior* 5, no. 9 (September 1976): 16-22.

Melendez, Winifred Albizu, and Rafael M. de Guzman. *Burnout: The New Academic Disease*. Association for the Study of Higher Education, Report 83-9. Washington, DC: ASHE, 1983.

Oncken, William. *Managing Management Time*. Englewood Cliffs, NJ: Prentice-Hall, 1984.

Oncken, William, and Donald L. Wass. "Management Time: Who's Got the Monkey?" *Harvard Business Review* 53 (November-December 1974): 75-80.

Pines, Ayala M., and Elliot Aronson. *Burnout: From Tedium to Personal Growth*. New York: Free Press, 1981.

Pines, Ayala M., and D. Dafry. "Occupational Tedium in the Services." *Social Work* 23 (November 1978): 506-8.

Preston, Paul, and Thomas W. Zimmerer. *Management for Supervisors*. Englewood Cliffs, NJ: Prentice-Hall, 1983.

Rosenbach, William E., and Robert L. Taylor. *Leadership: Challenges and Opportunities*. New York: Nichols, 1988.

Ross, Catherine, and Patricia Dewdney. *Communicating Professionally*. New York: Neal-Schuman, 1988.

Schuler, R. S. "Effective Use of Communication to Minimize Employee Stress." *Personnel Administration* 24 (June 1979): 40-44.

Servan-Schreiber, Jean-Louis. *The Art of Time*. Reading, MA: Addison-Wesley, 1988.

Spaniol, LeRoy, and Jennifer J. Caputo. *Professional Burn-Out: A Personal Survival Kit*. Lexington, MA: Human Services Associates, 1979.

Taylor, Harold L. *Making Time Work for You*. Toronto, Canada: Stoddart, 1986.

Van Fleet, James K. *The 22 Biggest Mistakes Managers Make and How to Correct Them*. West Nyack, NY: Parker Publishing, 1973.

Weiss, W. H. *Supervisor's Standard Reference Handbook*. 2d ed. Englewood Cliffs, NJ: Prentice-Hall, 1988.

Welch, I. David. *Beyond Burnout: How to Enjoy Your Job Again When You've Just about Had Enough*. Englewood Cliffs, NJ: Prentice-Hall, 1982.

White, Herbert S. "How to Cope with an Incompetent Supervisor." *Canadian Library Journal* 44 (December 1987): 381.

White, Herbert S. "Oh, Where Have All the Leaders Gone?" *Library Journal* 112 (1 October 1987): 68-69.

White, James. *Successful Supervision*. 2d ed. New York: McGraw-Hill, 1988.

Zaleznik, Abraham. "Managers and Leaders: Are They Different?" *Harvard Business Review* 55 (May-June 1977): 67-78.

Organizing for Student Employment

Even a journey of a thousand miles must begin with one step.
— Chinese proverb

ORGANIZING FUNCTION OF MANAGEMENT

The organizing function of management involves creating a structure for the unit or department in order to provide stability. That structuring requires that tasks be identified and grouped into jobs, and that relationships among the jobs be established in order to accomplish the objectives of the unit or department. In the academic library, the supervisor must know what has to be accomplished and have a well developed plan for getting the work done that includes both job descriptions and a system by which new employees are matched to jobs.

ORGANIZING A SYSTEM FOR STUDENT EMPLOYEE POSITIONS

The recruitment, screening, and hiring of student employees for the library is described in detail in the following chapter. Before any of those activities can take place, however, it is crucial that a foundation for employment exist. On the basis of that foundation, the supervisor should be able to respond positively to the following questions:

1. Do you know what tasks you will have each of the student employees perform?

2. Are the duties of each position documented in the form of approved job descriptions?

3. Are all of the tasks to be performed by each student employee included in the job descriptions? Have you made a decision on whether or not to include the statement "Other Duties as Assigned"?

4. Do the job descriptions contain enough information to describe the job? Are they concise, accurate, and complete?

5. Can the tasks described be evaluated?

6. Have you documented the desired and required experience and qualifications for each position?

7. Do you have positions that pay at different rates? Can you document the reasons for the differences in pay rates?

Job Design

Every job must be specifically created and named before an employee is selected to fill it. Creating jobs is an organizing task called job design—a process by which tasks to be performed are identified, methods for performing the work are delineated, and the relationships of these tasks to other jobs are described.

In determining the work to be accomplished, the job designer groups together a manageable number of similar tasks. In designing a job, it is important to keep the worker in mind. The following characteristics are important to employees:

1. Jobs should provide for a variety of activities.

2. Completion of tasks should produce identifiable final results.

3. Jobs should be seen as significant to other workers.

4. Employees want freedom in deciding the schedule and process for doing their jobs.

5. Workers want their completed tasks to provide feedback on how well the tasks have been performed.

Job Analysis

Because student employees' jobs change frequently, it is necessary to conduct ongoing job analysis—the process of gathering and studying information about existing jobs. Such data can be gathered by observing the worker on the job, interviewing the worker, or having the worker keep a log of tasks performed over a period of time. The job analysis process is designed to answer the following questions about each job to be performed:

1. What are the major duties and responsibilities?

2. What tools and procedures are used?

3. What skills, knowledge, and abilities are required?

4. What are the physical requirements of the job?

5. What are the environmental conditions of the job?

The data gathered from job design and job analysis are used to prepare or revise job descriptions.

PURPOSES OF JOB DESCRIPTIONS

A job description is a statement of the duties and functions to be performed by the persons holding the described job. The purpose of a job description is two-fold:

1. For the student employee or prospective student employee, the job description explains the duties and responsibilities of the position, as well as providing a written statement of what will be evaluated by the supervisor.

2. For the supervisor, the job description provides requirements and desired qualifications used in screening, interviewing, and hiring students for library positions and a method of evaluating the work performed.

The job description serves as the basis for all organizing activities. It provides information on what the personnel in a given unit or department should be doing and assists supervisors in organizing student employees on the basis of experience and expertise. Job descriptions permit the library to establish career ladders for student employees and to establish a system for differentiated pay.

Features of a Good Job Description

A job description is a list of things for which the student employee is responsible. It is a statement of the responsibilities of the job, not a list of activities. The following are some features of a good job description:

1. The job description contains factual statements about the job.

2. The job description is brief but concise.

3. The job description is easy to read and jargon-free.

4. The job description explains the environment in which the work is done.

5. The job description explains the relationship of the responsibilities to the rest of the department.

6. The job description lists the requirements for the position.

7. The job description explains the supervision to be received and given.

8. The job description contains the criteria for evaluation.

Uses of Job Descriptions

The job description can be useful to both the student employee and the supervisor. The information contained in the job description can be used in the following ways:

1. The job description can stimulate supervisory discussion concerning the necessity of each job.

2. The job description can help the supervisor screen and hire student employees.

3. The job description can help the new student employee become familiar with the nature and scope of the job.

4. The job description can be used as part of an orientation program.

5. The job description can serve as the basis for establishing performance standards.

6. The job description can serve as the basis for evaluating and comparing positions within a unit, department, or library.

7. The job description can serve as a communication device between supervisor and employee for discussion of job expectations and objectives.

GUIDELINES FOR PREPARING JOB DESCRIPTIONS

Most of the following suggestions for preparing good job descriptions emphasize brevity and clarity:

1. The sentence structure for job duties and responsibilities should be verb, object, and then explanatory phrase. The implied subject is always the incumbent occupying the job. For example, "responds to audio taping requests in a timely manner."

2. The present tense is to be used throughout.

3. Avoid words which are subject to varying interpretations, e.g., some, great, or occasionally.

4. Avoid proprietary names, e.g., WordPerfect, LOTUS, dBase. These references are subject to change and inclusion in the job description will necessitate change.

5. Avoid sexist terminology. Construct sentences in such a way that gender pronouns are not required.

6. Job descriptions should be kept to no more than two pages.

7. Describe the position as it is now and not as it will exist sometime in the future. (Not all anticipated changes take place.)

Job Descriptions for the Library

Job descriptions can be very useful organizational tools for student employee supervisors if they are carefully written and properly used. If you do not have them, you should. If you are writing or reviewing your student employee job descriptions, make certain the descriptions accurately reflect the jobs. If you are paying at different rates for different jobs, be sure you can justify the differential. Job descriptions must be revised and updated every year or two. Remember, that job descriptions have no value if they cannot be understood or are too general. Inadequate descriptions can lead to serious complaints about inequitable compensation or poor managerial decisions.

STUDENT EMPLOYEE JOB DESCRIPTIONS

Recognizing that libraries require that student employees perform a wide variety of tasks of differing levels of complexity, it is necessary to differentiate between different jobs in terms of the skills, knowledge, and experience required. The University of New Mexico General Library provides a good example of an organized system of job descriptions for student workers. The Student Employment Advisory Committee, composed primarily of staff who supervise student employees in departments, units, and branch libraries, developed a classification system for positions. Student positions are classed in one of three groups, the highest group subdivided into three levels.

Student employees in Group I and Group II positions are referred to as "aides" such as "catalog maintenance aide" or "government publications aide," or by more specific titles such as "shelver," "searcher," "typist," etc. Group I students work under general supervision and Group II students receive limited supervision. See figure 4.1 for Group I job description and figure 4.2 for Group II job description.

Group I Student Positions

Under general supervision, will perform routine duties which may include basic file maintenance; internal record-keeping; shelving; photocopying; word processing; typing; and telephone work. May handle cash, confidential circulation and archival records and information, and serve as a counter or desk attendant. May be required to provide basic referral and informational services.

Must have the ability to understand and execute basic procedural operations of the individual department and to understand the organizational structure of the library.

Group II Student Positions

Under limited supervision, provides specialized support to the individual department. As appropriate, must be acquainted with the duties and responsibilities of Group I. Responsibilities may include automated record-keeping; receiving, sorting, and distribution of library materials; preliminary processing of materials; basic duplicate and bibliographic searching; primary responsibility for on-going library operations (e.g., limited item maintenance, filing, searching, bindery functions, automated applications, basic bibliographic work, etc.) as well as limited reference and information services. May also provide limited support to area supervisors for training and supervision of other student employees.

Must exhibit a capacity for limited decision-making in consultation with area supervisors.

Fig. 4.1. Job Description: Group I Position

UNIVERSITY OF NEW MEXICO GENERAL LIBRARY

LIBRARY BRANCH ___Zimmerman Library___ DEPARTMENT ___Access___

HIRING SUPERVISOR _____ SECTION ___Circulation___

STUDENT POSITION TITLE ___Circulation Library Aide - Shelver I___

GROUP/PAY RATE ___Group I/$4.25___

TYPE OF SUPERVISION FOR THIS POSITION IS: (Check one)

GENERAL __X__ LIMITED _____ MINIMUM _____

DUTIES AND RESPONSIBILITIES: Use the generic job description as a guide.

Student will PERFORM these duties: (e.g., general office duties, telephone work, routine file maintenance, internal record keeping, shelving, specialized tasks as assigned, etc.)

___Shelve, shelfread and shift books. Must work at least two nights until the___
___library closes. Hours: Sunday - Thursday 8:00 a.m. - Midnight and Friday and___
___Saturday 9:00 a.m. - 9:00 p.m.___

REQUIRED ABILITIES: (e.g., computer literacy, good G.P.A., technical and supervisory experience, etc.)

___No special requirements___

PREFERRED SKILLS: (e.g., foreign language, technical or supervisory skills, previous library experience—be specific)

___No special skills___

DATE: _____

Fig. 4.2. Job Description: Group II Position

UNIVERSITY OF NEW MEXICO GENERAL LIBRARY

LIBRARY BRANCH ___Fine Arts Library___ DEPARTMENT ___Sound Room___

HIRING SUPERVISOR _____ SECTION _____

STUDENT POSITION TITLE ___Audio Recording Aide___

GROUP/PAY RATE ___Group II/$4.40___

TYPE OF SUPERVISION FOR THIS POSITION IS: (Check one)

GENERAL _____ LIMITED ___X___ MINIMUM _____

DUTIES AND RESPONSIBILITIES: Use the generic job description as a guide.

Student will PERFORM these duties: (e.g., general office duties, telephone work, routine file maintenance, internal record keeping, shelving, specialized tasks as assigned, etc.)

___Responds to taping requests in a timely manner. Prepares class tapes in the___
___prescribed format. Prepares tapes for performance as described by the requester.___
___Uses tape equipment in a responsible manner and monitors use of taping materials.___
___As necessary, researches items requested for taping.___

REQUIRED ABILITIES: (e.g., computer literacy, good G.P.A., technical and supervisory experience, etc.)

___Ability to work and communicate with faculty and library patrons. Must be able to___
___read music scores and have a knowledge of music history.___

_____

PREFERRED SKILLS: (e.g., foreign language, technical or supervisory skills, previous library experience—be specific)

___Must have previous experience with taping techniques and equipment. Foreign___
___language ability required.___

_____

DATE: _____

Group III Student Positions

Group III positions are subdivided into three levels: entry-level, mid-level, and high-level. Group III student employees are referred to as "assistants," such as "document delivery assistant" or "serials acquisitions assistant," or by specific titles, such as "counter attendant," "weekend supervisor," or "security supervisor." Group III students work under minimal supervision.

Entry-level Group III student employees perform basic operations, technical, security, and/or limited supervisory tasks. Level II Group III student employees perform back-up supervisory duties and/or specialized tasks requiring technical skills. The highest-level Group III students are supervisors of other students, may perform highly specialized tasks, and may substitute for library staff. Sample generic and specific job descriptions for each of the three levels of Group III appear in figures 4.3 and 4.4.

Generic Group III Description

Under minimum supervision, performs specialized instructional, operational, technical, supervisory, and/or security tasks. As appropriate, must be acquainted with duties and responsibilities of Group I and II. Has considerable latitude on a multitude of tasks as well as primary responsibility for independent/complex technical, reference, and/or information services. Is involved in the training, monitoring, and supervision of other student employees. May handle confidential records and information. May act as a liaison with other student employees, students, staff, faculty, and the general public. In the absence of regular staff may be responsible for staffing service areas and/or facilities. May provide input for establishing departmental priorities and implement related policies. May require knowledge of a second language.

Fig. 4.3. Job Description: Group III, Level II Position

UNIVERSITY OF NEW MEXICO GENERAL LIBRARY

LIBRARY BRANCH ___Parish Library___ DEPARTMENT _____

HIRING SUPERVISOR _____ SECTION _____

STUDENT POSITION TITLE ___Parish Library Student Supervisor___

GROUP/PAY RATE ___Group III, Level II/$4.90___

TYPE OF SUPERVISION FOR THIS POSITION IS: (Check one)

GENERAL _____ LIMITED _____ MINIMUM __X__

DUTIES AND RESPONSIBILITIES: Use the generic job description as a guide.

Student will PERFORM these duties: (e.g., general office duties, telephone work, routine file maintenance, internal record keeping, shelving, specialized tasks as assigned, etc.)

Will be involved in training, monitoring, and supervision of other student employees in areas of looseleaf filing, shelving, patron registration, etc; will handle confidential records and information; will liaise with student workers, faculty, staff, and general public; will provide input for establishing departmental priorities; other duties as assigned.

REQUIRED ABILITIES: (e.g., computer literacy, good G.P.A., technical and supervisory experience, etc.)

Must be familiar with Group I and Group II duties and responsibilities and exhibit ability to perform specialized technical, supervisory, operational, and instructional tasks. Must work at least one evening or weekend shift per week.

PREFERRED SKILLS: (e.g., foreign language, technical or supervisory skills, previous library experience—be specific)

Must have previous supervisory experience, good communication and typing skills.

DATE: _____

Fig. 4.4. Job Description: Group III, Level III Position

UNIVERSITY OF NEW MEXICO GENERAL LIBRARY

LIBRARY BRANCH ___Zimmerman Library___ DEPARTMENT __Mono. Cataloging__

HIRING SUPERVISOR _____ SECTION __General Cataloging__

STUDENT POSITION TITLE ___Cataloging Assistant II_____

GROUP/PAY RATE ___Group III, Level III/$5.60_____

TYPE OF SUPERVISION FOR THIS POSITION IS: (Check one)

GENERAL _____ LIMITED _____ MINIMUM __X___

DUTIES AND RESPONSIBILITIES: Use the generic job description as a guide.

Student will PERFORM these duties: (e.g., general office duties, telephone work, routine file maintenance, internal record keeping, shelving, specialized tasks as assigned, etc.)

Compare entries on Library of Congress authority records and entries in public catalog. Verify names/series in OCLC authority files. Make corrections made by cataloger to CIP records and after sufficient revision, produce the cataloging record.

REQUIRED ABILITIES: (e.g., computer literacy, good G.P.A., technical and supervisory experience, etc.)

Ability to handle detailed work. Need for accuracy and efficiency. Computer literacy, good typing skills. Must be hard worker and meticulous. Ability to work in a team environment.

PREFERRED SKILLS: (e.g., foreign language, technical or supervisory skills, previous library experience — be specific)

Reading knowledge of one or more modern European language other than Spanish/Portuguese. (See Ibero Cataloging listings for positions requiring Spanish/Portuguese language skills.)

DATE: _____

DIFFERENTIATED PAY

The compensation system for student employee is well established at most academic institutions. These guidelines will allow you only so much flexibility in setting your student employee pay rates. It is advisable, however, to examine also your library's internal compensation for student workers to assure that those rates you assign are fair. A fair compensation system should be logical, consistent, equitable, and competitive.

To be fair to all student employees, it is necessary to pay at different rates for different work. A compensation system which pays beginning searchers in acquisitions the same wage is fair. A system which pays the same wage to student employees who reshelve books and to those students who supervise circulation operations during late evening and weekend hours is illogical, inequitable, and inconsistent. There are good reasons to compensate different students for different work if the level of work differs.

One approach is to establish several groups of positions based on their levels of responsibility and difficulty. The system utilized by the University of New Mexico General Library is a good example of a differentiated pay system. Working closely with the student employment office, the General Library's Student Employment Advisory Committee developed the payrate structure in use at the University of New Mexico. The system was developed to improve the General Library's ability to fairly compensate and retain students who were leaving the library for better pay somewhere else on campus (see tables 4.1 and 4.2).

The steps in this schedule can be used for longevity increases to student employees. All Group II students, for example, would start work at $4.40 per hour and, after 500 hours (or two semesters) experience, be given an increase to $4.55 per hour. Longevity increases permit the library to reward students for staying in their positions. Of course, they could also be promoted to higher-level positions.

Table 4.1.

Pay Rate Structures for Student Employees

GROUP	STEP I (START RATE)	STEP II	STEP III	STEP IV
I	Base	Base + $.15	Base + $.30	Base + $.45
II	Base + $.15	Base + $.30	Base + $.45	Base + $.60
III				
Level 1	Base + $.30	Base + $.45	Base + $.60	Base + $.75
Level 2	Base + $.65	Base + $.80	Base + $.95	Base + $1.10
Level 3	Base + $.90	Base + $1.20	Base + $1.35	Base + $1.50

Table 4.2.

Sample Pay Rates

Where the Base is a minimum wage of $4.25 (effective April 1, 1991) the following schedule would apply:

GROUP	STEP I (START RATE)	STEP II	STEP III	STEP IV
I	$4.25	$4.40	$4.55	$4.70
II	$4.40	$4.55	$4.70	$4.85
III				
Level 1	$4.55	$4.70	$4.85	$5.00
Level 2	$4.90	$5.05	$5.20	$5.35
Level 3	$5.15	$5.45	$5.60	$5.75

STUDENT EMPLOYEE ALLOTMENTS

Methods of allocation of student work-study funds differ widely among academic libraries. The two primary means of setting allocations are (1) allocations of hours or dollars set by student employment offices for libraries, or (2) libraries own budgets for work-study students coordinated with the students' awards.

The student with a work-study award typically receives notification of the amount of the award and the period in which that amount can be earned, i.e., academic year, summer session, etc. The number of hours a work-study student can work, therefore, depends on the pay rate for the position. It is important for the student employee supervisor to know the total number of hours a student may work based on the award and pay rate. If there are twenty pay periods (bi-weekly payroll) in the fall and spring semesters, does the work-study student you are hiring have an award large enough to get through the entire academic year before exhausting the award? Will you be faced with having the student terminated because the award has run out, leaving desks unattended and hours not covered in your department's schedule? Constructing a schedule like table 4.3 is useful in determining how many hours per pay period may be worked in order for a work-study student to be able to work all year and earn the total award.

Table 4.3.

Number of Hours That Can Be Worked In Twenty Pay Periods
Note: Divide hours by two to determine hours per week.

AWARD	HOURLY PAY RATES									
	$4.25	$4.40	$4.55	$4.70	$4.85	$5.00	$5.20	$5.35	$5.60	$5.75
$1000	11.8	11.4	11.0	10.6	10.3	10.0	9.6	9.3	8.9	8.7
$1100	12.9	12.5	12.1	11.7	11.3	11.0	10.6	10.3	9.8	9.6
$1200	14.1	13.6	13.2	12.8	12.4	12.0	11.5	11.2	10.7	10.4
$1300	15.3	14.8	14.3	13.8	13.4	13.0	12.5	12.1	11.6	11.3
$1400	16.5	15.9	15.4	14.9	14.4	14.0	13.5	13.1	12.5	12.2
$1500	17.6	17.0	16.5	16.0	15.5	15.0	14.4	14.0	13.4	13.0
$1600	18.8	18.2	17.6	17.0	16.5	16.0	15.4	15.0	14.3	13.9
$1700	20.0	19.3	18.7	18.1	17.5	17.0	16.3	15.9	15.2	14.8
$1800	21.2	20.5	19.8	19.1	18.6	18.0	17.3	16.8	16.1	15.7
$1900	22.4	21.6	20.9	20.2	19.6	19.0	18.3	17.8	17.0	16.5
$2000	23.5	22.7	22.0	21.3	20.6	20.0	19.2	18.7	17.9	17.4
$2100	24.7	23.9	23.1	22.3	21.6	21.0	20.2	19.6	18.8	18.3
$2200	25.9	25.0	24.2	23.4	22.7	22.0	21.2	20.6	19.6	19.1
$2300	27.1	26.1	25.3	24.5	23.7	23.0	22.1	21.5	20.5	20.0
$2400	28.2	27.3	26.4	25.5	24.7	24.0	23.1	22.4	21.4	20.9
$2500	29.4	28.4	27.5	26.6	25.8	25.0	24.0	23.4	22.3	21.7
$2600	30.6	29.5	28.6	27.7	26.8	26.0	25.0	24.3	23.2	22.6
$2700	31.8	30.7	29.7	28.7	27.8	27.0	26.0	25.2	24.1	23.5
$2800	32.9	31.8	30.8	29.8	28.9	28.0	26.9	26.2	25.0	24.3
$2900	34.1	33.0	31.9	30.9	29.9	29.0	27.9	27.1	25.9	25.4
$3000	35.3	34.1	33.0	31.9	30.9	30.0	28.8	28.0	26.8	26.1
$3100	36.5	35.2	34.1	33.0	32.0	31.0	29.8	29.0	27.7	27.0
$3200	37.6	36.4	35.2	34.0	33.0	32.0	30.8	29.9	28.6	27.8
$3300	38.8	37.5	36.3	35.1	34.0	33.0	31.7	30.8	29.5	28.7
$3400	40.0	38.6	37.4	36.2	35.1	34.0	32.7	31.8	30.4	29.6
$3500	41.2	39.8	38.5	37.2	36.1	35.0	33.7	32.7	31.3	30.4
$3600	42.4	40.9	39.6	38.3	37.1	36.0	34.6	33.6	32.1	31.3
$3700	43.5	42.0	40.7	39.4	38.1	37.0	35.6	34.6	33.0	32.2
$3800	44.7	43.2	41.8	40.4	39.2	38.0	36.5	35.5	33.9	33.0
$3900	45.9	44.3	42.9	41.5	40.2	39.0	37.5	36.4	34.8	33.9
$4000	47.1	45.5	44.0	42.6	41.2	40.0	38.5	37.4	35.7	34.8
$4100	48.2	46.6	45.1	43.6	42.3	41.0	39.4	38.3	36.6	35.7
$4200	49.4	47.7	46.2	44.7	43.3	42.0	40.4	39.3	37.5	36.5
$4300	50.6	48.9	47.3	45.7	44.3	43.0	41.3	40.2	38.4	37.4
$4400	51.8	50.0	48.4	46.8	45.4	44.0	42.3	41.1	39.3	38.3
$4500	52.9	51.1	49.5	47.9	46.4	45.0	43.3	42.1	40.2	39.1
$4600	54.1	52.3	50.5	48.9	47.4	46.0	44.2	43.0	41.1	40.0
$4700	55.3	53.4	51.6	50.0	48.5	47.0	45.2	43.9	42.0	40.9
$4800	56.5	54.5	52.7	51.1	49.5	48.0	46.2	44.9	42.9	41.7
$4900	57.6	55.7	53.8	52.1	50.5	49.0	47.1	45.8	43.8	42.6
$5000	58.8	56.8	54.9	53.2	51.5	50.0	48.1	46.7	44.6	43.5

WORK-STUDY ELIGIBILITY

Just when you have established the work limits of your work-study student employees, their eligibility changes because of other grants, new information, or the courseloads. For example, a student completes both an application for a grant and the documentation required for work-study. After the student's need (work-study eligibility) is determined, you hire the student to work eighteen hours per week. Three months later a grant is awarded and the student's work-study award is reduced. You find that, in order to keep the student for the entire year, weekly hours must be reduced.

In another instance, a student may be awarded a small amount and, after several months, notice is received that the award has been increased far beyond the student's ability to earn in the time remaining. If it is any consolation, many students are unable to earn the amount of their awards. Student employment offices sometimes can redistribute work-study funds in that event.

The student employment office at the University of New Mexico uses a special form to notify students and their employers of remaining work-study eligibility when it appears that, at the present rate of expenditure, funds will lapse (see figure 4.5).

Fig. 4.5. Work-Study Eligibility Form

REMAINING WORK-STUDY ELIGIBILITY

FINANCIAL AID OFFICE   THE UNIVERSITY OF NEW MEXICO

DATE _____

TO: _____(STUDENT NAME)_____

DEPARTMENT _____   SSN: _____

FROM: Work-study Office

SUBJECT: Work-study Eligibility for Award Period: _____

Our records indicate that you (are approaching)/(have met) your allotted Work-study Award (Need) and must terminate by __(DATE)__ . *NOTE:* Calculations are based on 20/hrs. wk. This award was based on the information which you supplied on your Financial Aid Application. If your financial status has changed, it may be possible to raise your award.

If you have any questions or would like to provide additional information that might change your current status, please contact the Financial Aid Office.

Your Award: $_____

Your Balance: $_____ / _____ hours, as of __(DATE)_____

Distribution: Copies to Student file, Department, and Student

JOB MATCHING

Job matching is simply the process of bringing together the work and the people in such a way that the requirements of the work are matched with the skills and abilities of the persons available to do that work. Some student employees are extremely good at detailed work such as those tasks required in academic library cataloging and acquisitions departments. Others are extremely well organized and can coordinate the activities of other student workers, while still others prefer the routine or physical work of shelving, while others like the challenges and diversity of a service desk. No one is good at everything but most people have one or two skills or abilities which are higher than average. If the right student is matched with the right job, the library will function more efficiently and each student employee will have an opportunity to excel.

Student Employment Application Form

In order to effectively match student applicants to student jobs, it is necessary to have an application form which solicits the kind of information you need to screen applicants. The following form is in use at the University of New Mexico General Library (see figure 4.6).

Fig. 4.6. Student Employment Application

UNM GENERAL LIBRARY STUDENT EMPLOYMENT APPLICATION

Application for work-study and non-work-study student positions in the UNM main campus libraries: Zimmerman Library, Centennial Science and Engineering Library, Parish Business Library, Fine Arts Library, and Tireman Learning Materials Library. Applications will remain on file for one semester only.

PLEASE PRINT

DATE: _____

_____
Last Name   First Name   M.I.   Social Security No.

Current   Address _____

Current Phone No. _____ Best time to call weekdays _____

Person to notify in case of emergency _____

Phone No. _____

Academic Major _____ Minor _____

Presently enrolled for _____ semester hours for the

Fall/Spring/Summer (circle one) semester, 19____. Anticipated graduation date _____

Please list any preferences as to which library/libraries and/or position(s) you would like to be considered for:
_____

(Please consult the UNM General Library Student Job Descriptions for the requirements for currently open positions.)

List the times when you will be available for work. Notify this office of any changes in your schedule *prior* to hiring. Thank you.

Mondays _____

Tuesdays _____

Wednesdays _____

Thursdays _____

Fridays _____

Saturdays _____

Sundays _____

For Library Personnel Office Use only

Work-study qualified? _____

Amount of award _____

Verified by _____

ORGANIZING STUDENT EMPLOYEES

The organizing function is extremely important to supervision. You must know what you expect of the employees, just as they must know what you expect of them. The job description provides the structure for positions and the pay system provides for equitable compensation for work accomplished. It is important to be continually reevaluating the tasks performed and the work distribution and to keep job descriptions up to date. Changes in the work may necessitate a change in level and pay rate.

BIBLIOGRAPHY

American Library Association. Ad Hoc Committee to Revise the ALA Personnel Organization and Procedures Manuals. *The Personnel Manual*. Chicago: ALA, 1977.

Armstrong, Michael. *A Handbook of Personnel Management Practice*. 3d ed. New York: Nichols, 1986.

Cargill, Jennifer, and Gisela M. Webb. *Managing Libraries in Transition*. Phoenix, AZ: Oryx, 1987.

Creth, Sheila. "Personnel Planning, Job Analysis, and Job Evaluation with Special Reference to Academic Libraries." *Advances in Librarianship* 12 (1982): 47-97.

Creth, Sheila, and Frederick Duda. *Personnel Administration in Libraries*. 2d ed. New York: Neal-Schuman, 1989.

Drucker, Peter. "Effective Structures for the Management of Human Resources." *Australian Academic and Research Libraries* 16 (June 1985): 88-96.

Famularo, Joseph J., ed. *Handbook of Human Resources Administration*. 2d ed. New York: McGraw-Hill, 1986.

Gael, S. *Job Analysis: A Guide to Assessing Work Activities*. San Francisco, CA: Jossey-Bass, 1983.

Hall, H. Palmer, Jr. "Personnel Administration in the College Library." In *College Librarianship*, edited by William Miller and D. Stephen Rockwood, 79-86. Metuchen, NJ: Scarecrow Press, 1981.

Handbook of Wage and Salary Administration. 2d ed. New York: McGraw-Hill, 1984.

Hill, Virginia S., and Tom G. Watson. "Job Analysis: Process and Benefits." *Advances in Library Administration and Organization* 3 (1984): 209-19.

Howard, Helen. "Organization Theory and Its Applications to Research in Librarianship." *Library Trends* 32, no. 4 (Spring 1984): 477-93.

Job Analysis in ARL Libraries. Washington, DC: ARL/OMS, 1987.

Kanter, Rosabeth M. "From Status to Contribution: Some Organizational Implications of the Changing Basis for Pay." *Personnel* 64, no. 1 (January 1987): 12-37.

Klingner, Donald E. "When the Traditional Job Description is Not Enough." *Personnel Journal* 58 (April 1979): 243-48.

Lawrence, Paul R., and Jay W. Lorsch. *Organization and Environment: Managing Differentiation and Integration*. Rev. ed. Boston: Harvard Business School Press, 1986.

Lewis, David W. "An Organizational Paradigm for Effective Academic Libraries." *College & Research Libraries* 47, no. 4 (July 1986): 337-53.

Martell, Charles R. *The Client-Centered Academic Library: An Organizational Model*. Westport, CT: Greenwood Press, 1983.

Martin, Lowell A. *Organizational Structure of Libraries*. Library Administration Series, 5. Metuchen, NJ: Scarecrow Press, 1984.

McCabe, Gerard B. "Contemporary Trends in Academic Library Administration and Organization." In *Issues in Academic Librarianship: Views and Case Studies for the 1980's and 1990's*, edited by Peter Spyers-Duran and Thomas W. Mann, Jr., 21-35. Westport, CT: Greenwood, 1985.

McCormick, Ernest J. *Job Analysis: Methods and Applications*. New York: AMACOM, 1979.

Metcalf, Keyes D. "Departmental Organization in Libraries." In *Current Issues in Library Administration*, edited by Carlton B. Joeckel, 90-110. Chicago: University of Chicago Press, 1939.

Mussman, K. "Socio-technical Theory and Job Design in Libraries." *College & Research Libraries* 39 (January 1978): 20-28.

Personnel Classification Schemes. Washington, DC: ARL/OMS, 1978.

Personnel Policies in Libraries, edited by Nancy Patton Van Zant. New York: Neal-Schuman Publishers, 1980.

Ricking, Myrl, and Robert E. Booth. *Personnel Utilization in Libraries: A Systems Approach*. Chicago: ALA, 1974.

Treiman, Donald J., and H. I. Hartmann. *Women, Work, and Wages—Equal Pay for Jobs of Equal Value*. Washington, DC: National Academy Press, 1981.

Tunley, Malcolm. *Library Structures and Staffing Systems*. London: Library Association, 1979.

Van Horn, Charles W. G. "The Hay Guide—Chart Profile Method." In *Handbook of Wage and Salary Administration*, edited by Milton L. Rock, 286-97. New York: McGraw-Hill, 1972.

Van Rijn, Paul. *Job Analysis for Selection: An Overview*. Washington, DC: U.S. Office of Personnel Management, Staffing Services Group, 1979.

Hiring Student Employees

If you suspect a man, don't employ him; if you employ a man, don't suspect him.

—Chinese Proverb

HIRING AND FIRING

Probably the single most important part of your job as a supervisor is hiring the right persons for the work. Any supervisor who has fired student employees realizes how important it is to hire the right people and train them well in the first place.

In this chapter, we will discuss how to effectively recruit, screen, and interview student employees. Suggestions on handling corrective discipline and termination are offered in chapter 12.

REFERRAL OF STUDENT WORKERS

The referral of student workers to the library has been improved in recent years. Thankfully, gone are the days when this exchange was common in university financial aid offices:

Student Employment Counselor: Do you have any preference as to where you'd like to work?

Student: No.

Counselor: Do you have any special skills?

Student: No, but I am carrying 17 hours.

Counselor: Oh, O.K., Go to the library. They don't need special skills and they let you study.

Student: Where's the library?

Today, you are more likely to hear a conversation such as this in the student financial aid office:

Student Employment Counselor: Do you have any preference as to where you'd like to work?

Student: Not really.

Counselor: Do you know any languages?

Student: Besides English?

Counselor: Spanish, German, French?

Student: Yes, I am fluent in German and can read Spanish.

Counselor: How about computer keyboard skills?

Student: Yes, I'm pretty good at that.

Counselor: Good, I have a request from the acquisitions department in the library for someone who can read German and can learn their automated system. It pays $4.40 to start. Interested?

Student: Yes, where's the library?

Well, even though a slight improvement in the college-wide orientation program is obviously still needed, an appropriately skilled student can now be interviewed by a hiring supervisor in the library.

RECRUITING STUDENT WORKERS

The recruitment and screening of student employees for library employment varies greatly from one university to another. Recruitment depends on the available pool of student workers, their funding sources, and the way prospective employees get to the library's hiring supervisors. On some campuses, the library has a part-time employee budget which does not depend on work-study students; it may even allow the employment of other than current students. Most campuses rely very heavily on work-study funding, or have a combination of work-study and other part-time employee budgets.

One aspect of recruitment involves keeping the student employment office up to date on the skills needed by prospective library student employees. Work in the library can be made quite attractive to students looking for employment. Night and weekend hours are a selling point as are the opportunities for students to set their own schedules in some jobs. Some students are attracted by the prospect of learning more about the library which they hope will help them in their coursework. Capitalize on that interest if you can.

Recruitment for library work can be quite extensive. Some libraries take part in job fairs on campus, advertise in the student newspaper, post job openings around campus, post "help wanted" signs on bulletin boards, or ask present student employees to recruit their friends. The hope is that libraries are such attractive places to work, that you will have many more applications for jobs than you have openings.

SCREENING PROSPECTIVE STUDENT WORKERS

The initial screening process begins when a student completes an application. In some universities, the student employment office screens students for jobs throughout campus. Sometimes, students who seem to have no usable skills may be sent to the library, thus making the library's hiring process more difficult. At other universities, the student employment office carefully reviews the library's needs and refers highly skilled students to the library. Many libraries also have their own personnel office, which screen student employee applicants for departments of the library.

It is essential that the hiring supervisors provide those who screen applicants with job descriptions which describe not only the work but also the skills required to do that work. The screening process is nothing more than a comparison of applications with the skills required for the job available. Effective screening will greatly improve the hiring supervisor's ability to hire qualified people.

Preparing for the Interview

It is desirable for students who have gone through the screening process and met the qualifications for the job to be asked to meet the hiring supervisor. The best place for students to meet the interviewer is in the dean's or director's office area, branch library office, the personnel office, conference room, etc.

The supervisor as well as the applicant must prepare for the interview. The following are suggestions for preparing for the interview:

1. Review the job description for the position as well as the job application.

2. Set the stage for the interview by planning to conduct the interview in a comfortable private office or conference room. Keep in mind that the interview is a two-way street: you want to give the interviewee a good first impression of the library just as much as the interviewee wants to make a good impression on you.

3. Be sure to set aside enough time for the interview; and make certain that there will be no interruptions.

4. Review the application. Is it filled out completely, with no blanks? Is it legible? Does it present a sequential outline of the applicant's work history and education? Does it tell why the applicant left each job?

5. Don't include questions that are answered on the application.

6. Prepare most of the questions which will be asked in the interview. These should focus on the applicant's employment history, education, schedule, outside activities and interests, and strengths and weaknesses. (A list of possible questions, as well as questions which are inappropriate, is presented later in this chapter.)

7. Make certain you are prepared to answer any questions the interviewee has about the job, the department, and the library. Know ahead of time how soon you will make a decision about hiring for the position.

Interview Types

There are three different types of interviews: the directed interview, the nondirected interview, and the stress interview.

The directed interview usually involves use of a predetermined set of questions which are asked of the interviewee. The primary advantage is that of thoroughness and consistency. All interviewees are asked the same questions, usually in the same order. The disadvantages of directed interviews are that interviewers sometimes get caught up in asking questions without listening to the answers, and structured interviews tend to cause anxiety in applicants.

The nondirected interview is usually unstructured. The purpose is to allow the interviewees to talk more freely. The interviewer knows what information needs to be obtained and does so by skilled questioning. The use of the nondirected approach by skilled interviewers can be very effective, but much less so for unskilled interviewers.

The stress interview technique is seldom used. It relies on a series of tough, unexpected, anxiety-producing questions designed to place the interviewee in an uncomfortable situation and force instinctive reactions. Its purpose is to determine how an individual reacts under pressure. It is a technique sometimes used to screen people for higher-level management positions.

Probably the best approach is a combination of the directed and nondirected interview techniques. Using this approach, the interviewer uses a broad list of prepared questions, asking them in no particular sequence. The interviewee is given latitude in responding to questions, some of which are not scripted. The interviewee feels more at ease and yet it provides the interviewer with some structure. It is still necessary to ask essentially the same questions of all applicants for a position.

Conducting the Interview

The following are suggestions on how to conduct the interview meeting:

1. Begin the interview by putting the interviewee at ease: spend a few moments in small talk but be careful to avoid asking questions which might be considered discriminatory.

2. Let the applicant know the purpose of the interview—to determine if there is a fit between the applicant and the position opening in the department.

3. Keep in mind that the interview should provide you with information about the applicant that may not be completely covered in the application and provide the applicant with more complete information about the job.

4. Listen to the interviewee's answers: one of the most common mistakes made by interviewers is to concentrate so much on the questions they ask, that they forget to listen to the answers.

5. Maintain control of the interview by establishing the direction of the questions and not allow the interviewee to wander off in other directions.

6. Never help an interviewee by suggesting the answer to a question but don't use brutal interrogation techniques either.

7. Keep the interview friendly and comfortable.

8. Take notes during the interview to refresh your memory when making a decision. Some people claim that taking notes disrupts the interview and that the interviewer should develop the ability to remember responses and make notes after the interview.

9. End the interview when you are sure that you have gotten the information you need to make a decision and when all of the interviewee's questions have been answered.

10. Close the interview by thanking the interviewee and providing information regarding when a decision will be made. If you are able to hire on the spot, discuss schedules, pay rates, starting date, etc.

11. Check references. This step is sometimes left out when hiring student employees, but it is good practice nonetheless.

Sample Questions Which May Be Asked

The following are suggested questions which may be asked in the interview. Job-specific questions should be prepared for specific positions in the library.

WORK EXPERIENCE:

Describe your work experience at your last job.

What was the most fulfilling aspect of the job? What was the least fulfilling?

Why did you leave?

What skills did you develop in your previous job?

EDUCATION:

What is your major? (This will probably be on the application.)

Why did you select that major?

What is your minor?

What courses do you prefer? Why?

What courses do you dislike? Why?

What courses do you find most and least valuable? Why?

What extra curricular activities are you involved in?

What are your short-term goals?

What are your long-term goals?

LEADERSHIP, INITIATIVE, AND PERSISTENCE:

How do you feel about making decisions? Why?

How do you feel about supervising others? Why?

What is your idea of challenging work?

How do you feel about working in an unstructured environment?

How do you feel about increasing your job responsibilities?

How do you feel about working in a high-pressure area?

How would you react if given an unpleasant task?

LIBRARY WORK AND SPECIFIC:

Tell me about experience you have had with computers.

Tell me about experience you have had in working with customers or patrons.

Describe your experience in using libraries.

What times during the day and week are you available to work?

Types of Questions to Be Avoided

To gain the type of information you need from an interviewee, you should avoid the following types of questions:

1. Questions which can be answered with a "Yes" or "No" should be changed to open-ended questions which allow the interviewee to demonstrate communication skills.

2. Leading questions which telegraph the expected answers are of little use. For example, "Would you say that you have good interpersonal skills?" definitely calls for a positive response.

3. Obvious questions are to be avoided. "So you graduated from Midvale High School?" is a question which is answered on the application and a waste of time. Ask only questions which the application does not answer.

4. Questions that are not related to the job waste time and accomplish nothing. "Do you think the Chicago Cubs will win the pennant?" has nothing to do with the job, even if you are a Cubs fan.

5. Questions that may be considered discriminatory are both ill-advised and likely to be illegal. (Examples are given later in this chapter.)

LEGAL IMPLICATIONS OF EMPLOYMENT DECISIONS

All employment decisions, including hiring, promotion, transfer, and termination, must be made on the qualifications of the individual, not on race, creed, sex, age, sexual preference, national origin, or handicap. In order to avoid charges of discrimination in employment, supervisors must be aware of laws that protect certain groups from discriminatory practices. At the federal level, there are laws governing equal employment opportunity and protection of employees:

1. Title VII of the 1964 Civil Rights Act, as amended, outlaws discrimination in employment decisions which is based on race, color, religion, sex, or national origin.

2. The Equal Pay Act of 1963 makes it unlawful to pay females less than males who do similar work.

3. The Age Discrimination in Employment Act of 1967, as amended, outlaws discrimination on the basis of age. It specifically protects all persons over the age of 40.

4. The Rehabilitation Act of 1973, enforced by the Americans with Disabilities Act of 1990, prohibits discrimination in employment on the basis of a mental or physical handicap.

5. The Vietnam Era Veterans' Readjustment Assistance Act of 1974 requires federal contractors and subcontractors to take affirmative action to employ, and advance in employment, qualified disabled veterans and veterans of the Vietnam era.

6. The Pregnancy Discrimination Act of 1978 protects against discrimination in employment because of pregnancy. Pregnancy must be treated as any other temporary disability; an employer may not refuse to hire a qualified female because she is pregnant.

7. The Immigration Reform and Control Act of 1986 (IRCA) makes it illegal to recruit, hire, or refer for hire any unauthorized alien; requires documentation of identity and eligiblity of worker to work in the United States; and prohibits discrimination on the basis of national origin or citizenship status.

8. The Employee Polygraph Protection Act of 1988 protects employees from wrongfully being subjected to polygraphs in pre-hiring or employment.

The Supervisor's Responsibility

As a supervisor, it is your responsibility to assure that discrimination does not occur in hiring or employment. It is also your responsibility to report any instances of discrimination to the appropriate person. Even the perception of discrimination based on race, creed, sex, age, sexual preference, national origin, or handicap in the library must be avoided at all costs. Although it is not expected that supervisors will become experts in employment law, it is the responsibility of supervisors to be familiar with applicable laws.

Student employees who believe that they are victims of employment discrimination have the right to avail themselves of the library's grievance process. The student may also file a complaint with the local or regional office of the Equal Employment Opportunity Commission. If you are named in a discrimination grievance, be prepared to present documentary evidence that will clearly show nondiscriminatory intent or action. The grievance procedure is described in chapter 11.

Nondiscriminatory Interviewing

Nondiscriminatory interviewing simply means asking only questions which are job related. Supervisors must be aware of the types of questions which cannot be asked in the interview. The following are some guidelines:

1. Do not discuss age.

2. Do not ask female applicants about child care arrangements.

3. Do not ask about religious preferences.

4. Do not ask about the employment of a spouse.

5. Do not discuss matters relating to the applicant's race, ancestry, or national origin.

6. Do not attempt jokes related to race, national origin, religion, or sex.

7. Do not ask about military discharge or rank at time of discharge.

8. Do not ask a handicapped applicant about the severity of the handicap.

9. Do not ask questions about civil rights litigation with former employers.

10. Do not ask questions about arrests: a person is not judged guilty simply because of an arrest.

11. Do not discuss political affiliation or membership.

REFERENCE CHECKS

You have a right to collect information about prospective student employees regarding past employment, including duration, absences, punctuality, skills, and reasons for leaving previous positions. In most instances, the references provided by the employee will confirm your impressions of the applicant. There are times, however, when contacting those references will help you choose between two applicants, or even avoid a hiring mistake. When you contact references supplied by the applicants, you must ask the same questions about all applicants for a particular position and you must have a good business reason for seeking the information. The following are suggested areas for reference check questions:

1. Relationship to the applicant

2. Length of time the reference has known the applicant

3. Length of time the reference has supervised the applicant

4. Applicant's employment dates

5. First and last position held

6. Starting and leaving salary

7. Duties and responsibilities

8. Quality of work

9. Quantity of work

10. Attendance and punctuality

11. Cooperation with other employees and supervisors

12. General work habits

13. Amount of time required to learn new jobs

14. Willingness to accept responsibility

15. Reason for leaving position

16. Eligibility for rehire

COMMUNICATING THE HIRING DECISION

The final step in hiring is the offer. Communicating your decision to applicants is important and should not be unnecessarily delayed. Your choice for the position may well find another job if you do not act within a reasonable time period, and it is unfair to all applicants to be kept waiting.

Care should be exercised in communicating either acceptance or rejection. It is always easier to give someone good news than bad news. Whether you communicate the bad news in person, by phone, or in writing, you may consider beginning with, "we have a very strong pool of applicants for this position" and mention this individual's strengths. It is possible to reject people in a kind way, without adding to the disappointment unsuccessful applicants already feel. Too often, hiring supervisors forget to consider the feelings of the persons being rejected. Consider how you would like to be informed that you were not the successful applicant.

INTERVIEW SITUATIONS

The hiring interview is only one of the many face-to-face situations a supervisor experiences. Interviewing isn't just talking with someone; it is a process with a purpose and structure. Interviews are also used in performance appraisal, termination, and some problem-solving situations. Interviewing, if done well, is a very important skill to possess. The resources provided in the bibliography will help you develop hiring skills.

BIBLIOGRAPHY

American Library Association, Office for Library Personnel Resources. *Hiring Library Staff*. Chicago: ALA, 1986.

American Society for Personnel Administration. *Reference Checking Handbook*. Alexandria, VA: ASPA, 1985.

Arthur, Diane. *Recruiting, Interviewing, Selecting and Orienting New Employees*. Saranac Lake, NY: AMACOM, 1986.

Arvey, Richard D., and Robert Faley. *Fairness in Selecting Employees*. 2d ed. Reading, MA: Addison-Wesley, 1988.

Association of Research Libraries, Office of Management Studies. *Recruitment and Selection Practices*. Washington, DC: ARL, 1981.

Biggs, Debra R., and Cheryl T. Naslund. "Proactive Interviewing." *College & Research Libraries News* 48, no. 1 (January 1987): 13-17.

Bingham, Walter Van Dyke, and Bruce Victor Moore. *How to Interview*. 4th rev. ed. New York: Harper, 1959.

Black, James Menzies. *How to Get Results from Interviewing*. New York: McGraw-Hill, 1970.

Bowes, Lee. *No One Need Apply: Getting and Keeping the Best Workers*. Boston: Harvard Business School Press, 1987.

Creth, Sheila. "Conducting an Effective Employment Interview." *Journal of Academic Librarianship* 4, no. 5 (November 1978): 356-60.

Creth, Sheila. *Interviewing Skills: Finding the Right Person for the Job*. Chicago: ACRL, 1984.

Daughtrey, Anne Scott, and Betty Roper Ricks. *Contemporary Supervision: Managing People and Technology*. New York: McGraw-Hill, 1988.

Dewey, Barbara I. *Library Jobs: How to Fill Them, How to Find Them*. Phoenix, AZ: Oryx, 1987.

Evered, James F. *Shirt-Sleeves Management*. New York: AMACOM, 1981.

Fallon, William K., ed. *Leadership on the Job: Guides to Good Supervision*. New York: AMACOM, 1981.

Farrell, Barry M. "The Art and Science of Employment Interviews." *Personnel Journal* 65 (May 1986): 91-94.

Flippo, Edwin B. *Principles of Personnel Management*. 4th ed. New York: McGraw-Hill, 1976.

Gorden, Raymond L. *Interviewing: Strategy, Techniques and Tactics*. 4th ed. Homewood, IL: Dorsey, 1987.

Guy, Jeniece. "Equal Employment Opportunity and the College Library Administrator." In *College Librarianship*, edited by William Miller and D. Stephen Rockwood, 87-96. Metuchen, NJ: Scarecrow Press, 1981.

Hellman, Paul. *Ready, Aim, You're Hired! How to Job-Interview Successfully Anytime, Anywhere with Anyone*. New York: AMACOM, 1986.

Hodgetts, Richard M. *Effective Supervision: A Practical Approach*. New York: McGraw-Hill, 1987.

Hodgson, Philip. *A Practical Guide to Successful Interviewing*. New York: McGraw-Hill, 1988.

Imundo, Louis V. *The Effective Supervisor's Handbook*. New York: AMACOM, 1980.

Kahn, Robert L., and Charles F. Cannel. *The Dynamics of Interviewing: Theory, Techniques, and Cases*. New York: Wiley, 1966.

Kelly, John G. *Equal Opportunity Management: Understanding Affirmative Action and Employment Equity*. Don Mills, Ontario: CCH Canadian, Ltd., 1986.

Lefkowitz, J., and M. L. Katz. "Validity of Exit Interviews." *Personnel Psychology* 22 (1969): 445-55.

Library Administration and Management Association, Personnel Administration Section. *A Discussion and Annotated Bibliography on the Selection Interview for Interviewers and Interviewees*. Chicago: LAMA, 1981.

Lopez, Felix M. *Personnel Interviewing: Theory and Practice*. New York: McGraw-Hill, 1975.

Loretto, Vincent. "Effective Interviewing Is Based on More Than Intuition." *Personnel Journal* 65 (December 1986): 101-7.

Medley, H. A. *Sweaty Palms: The Neglected Art of Being Interviewed*. Berkeley, CA: Ten Speed Press, 1984.

Mika, Joseph J., and Bruce A. Shuman. "Legal Issues Affecting Libraries and Librarians." *American Libraries* 19, no. 2 (February 1988): 108-12.

Minter, Robert L. "The Hiring Interview." *Supervisory Management* (December 1974): 2-10.

Peskin, Dean B. *Human Behavior and Employment Interviewing*. New York: American Management Association, 1971.

Potter, Edward E., ed. *Employee Selection, Legal and Practical Alternatives to Compliance and Litigation*. Washington, DC: Equal Employment Advisory Council, 1983.

Preston, Paul, and Thomas Zimmerer. *Management for Supervisors*. 2d ed. Englewood Cliffs, NJ: Prentice-Hall, 1983.

Rae, Leslie. *The Skills of Interviewing*. New York: Nichols, 1988.

Sanders, Nancy, comp. *Guidelines for Interviewing for the Entry Level Position*. Chicago: LAMA, 1981.

Schuster, Frederick E. *Human Resource Management: Concepts, Cases and Readings*. 2d ed. Reston, VA: Reston Publishing, 1985.

Sidney, E., and M. Brown. *The Skills of Interviewing*. London: Tavistock, 1961.

Simon, Barry. "Personnel Selection Practices: Applications and Interviews." *American Libraries* 9, no. 3 (March 1978): 141-43.

Steinmetz, Lawrence L. *Interviewing Skills for Supervisory Personnel*. Reading, MA: Addison-Wesley Publishing, 1971.

Uris, Auren. *The Executive Interviewer's Deskbook*. Houston, TX: Gulf Press, 1978.

Uris, Auren. *88 Mistakes Interviewers Make ... and How to Avoid Them*. New York: AMACOM, 1988.

Volluck, Philip R. "Recruiting, Interviewing and Hiring: Staying within the [Legal] Boundaries." *Personnel Administrator* 32, no. 5 (1987): 45-52.

Wanous, John P. *Organizational Entry: Recruitment, Selection, and Socialization of Newcomers*. Reading, MA: Addison-Wesley, 1980.

Weiss, W. H. *Supervisor's Standard Reference Handbook*. 2d ed. Englewood Cliffs, NJ: Prentice-Hall, 1988.

Understanding Federal Student Financial Aid

For every complex problem there's a simple answer, and it's wrong.
—H. L. Mencken

FEDERAL AID FOR STUDENT EMPLOYMENT

The predominant source of funding for student employees in academic libraries is federally funded aid administered by each university, normally by a student financial aid or student employment office. More than 8,600 schools take part in one or more of the federal programs offered by the U.S. Department of Education; however, some schools do not take part in all programs.

Academic libraries are usually one of the largest—if not the largest—employers of both undergraduate and graduate students on university campuses. Supervisors of student employees need to have a basic understanding of the student financial aid system as administered at their university, especially how students qualify for and receive financial aid.

In this chapter, the various federal student financial aid programs will be described. While the basic provisions of the programs usually remain intact, the reader is cautioned that frequent revisions are made in the programs by the Department of Education and Congress. Before advising any of your student employees about federal student aid programs, check with your student employment office.

FEDERAL STUDENT AID PROGRAMS

The U.S. Congress established the foundation for student financial aid with Title IV of the Higher Education Act of 1965 and has made changes, through amendment, in the ensuing years. The Office of Student Financial Assistance (OSFA) of the Department of Education administers the Pell Grants, Stafford Loan Program (formerly the Guaranteed Student Loan [GSL] Program), Supplemental Educational Opportunity Grants (SEOG), the College Work-Study (CWS) Program, and Perkins Loan Program (formerly the National Direct Student Loan [NDSL] Program). The Parent Loans to Undergraduate Students (PLUS) Program was established in the Higher Education Amendments of 1980, and the Supplemental Loans to Students (SLS) Program was established in the Education Amendments of 1986, both being forms of guaranteed student loans. Each of these programs is described in this chapter. With the exception of the PLUS and SLS programs, a student must demonstrate financial need to receive aid from OSFA programs.

FINANCIAL NEED

Financial need is defined as the difference between the cost of a student's education and the student's ability to pay those costs. Unlike scholarship programs which may award funds based on academic merit or area of study, OSFA financial aid is based on a student's need for assistance. The concept of need-based aid has been used by colleges and universities for many years to award their own aid to students and is also a requirement for federal aid.

The student financial aid office on each campus is charged with the responsibility of administering OSFA programs and conducting a "needs analysis" to determine financial need for each student who applies. Needs analysis technically refers only to calculating the expected family contribution, but also can be used to describe the entire process of determining financial need (i.e., cost of attendance minus expected family contribution).

Cost of Attendance in Determining Financial Need

Cost of attendance is an estimate of the student's educational expenses for the year. Statutes define which educational costs may be included for OSFA programs, based on the student's tuition and fee charges, living situation (on-campus, off-campus, off-campus with parents), and other factors, including books and supplies. In addition, some students may have additional expenses, such as a physically impaired person's need for special equipment or services. There are two different methods for determining costs of attendance for the OSFA programs: that used in the Pell Grant Program and that for all other programs.

Family Contribution in Determining Financial Need

There are two need analysis methodologies, as defined in the Higher Education Amendments of 1986, for calculating family contribution figures for the OSFA programs. The Pell Grant formula produces a student aid index (SAI) and the congressional methodology produces a family contribution (FC) amount used in all other federal aid programs. The Pell Grant and the congressional methodology formulas are similar in that they analyze a family's income, expenses, and assets to arrive at an expected family contribution.

The Higher Education Amendments of 1986 also established a "simplified formula" for certain low income families, used to calculate either the SAI or FC if the total family income is $15,000 or less. For more about how the SAI and FC are calculated, see *The Pell Grant Formula 1988-89* or the *1988-89 Congressional Methodology*.[1]

There are different versions of both formulas for calculating need for dependent and independent students. Many students feel that they should be considered independent of their families and should be awarded aid on those grounds, but specific guidelines are provided in the statute to answer that question.

Independent Student Definition in Determining Financial Need

Traditionally, in needs analysis, it has been assumed that parents have the primary responsibility for paying for their children's education. There are exceptions to the rule, however; for example, students who no longer have contact with their parents, or older nontraditional students. The Higher Education Amendments of 1986 redefined the concept of an independent student and also gave student aid administrators the authority to make exceptions for students who have individual circumstance that make them independent, even though they do not meet the definition in the law. The following is the standard by which independence is judged:[2]

For the 1988-89 award year, a student is automatically considered independent if he or she:

1. Is over 23 years of age, or

2. Is a veteran of the U.S. Armed Forces, or

3. Is an orphan or ward of the court, or

4. Has legal dependents other than a spouse.

The student will also be considered to be independent if the school documents that either of the following circumstances exists:

1. The student is married, or a graduate or professional student, and will not be claimed as an income tax exemption by his or her parents, or

2. The student is a single undergraduate student, was not claimed as an income tax exemption by his or her parents in either 1986 or 1987, and has demonstrated self-sufficiency for two years. The student is considered self-sufficient if he or she had total income and other resources of at least $4,000. If the student received aid in the 1987-88 award year, the two years used to show self-sufficiency are 1985 and 1986. If the student did not receive aid in 1987-88, the two years are 1986 and 1987. (The two years used to demonstrate self-sufficiency are the two years before the student first received federal student aid, beginning with the 1987-88 award year.)

Terms used in the independent student definition:

LEGAL DEPENDENT: Any person who lives with the student, receives more than half-support from the student, and will continue to receive more than half-support from the student during the award year; also, the natural or adopted child of the student, or a child for whom the student is legal guardian, if the child receives more than half-support from the student (the child does not have to live with the student).

OVER 23 YEARS OF AGE: A student who is at least 24 years old on December 31, 1988.

PARENT: A natural or adoptive parent, or a legal guardian who has been appointed by a court and specifically directed by the court to support the student.

RESOURCES: Includes not only traditional sources of income (such as wages, salaries, tips, interest and dividend income, untaxed income and benefits, fellowships and veteran's cash benefits), but also any student financial aid (except PLUS loans), and personal long-term cash loans used for educational purposes. These resources, of course, do not include any support from the student's parents.

Citizenship Requirements for Financial Aid

OSFA programs are intended to provide student financial aid to needy students who are in one of the following categories:[3]

1. A U.S. citizen or national. The term "national" includes not only all U.S. citizens but also natives of American Samoa or Swains.

2. A permanent resident of the U.S. A permanent resident of the U.S. must provide documentation from the Immigration and Naturalization Service (INS).

3. Certain residents of the Pacific Islands. In some cases, residents of Palau, the Marshall Islands, and the Federated States of Micronesia (former Trust Territories) continue to be eligible for aid from Pell, SEOG, and CWS programs.

4. Other eligible noncitizens. An individual who can provide documentation from the INS that he or she is in the U.S. for other than a temporary purpose and has the intention of becoming a citizen or permanent resident may be eligible, including refugees, persons granted asylum, Cuban and Haitian Entrants, temporary residents as defined in the Immigration Reform and Control Act of 1986, and others.

ELIGIBILITY REQUIREMENTS

Table 6.1, following, describes the eligibility requirements for the five federal student financial aid programs:[4]

Table 6.1.

Eligibility Requirements for Federal Student Financial Aid Programs

REQUIREMENTS	PELL	STAFFORD	SEOG	CWS	PERKINS
Undergraduate	YES	YES	YES	YES	YES
Graduate	NO	YES	NO	YES	YES
At least ½-time	YES	YES	YES	YES	YES
Must pay back	NO	YES	NO	NO	YES
U.S. citizen or eligible non-citizen	YES	YES	YES	YES	YES
Registered with Selective Service (if applicable)	YES	YES	YES	YES	YES
Have financial need	YES	YES	YES	YES	YES
Attend participating school	YES	YES	YES	YES	YES
Working toward a degree or certificate	YES	YES	YES	YES	YES
Making satisfactory academic progress	YES	YES	YES	YES	YES
Not in default or owe a refund on a federal grant or loan	YES	YES	YES	YES	YES
Having a bachelor's degree makes student ineligible	YES	NO	YES	NO	NO
Conviction of drug distribution or possession may make student ineligible	YES	YES	YES	YES	YES

PELL—Pell Grants

STAFFORD—Stafford Loan Program (formerly the Guaranteed Student Loan [GSL] Program)

CWS—College Work-Study Program

SEOG—Supplemental Educational Opportunity Grants (SEOG)

PERKINS—Perkins Loan Program (formerly the National Direct Student Loan [NDSL] Program)

PELL GRANTS

The Department of Education provides funds to each participating institution to pay eligible students, and so, unlike the campus-based programs such as the College Work-Study Program, a student's eligibility for Pell Grants does not depend on the availability of funds at the institution. The institution does not select Pell Grant recipients, but does have the responsibility to ensure that the recipients meet the eligibility requirements. Pell Grants are available only to undergraduate students who have an eligible student aid index (SAI). This number is an index of the student's ability to contribute to the cost of education. To apply, the student must complete a financial aid form.[5]

STAFFORD LOAN PROGRAM

The Guaranteed Student Loan (GSL) Program was renamed the Stafford Loan Program by Congress in 1988 in honor of Senator Robert T. Stafford of Vermont. The program was established by Title IV of the Higher Education Act of 1965 in order to make low-interest loans available to students. As a means of encouraging participation in the program, the federal government subsidizes a portion of the interest on Stafford Loans, thus enabling lenders to obtain competitive interest rates on loans, while, at the same time, providing students with loans at below-market rates. Approximately 7,300 schools participate in the Stafford Loan Program.

Stafford Loans are unique in that they operate through state and private nonprofit agencies, requiring interaction among the federal government, private lending institutions, colleges and universities, state and private nonprofit guarantee agencies, and students. Either state guarantee agencies or private institutions insure the loans and are reimbursed by the federal government for all or part of any insurance claims they pay to lenders. This guarantee takes the place of the security or collateral usually required when making long-term consumer loans. For the latest information on terms and limits on Stafford Loans, consult with your student financial aid office.

PLUS AND SLS PROGRAMS

Congress established the Parent Loans to Undergraduate Students (PLUS) Program with the Education Amendments of 1980. PLUS is a type of guaranteed student loan, originally established to provide parents of dependent undergraduate students with additional funds. Congress extended the PLUS program in 1986 to graduate students.

The Supplemental Loans to Students (SLS) Program, established by the Education Amendments of 1986, provides loans directly to students. As noted earlier, students do not have to demonstrate financial need to receive aid from either the PLUS and SLS programs. For the latest information on terms and limits on PLUS and SLS loans, consult with your student financial aid office.

CAMPUS-BASED STUDENT FINANCIAL AID PROGRAMS

The campus-based programs are the Supplemental Educational Opportunity Grants (SEOG), the College Work-Study (CWS) Program, and the Perkins Loan Program (formerly the National Direct Student Loan [NDSL] Program). They are called campus-based because each participating school or university is responsible for administering the programs on its own campus. The financial aid administrator ensures that funds are provided to students in accordance with the provisions of the law and regulations, in cooperation with the Secretary of Education and the Department of Education. Unlike the Pell Grants, Stafford Loans, PLUS, and SLS, student eligibility does depend on the availability of funds at the university.

SUPPLEMENTAL EDUCATIONAL OPPORTUNITY GRANTS (SEOG)

The SEOG Program is another of the major Federal student financial aid programs authorized under Title IV of the Higher Education Act of 1965 and its amendments. The Supplemental Educational Opportunity Grants (SEOG) program provides grants not loans, to undergraduate students only. Eligible students are selected by the school's financial aid office and based on financial need as determined by the family contribution (FC) figure. SEOG awards range from $100 to $4,000 per year (1990).

A student's eligibility for SEOG Grants has not, until recently, depended on the availability of funds at the institution. Historically, the SEOG Program has been funded completely with federal funds; however the federal share for 1989-90 was reduced to 95 percent; for 1990-91, 90 percent; and, for 1991-92 and subsequent years, 85 percent.

THE COLLEGE WORK-STUDY PROGRAM (CWS)

The most common source of funding for student employees in academic libraries is the College Work-Study Program (CWS). College Work-Study gives needy undergraduate and graduate students the opportunity to work part-time to help meet the costs of postsecondary education. Students must meet all eligibility requirements including demonstration of financial need in order to receive a work-study job.

To the extent practical, the university must provide work-study jobs which will complement each student's educational or career goals. Every work-study position is required to have a job description which has the following purposes:

1. Defines whether or not the job qualifies as a work-study job

2. Explains the position to students to help them select the type of employment closest to their educational objectives

3. States the number of hours of work required and the wage rate

4. Provides a written record of the job's duties and responsibilities

Universities must also make available "equivalent employment" (nonwork-study jobs)—to the extent of available funds—to all students who want to work.

In assigning a work-study job, the university must consider the student's financial need, the number of hours a student can work, the length of the academic period or period of employment, the anticipated wage rate, and the amount of other assistance available to the student. There is no minimum or maximum amount of award, but it, together with other sources of financial aid, may not exceed the student's financial need.

Work-Study Employment Conditions and Limitations

The following conditions and limitations apply to all College Work-Study Program jobs:

1. Work-study jobs may be either on-campus or off-campus. Off-campus jobs must be in the public interest for private, nonprofit organizations or for federal, state, or local public agencies.

2. Work-study employment must be governed by employment conditions that are reasonable according to the type of work performed, the geographic region, the employee's proficiency, and any applicable federal, state, or local law.

3. Work-study employers must pay students at least the current Federal minimum wage.

4. Work-study employees may not displace other employees. The intent of Work-study is to create new job opportunities.

5. Work-study positions must not involve constructing, operating, or maintaining any part of a building used for religious worship or sectarian instruction.

6. The university may not accept, solicit, accept, or permit solicitation of any fee, commission, contribution, or gift as a condition for gaining work-study employment. A student may pay union dues if they are a condition of employment and if nonwork-study students must also pay dues.

7. Work-study students must be paid for all hours worked. The Fair Labor Standards Act of 1938, as amended, prohibits employers from accepting voluntary services from any paid employee.

8. Work-study students may not be paid for receiving instruction for academic credit in a classroom, laboratory, or other academic setting.

9. Work-study student wages may be garnished only to pay any tuition or fee costs the student owes the university.

10. Work-study jobs at proprietary schools (as of October 1, 1986) must be on campus and must provide student services. Generally, work which primarily benefits the school rather than the students is not permitted.

11. Work-study students employed by a federal, state, or local public agency, or by a private nonprofit organization must perform work which is in the public interest. Work which in any way involves political activity is not permitted.

Paying Work-Study Student Employees

Undergraduate students are paid work-study wages on an hourly basis only. Graduate students may be paid by the hour or may be paid a salary. The university is required to base the number of hours a student may work on the student's financial need and on how the combination of work and study hours will affect the student's health and academic progress. The law provides no limits on the number of hours per week or pay period a student can work.

A student must be paid at least the federal minimum wage, but there is no maximum wage rate. It is unacceptable to base a wage rate on need or any other factor not related to the skills required for the position. If the student's skill level depends on academic achievement, the university may set the wage on that basis. A junior lab student, for example, may be paid a higher rate than a sophomore lab student if the job requires academic achievement. Generally, however, students performing comparable jobs should be paid comparable wages. This applies to students at different class levels and to students performing the same work as regular employees. The university may use any payroll period it chooses, but work-study students must be paid at least monthly.

The federal share of the College Work-Study Program as of the 1988-89 academic year was 80 percent. The federal share may not include fringe benefits such as sick leave, vacation pay, and holiday pay, nor the employer's contributions to social security, worker's compensation, retirement, or any other welfare or insurance program. Universities may extend the work-study benefits to more students by contributing more than 20 percent to the federal share.

Work-Study Employment During Nonenrollment Periods

Work-study students may be employed during summer, or equivalent vacation periods, if the student is planning to enroll for the next regular session. Some universities require, however, that work-study students enroll for at least three hours of credit during the summer in order to be eligible. During the regular academic year, students must be at least half-time students in order to qualify for work-study jobs.

PERKINS LOAN PROGRAM

Perkins Loans are low-interest long-term loans made through university financial aid offices to help needy undergraduate and graduate students pay their educational costs. The Perkins Loan Program is the new name for the National Direct Student Loan (NDSL) Program. It had been established as the National Defense Student Loan Program in 1958 and was renamed beginning with the 1987-88 award year to honor the late Carl D. Perkins, former chairman of the House Education and Labor Committee. Defense Loans were those made before July 1, 1972; Direct Loans were made between July 1, 1972 and June 30, 1987; Perkins Loans are those made on or after July 1, 1987.

To be eligible, students must meet all eligibility requirements, and in addition, priority must be given by the university to students with exceptional financial need. The university must also consider evidence relating to the student's willingness to repay the loan: default on a previous loan or a history of unpaid debts can make a student ineligible. Loans must be available to all levels of students, without discrimination.

The primary difference between Perkins Loans and other loan programs is that the university makes the loans to students while financial institutions provide Stafford, PLUS, and SLS Loans. For the latest information on terms and limits on Perkins Loans, consult with your student financial aid office.

STATE STUDENT INCENTIVE GRANT (SSIG) PROGRAM

The State Student Incentive Grant (SSIG) Program assists states in providing community service or learning job programs to eligible postsecondary students. To be eligible, students must have substantial financial need and attend institutions of higher education. The programs vary from state to state and are called by different names. Generally, states receive annual SSIG allotments from the Department of Education. The Federal allotments must be matched by state-appropriated funds. For inquiries about SSIG programs in your state, consult with your student financial aid office.

ROBERT C. BYRD HONORS SCHOLARSHIP PROGRAM

The Robert C. Byrd Honors Scholarship Program is a federally funded program of grants to states to promote student excellence with scholarships to outstanding high school graduates for the first year of study. Authorized by Title IV of the Higher Education Act of 1965, as amended, the Secretary of Education makes grants to individual states and those states establish specific scholar selection criteria in cooperation with school administrators, school boards, teachers, and parents.

COUNSELING THE STUDENT ON FINANCIAL AID

By reviewing information on the various financial aid available to students, you will gain a basic understanding of how those programs work. For example, if one of your student employees receives a grant, any work-study award will quite probably be reduced, changing the total number of hours that student can work.

Supervisors are often surprised by the circumstances of the individual and interconnected financial programs: a student who has received a work-study allocation subsequently is awarded a grant from another program and, suddenly, the work-study monies have been reduced. A supervisor who understands how these programs work can deal with these and similar situations easily.

The Department of Education provides suggestions on loan counseling for financial aid administrators:[6]

1. Explore all sources of aid.

2. Stress constraints on aid.

3. Urge students to read and save all loan documents.

4. Review requirements for satisfactory academic progress.

5. Remind students to keep lender informed.

6. Review loan terms and conditions.

7. Describe consequences of multiple borrowing.

8. Review student rights and responsibilities.

9. Review deferment and forbearance conditions.

10. Review loan repayment obligations.

11. Provide general information on average indebtedness of students.

12. Provide data on average, anticipated monthly repayment.

13. Provide information on debt management strategies.

14. Counsel on personal financial planning.

WHAT YOU CAN DO

As the supervisor of student employees in an academic library, you have frequent contact with students who receive some form of financial aid. Understanding the workings of, for instance, the College Work-Study Program will help you deal with awards and allotments and abide by the program's regulations and requirements. As supervisors, we often forget that many of our student employees are also paying on student loans. In recognition of their financial obligations, we as supervisors should do what we can to allow student employees to make up missed work time and attempt to provide sustained employment. It may be easier, for example, to tell your student employees to take vacation periods off, but, in fact, they may well have loan payments which cannot be made without regular paychecks.

Remember, before advising any of your student employees on federal student aid programs, check with your student employment office to be certain you know your university's regulations and to assure that you have the latest information available.

NOTES

[1]U.S. Department of Education, Office of Student Financial Aid, *The Pell Grant Formula, 1988-89* (Washington, DC: GPO, 1988); U.S. Department of Education, Office of Student Financial Aid, *1988-89 Congressional Methodology* (Washington, DC: GPO, 1988).

[2]U.S. Department of Education, Office of Student Financial Aid, *The Federal Student Financial Aid Handbook, 1988-89* (Washington, DC: GPO, 1989), 69.

[3]Ibid, 156.

[4]College Entrance Examination Board, *FAF: Financial Aid Form, School Year 1990-91* (Princeton, NJ: CEEB, 1990), 2.

[5]Ibid.

[6]*Federal Student Financial Aid Handbook, 1988-89*, 451.

BIBLIOGRAPHY

Chandler, Lana J., and Michael D. Boggs. *The Student Loan Handbook*. White Hall, VA: Betterway Publications, 1987.

College Entrance Examination Board. *FAF: Financial Aid Form, School Year 1990-91*. Princeton, NJ: CEEB, 1990.

Cronin, Joseph Marr, and Sylvia Quarles Simmons, eds. *Student Loans: Risks and Realities*. Dover, MA: Auburn House, 1987.

Dennis, Marguerite J. *Mortgaged Futures: How to Graduate from School without Going Broke*. Washington, DC: Hope Press, 1986.

Ehrhart, Julie Kuhn, and Shelagh Meehan, eds. *Financial Aid: A Partial List of Resources for Women*. 5th ed. Washington, DC: Project on the Status and Education of Women, Association of American Colleges, 1989.

Fenske, Robert H., and Robert P. Huff and associates. *Handbook of Student Financial Aid*. San Francisco: Jossey-Bass, 1983.

Financial Aid for Minorities: Awards to Students with Any Major. Garrett Park, MD: Garrett Park Press, 1989.

Institute of International Education. *Financial Resources for International Study: A Definitive Guide to Organizations Offering Awards for Overseas Study*. Princeton, NJ: Peterson's Guides, 1989.

Lehman, Andrea E., ed. *The 1988 College Money Handbook: The Only Complete Guide to Scholarships, College Costs, and Financial Aid*. 5th ed. Princeton, NJ: Peterson's Guides, 1987.

Leider, Robert, and Anna Leider. *Don't Miss Out: The Ambitious Student's Guide to Financial Aid*. 13th ed. Alexandria, VA: Octameron Press, 1988.

Maintaining Balances: The Relationship between Student Financial Aid and Institutional Finance. Sacramento, CA: The Eureka Project, 1988.

Margolin, Judith B. *Financing a College Education: The Essential Guide for the 90's*. New York: Plenum, 1989.

Paying for College: Student Loans and Alternative Financing Mechanisms. Sacramento, CA: The Eureka Project, 1988.

Schlachter, Gail A. *Directory of Financial Aids for Minorities, 1989-90*. Los Angeles: Reference Service Press, 1989.

Schlachter, Gail A. *How to Find Out about Financial Aid: A Guide to Over 700 Directories Listing Scholarships, Fellowships, Loans, Grants, Awards, Internships*. Los Angeles: Reference Service Press, 1987.

Stewart, Alva W. *College Student Aid: Problems and Prospects: A Bibliographical Checklist*. Monticello, IL: Vance Bibliographies, 1987.

U.S. Department of Education, Office of Student Financial Assistance. *1988-89 Congressional Methodology*. Washington, DC: GPO, 1988.

U.S. Department of Education, Office of Student Financial Assistance. *The Federal Student Financial Aid Handbook, 1988-89*. Washington, DC: GPO, 1989.

U.S. Department of Education, Office of Student Financial Assistance. *The Pell Grant Formula, 1988-89*. Washington, DC: GPO, 1988.

U.S. General Accounting Office. *Supplemental Student Loans: Who Borrows and Who Defaults: Fact Sheet for Congressional Requesters*. Washington, DC: U.S. General Accounting Office, 1989.

Orientation and Training of Student Employees

Training is everything. The peach was once a bitter almond; cauliflower is nothing but cabbage with a college education.

— Samuel Langhorne Clemens

TRAINING IS EVERYTHING

Why is good training necessary? Won't employees learn without being trained? Yes, they will, but not necessarily the right things. Some people cringe at the word "training." "Training is what you give to monkeys; development is for people." In fact, training for a job is a very specialized and practical form of education which prepares employees to do that job well. In academic libraries, supervisors have an obligation not only to train student employees to do their jobs but also to develop student workers by providing them with experiences designed to enhance their strengths and give them positive work experiences.

In this chapter we will discuss the first step in training, orientation, as well as training and development programs.

WHY PROVIDE ORIENTATION?

Oriented workers do a better job and stay with the library longer than do those who are not given an orientation. Orientation reduces the anxiety associated with a new job and saves time for supervisors and co-workers. The better the orientation, the less time the new employee will spend asking questions of others. An effective orientation helps the new employee develop a positive attitude toward the library and the job. The result is higher job satisfaction and better performance.

First Impressions

Orientation training (or induction training in industry) actually begins the minute an applicant comes to the library to fill out an application or appears for an interview. First impressions, often as a library user, will determine the student's initial feelings about the library. It is important to establish a central point for student employee applicants to report, for instance, the office of the dean or director, branch library office, or the library's personnel office. The hiring supervisors should be scheduled to meet the students and escort them to the department office or work area. If handled properly, new employees will have more positive attitudes toward the library as well as toward their jobs.

The New Student Employee

It is essential that you recognize how the student feels when reporting for work on the first day. Think about your first day on a new job: did you feel anxious, out of place, concerned about how others would accept you, confused, and worried about how you would perform? Almost everyone has those feelings, including your new student employees. It is important that an employee orientation system is followed which will ease the new student employees' anxiety and which makes them feel welcome.

Orientation of Student Employees

Effective orientation of new student employees paves the way for good relations between the employees and the library in the future. The time and personal attention given by the supervisor during the first few days on the job go a long way toward making the student employees feel wanted and important. Your personal attention to orientation gives new employees a sense of security and demonstrates that the library is interested in the employees as individuals.

Orientation begins with introductions and a tour of the department. Explain what other employees do and how they work together in the department or unit. You should explain how the job will be learned and who will provide the training. Orienting new employees includes discussing library rules, procedures, and policies, usually included in a student handbook. It is not advisable to simply hand the book to new employees and tell them to read it. Even if you do have a handbook, you should sit down with new student employees and review it with them.

A student employee handbook should include the following information:

1. Eligibility for student employment. Included is a statement of the number of credit hours required in order to qualify for employment. Students must be made aware that if the number of credit hours falls below the required number, they will be terminated. (Different libraries have different policies.)

2. Hours of work allowed. Many libraries limit the number of hours a student may work each week (normally twenty).

3. Time sheets or time clock. Describe how time worked is to be reported.

4. Pay periods. Describe how, when, and where student employees receive their paychecks and provide a schedule of paydays.

5. Absences. Describe the library's policy on reporting absences and what to do when an employee will be or is late.

6. Transfer policy. Some libraries require that students work a certain number of months before they may request a transfer to another department or campus job.

7. Personnel records. Inform student employees about employment records which are maintained and clarify how they are used.

8. Telephones. Describe the library's policy on personal use of telephones.

9. Socializing and studying. Describe the library's policy on socializing and studying on the job or in the work area.

10. Library equipment. Describe the library's policy on the use of university equipment for personal use.

11. Security, safety, and emergencies. Describe the library's policies on the issuance of keys, the reporting of emergencies, and the locations of alarms, extinguishers, and fire exits.

12. Termination. Describe what length of notice is required or desired when terminating employment. Describe also the process used for termination for disciplinary reasons.

13. Grievance procedures. Describe employee rights and the library or university grievance procedures.

14. Training. Note that the students' supervisor will provide further orientation and training.

If your library does not presently have a handbook for student employees, you should consider developing one. A handbook guarantees that all employees are given the same information, regardless of how thorough the supervisors are in providing new employee orientation. Of course, there is no guarantee that the handbook will be read, but if you review the handbook with each new employee, later claims of ignorance about these policies and procedures will be without foundation.

Orientation Checklist

Does your new student orientation provide answers to the following questions?

- What does the organization do?

- How does the student's work group or job fit into the overall library organization?

- How important is the work to the library?

- What do the other departments do?

- What do the other libraries on campus do?

- What is the chain of command?

- What exactly will the student do?

- What equipment will the student employee be using?

- What other employees will the student be working with daily?

- What are the work hours?

- Are there scheduled breaks?

- How long is the employee's probationary period?

- When and how will the student employee be evaluated?

- How and how much will the student be paid?

- When is payday?

- Will the employee be paid after the first pay period or is there a delay of one pay period?

- What will be deducted from paychecks?

- How will time worked be reported?

- If a time clock is used, where is it and how do you use it?

- If time sheets are used, how are they filled out, and when are they due?

- How are pay increases determined?

- When the student employee has questions, whom should the student ask?

If your new student employees have the answers to these questions, whether provided by a library-wide orientation program or by you, your employees will be ready for job training.

TRAINING AND DEVELOPMENT ARE NOT THE SAME

We have all heard the terms "training" and "development" used interchangeably, but the terms do not mean the same thing: it is important to know the difference. Training for a job emphasizes the skills and knowledge necessary to achieve and maintain an acceptable level of performance, whereas development focuses on the growth and improvement of employees as human beings and as members of the organization. The payoffs for training tend to be for the short-run, while the benefits of development programs are felt over the long-run.

Role of the Student Employee Supervisor in Training

While your job description may say simply, "supervises student employees," or "hires, trains, supervises, and evaluates student workers," training is, in fact, a most important part of your supervisory role. The role of the supervisor in training can vary with different organizations. In industry, the personnel department is often charged with the responsibility for training new employees, or there may even be a separate training division. In libraries, the student employee supervisor is usually directly responsible for teaching new employees all of the skills and information necessary to become full contributing members of the department. Typically, the supervisor is given latitude in developing a training program as long as it has the desired results. Frequently, the student employee supervisor inherits a training program from a previous supervisor who may no longer be in the department.

Two Types of Training

There are two types of training which you may use in preparing student employees for their jobs: off-the-job, or vestibule training, and on-the-job training.

Vestibule training takes place away from the site where the actual work will be done, for instance, in a classroom or at a desk away from the work station. The advantage is that the new employee is given "hands-on" experience without interferring with the flow of work in the department.

On-the-job training is conducted in the department at the actual assigned work station. Most library training is done on the job.

Should the Supervisor Do All the Training?

Supervisors approach training in one of two ways: by doing all the training personally, or by placing the new student with an experienced employee. By doing all of the training personally, the supervisor can be assured all employees are trained the same way. The training is very time-consuming, however, and takes time from other responsibilities. Having another experienced employee handle the training can be effective also, but the best approach is probably a combination of the two.

WHAT DO YOU TRAIN FOR?

Since you cannot train immediately for everything there is to do on the job, teach those things that are vital to the job and that will protect the employee and equipment from harm. You should divide the knowledge and skills into groups: "have to know now," "have to know soon," and "have to know one of these days." The "have to know now" are those things without which nothing can be done. If they are not learned now, employees could hurt themselves, turn away a patron with an incorrect or improper response, or damage a piece of equipment. You can avoid some training by determining, in advance, what a student employee already knows.

FOUR-STEP METHOD FOR TRAINING

For supervisors, training can be either very simple or very difficult. The foundation of systematic, structured job training is a four-step procedure called Job Instruction Training. Developed during World War II, the system has been in wide use ever since. If you do not use this approach, training will always be difficult and may not be effective.

1. Preparation: Get the workers ready to learn.

2. Presentation: Demonstrate how the job should be done.

3. Performance Tryout: Try the workers out by letting them do the job.

4. Follow-up: Put the workers on their own gradually.

Step 1. Preparation of the Learner

Until individuals are psychologically and emotionally ready to learn, it is almost impossible to teach them. It is the supervisor's responsibility to help the trainee prepare to learn. The following suggestions will help get the trainee ready to learn the job:

1. Put the student employee at ease: relieve the tension.

2. Explain why the trainee is being taught.

3. Create interest, encourage questions, and find out what the student employee already knows about the job.

4. Explain the why of the whole job and relate it to some job the trainee already knows.

5. Place the student employee as close to the normal working position as possible.

6. Familiarize the trainee with the work area and equipment and materials which will be used.

Step 2. Presentation of the Operation

After preparing the student employee to learn, you are ready to begin demonstrating how the job should be done. Describe and demonstrate, one step at a time: stress each key point of the job and, patiently, without giving the trainee more than can be mastered, teach the steps of the job in sequence. The following steps are followed in presentation:

1. Explain requirements for quantity and quality.

2. Go through the job at the normal work pace.

3. Go through the job at a slow pace several times, explaining each step. Between operations, explain the difficult parts, or those in which errors are likely to be made. Repeat several times.

4. Have the trainee explain the steps and key points as you go through the job at a slow pace.

Step 3. Performance Tryout

You now give the trainee the opportunity to actually perform the job while you observe. Performance try-out includes the following:

1. Have the student employees go through the job several times, slowly, explaining to you each step. Correct trainee mistakes, and, if necessary, do some of the complicated steps for them the first few times.

2. You, the trainer, run the job at the normal pace.

3. Have the trainees do the job, gradually building up skill and speed.

4. As soon as the trainees demonstrate proficiency, put the trainees on their own but don't abandon them.

Step 4. Follow-up

The most difficult step is the last because there is a tendency to think that, once the employee is trained, you're done. To guarantee long-term quality performance, you need to be sure the employee knows where to go for help and you must check frequently to see if all is going well. During this step, you will taper off coaching so the employees don't feel you're watching over their shoulders. Follow-up entails these activities.

1. Designate to whom the trainees should go for help or to ask questions.

2. Gradually decrease supervision, checking student employees' work occasionally against quantity and quality standards.

3. Correct faulty work patterns before they develop into habits. Demonstrate why the method taught is superior.

4. Compliment good work and provide encouragement until the trainees are able to meet quantity and quality standards.

EXTENDING THE TRAINING

Some libraries use the mentor or buddy system to extend the training of student employees after the initial training. Experienced student employees are assigned to new employees to serve as role models and as sources of help after new employees are put on their own in their jobs. If the mentor or buddy is a willing participant in the training process, the relationship can be a positive training support system. It goes without saying that care must be taken to assure that the assigned mentor or buddy will be a positive influence on the new student employee.

COMMON TRAINING ERRORS

Experience, like practice, makes us perfect only if we are doing the correct thing. Many of us do things incorrectly day-in and day-out, simply because we learned them that way in the first place. If you follow the four-step training method, but discover that your training is not effective, the cause may be one of the following common training errors:

1. Failure to devote enough time to teaching. A common error for supervisors is to let other responsibilities hurry their training. Remember that the time devoted to training new employees properly is time well spent if the workers are to be productive.

2. Failure to follow the system step by step. The four-step system takes time, but, if followed precisely, it works. If you skip a step, the system will break down and you may fail. Don't cut corners.

3. Failure to show enough patience with the slow learner. When you teach someone who learns more slowly than others, you must slow your own pace or you will surely be disappointed in the results. Cover each of the four steps, even if it takes you twice as long. Keep in mind that many slow learners make excellent workers once they master a job, so your time will not be wasted.

TIPS TO IMPROVE TRAINING

Don'ts

*   Don't assume that everyone you train will learn at the same pace. We all learn at different rates. Be patient.

*   Don't assume a task is easy because you found it easy. We all find different tasks easy to learn.

*   Don't assume that, because employees are trained, they will continue to do things the way they were taught. Skills slip, and you will have to retrain some people.

- Don't assume that, because employees have experience, they know how to perform some tasks. They may have experience performing tasks incorrectly.

- Don't forget that it takes time for good habits to develop.

- Don't just act interested in your student employees' learning; be interested in their learning.

- Don't make fun of employees who make mistakes. We all learn from our mistakes.

Do's

- Do follow the four-step training method.

- Do let your student employees know that you expect them to continue doing things correctly.

- Do let them know you are always willing to help them learn.

- Do give encouragement and recognition for work done well.

- Do keep student employees informed on how well they are doing and where they need improvement.

- Do ask your student employees what you can do to help them do a better job. Ask them often.

ACTIVE VERSUS PASSIVE LEARNING

We assume our student employees are adults and need to be treated as such. In planning training programs, it is important that your training program is aimed at adults who learn differently from children. Children are passive learners who are taught to sit quietly, absorb what they are told, and repeat it on command. Adults, on the other hand, demand active learning that is relevant and participative.

Your student employees have learned how to learn, and are in fact engaged in learning as part of their daily undergraduate or graduate experience. Unless student employees see relevance of your training, you will not accomplish much. You can establish the relevancy of training by explaining why it is given, how it will benefit them, and why it is important to the work group's productivity.

Adults learn by doing so there should be as much activity as possible throughout the learning process. Further student employees are lectured to all day; they will respond better to doing than to hearing about doing. Student employees can absorb far more by actively participating than from studying manuals. Do not use the same teaching methods you use with children to teach your student employees: remember, your student employees are adults.

IMPLEMENTING YOUR TRAINING PROGRAM

The following are suggestions on how to prepare and implement your training program:

1. Be sure that you have done your homework. Do some reading in the psychology of learning and motivation.

2. Make notes to yourself about the four-step training process and resolve to follow the system.

3. Develop a plan for training and write it down.

4. Prepare a checklist of tasks to be taught and describe how proficiency will be measured.

5. Use your checklist to be sure everything is taught.

6. Recognize that training takes time and that retraining is an integral part of your job. At times you will feel that all you accomplish is training, but remember, don't cut corners.

7. Identify experienced student employees in the department who can help you and possibly act as mentors to new student employees.

8. Discuss your training plan with your supervisor, ask for suggestions, and get support.

9. Discuss training plans with other student employee supervisors and consider using their ideas.

DEVELOPMENTAL TRAINING

A part of your training responsibility as supervisor is developmental training. Developmental training usually refers to long-term growth: training to improve performance and preparation of employees for higher level positions. In libraries, the emphasis is normally on preparing regular staff for managerial positions or for other types of advancement. For student employees, developmental training usually is limited to preparing them for supervisory duties within the department—night supervisor, for example—or for higher-level positions in the same or other departments of the library.

Determine what kinds of training your student employees need. Developmental training is designed primarily for experienced employees and must meet one of two needs: training to improve performance on the present job, or training to prepare for higher-level jobs. Both types of training are needed for all employees.

Training Present Employees to Improve Performance

Training to improve performance hinges on the difference between "can do" and "will do." If a student employee "cannot do" a task, ask yourself these questions: Has this employee ever done the task correctly? Has this employee been taught to do it correctly? If offered a reward to do the task correctly, could the employee do it? If the answer to any of the questions is "no," you have a training problem—the employee in reality "cannot do" the task.

If you can answer "yes" to the previous questions, you must determine if you have a "will not do" problem on your hands. If the employee can do the task but will not do it, it is a managerial, not a training, problem. The way the employee is supervised, the way the job is organized, or the employee's attitude must be examined. No amount of training will solve the "will not do" problem.

To attack the "cannot do" problem, the trainer must isolate the task which cannot be performed. Having the employee perform the task under your observation is the best way to separate the employee's abilities from inabilities. Once identified, the task which is not performed properly can be taught using the four-step training procedure described earlier.

Training to Prepare Student Employees for Higher-Level Work

Training to prepare student employees for higher-level jobs depends greatly on what those jobs are. Provide opportunities for student employees to learn a wide range of jobs and to develop skills which will help them in any future work situation, such as keyboard skills, telephone skills, interpersonal relations skills, and the development of good work habits. This may also be an opportunity to mentor student employees who express interest in librarianship as a career.

Opportunities for student employees to take advantage of staff development programs in the library or development programs offered by the university should also be investigated. Find out whether or not student employees can avail themselves of programs offered to library staff. If so, make every effort to communicate those opportunities to your student employees.

Developmental Training Methods

Libraries with active staff development programs often invite student employees to participate. You, as their supervisor, should encourage participation in those programs which will provide enrichment to their jobs and help them prepare for future careers. There are at least a dozen developmental training methods used in industry and education. The most common methods used by libraries are:

1. Conference: verbal interaction between an instructor and participants.

2. Lecture: presentation by a knowledgeable person given to a group of employees.

3. Programmed or computer-assisted instruction: instruction in which the learner must respond correctly to each part before proceeding to the next.

4. Case study: a written description of a situation that the trainee must read and analyze.

5. Role playing: assuming the role of other people and interacting with other learners in acting out a situation.

Talk to your supervisor and to other student supervisors to learn how they provide developmental training for staff and student employees. Ask questions about programs offered and find out how your student employees can participate. Remember that one of your responsibilities as a supervisor of student employees is to help them grow and develop. Through counseling and coaching, you can provide the ongoing, informal training intended to refine skills and give assistance for personal growth.

SUPERVISOR'S TRAINING CHECKLIST

If you can honestly answer "yes" to all of the following questions, you are well on your way to becoming an effective trainer of student employees:

1. Do you accept full responsibility for training your student employees?

2. Do you consider training to be a continuous, ongoing activity?

3. Do you have an orientation checklist and religiously cover each item on the list?

4. Do you have a training checklist and use it every time you train a new student employee?

5. Do you use the four-step training process without skipping any steps?

6. Do you recognize that individuals learn at different rates and are you patient with those who learn more slowly than others?

7. Do you stay in touch with new employees to be sure they know they can ask questions?

8. Do you have a way to identify present employee performance deficiencies and can you differentiate between "cannot do" and "will not do" problems?

9. Do you have a developmental training program for your student employees?

ORIENTATION, TRAINING, AND DEVELOPMENT

The supervisor's responsibility for preparing workers, training them to perform their jobs, and developing employees can not be understated. How well these are accomplished may well determine whether supervisor succeeds or fails.

BIBLIOGRAPHY

Bittel, Lester R. *What Every Supervisor Should Know*. New York: McGraw-Hill, 1980.

Casner-Lotto, Jill. *Successful Training Strategies*. San Francisco: Jossey-Bass, 1988.

Collins, Eliza G. V., and Patricia Scott. "Everyone Who Makes It Has a Mentor." *Harvard Business Review* 56 (July-August 1978): 89-100.

Conroy, B. "Human Element: Staff Development in the Electronic Library." *Drexel Library Quarterly* 17 (Fall 1981): 91-106.

Creth, Sheila. *Effective On-the-Job Training: Developing Library Human Resources*. Chicago: ALA, 1986.

Creth, Sheila. *Job Training: Developing Training Plans for Your Staff*. Chicago: ACRL, 1984.

Creth, Sheila. "Staff Development and Continuing Education." In *Personnel Administration in Libraries*, edited by Sheila Creth and Frederick Duda, 189-225. New York: Neal-Schuman, 1981.

Daughtrey, Anne Scott, and Betty Roper Ricks. *Contemporary Supervision: Managing People and Technology*. New York: McGraw-Hill, 1988.

Evered, James F. *Shirt-Sleeves Management*. New York: AMACOM, 1981.

Fallon, William K., ed. *Leadership on the Job: Guides to Good Supervision*. New York: AMACOM, 1981.

Friedman, Paul, and Elaine A. Yarbrough. *Training Strategies from Start to Finish*. Englewood Cliffs, NJ: Prentice-Hall, 1985.

Gardner, James E. *Training the New Supervisor*. New York: AMACOM, 1980.

Hunt, Suellyn. "Staff Development: Your Number One Investment in the Future." *Library Personnel News* 1, no. 1 (1987): 5-6.

Imundo, Louis V. *The Effective Supervisor's Handbook*. New York: AMACOM, 1980.

Library Administration and Management Association. *Staff Development in Libraries: Bibliography*. Chicago: LAMA, 1983.

Lipow, Ann Grodzins. *Staff Development: A Practical Guide*. Chicago: LAMA, 1988.

Preston, Paul, and Thomas Zimmerer. *Management for Supervisors*. 2d ed. Englewood Cliffs, NJ: Prentice-Hall, 1983.

Rader, Hannelore. "Library Orientation and Instruction, 1987." *Reference Services Review* 16, no. 3 (1988): 57-68.

Rae, Leslie. *How to Measure Training Effectiveness*. New York: Nichols, 1986.

Robinson, Dana Gaines, and James C. Robinson. *Training for Impact: How to Link Training to Business Needs and Measure the Results*. San Francisco: Jossey-Bass, 1989.

Rosow, Jerome M., and Robert Zager. *Training, the Competitive Edge*. San Francisco: Jossey-Bass, 1988.

Schuster, Frederick E. *Human Resource Management: Concepts, Cases and Readings*. 2d ed. Reston, VA: Reston Publishing Company, 1985.

Shaughnessy, Thomas W. "Staff Development in Libraries: Why It Frequently Doesn't Take." *Journal of Library Administration* 9, no. 2 (1988): 5-12.

Shea, Gordon F. *The New Employee: Developing a Productive Human Resource*. Reading, MA: Addison-Wesley, 1981.

Siegel, Laurence, and Irving M. Lane. *Personnel and Organizational Psychology*. 2d ed. Homewood, IL: Richard D. Irwin, 1987.

Skitt, John. "Setting Up a Staff Development Scheme; Staff Appraisal and Training Needs." In *Management Issues in Academic Libraries*, edited by Tim Lomas, 67-77. London: Rossendale, 1986.

Sullivan, Maureen. *Resource Notebook on Staff Development*. Washington, DC: ARL, 1983.

Weiss, W. H. *Supervisor's Standard Reference Handbook*. 2d ed. Englewood Cliffs, NJ: Prentice-Hall, 1988.

Supervision Techniques for Student Employee Supervisors

We all learn from the mistakes of others. After all, we haven't got the time
to make them all ourselves.

— Proverb

MANAGING AND BEING MANAGED

Every person manages, is managed, and is affected by management. The largest group of managers in organizations are the first-line managers, or supervisors. As the term implies, first-line managers are those who are in closest contact with workers. In libraries, there may be two groups of first-line managers: supervisors of student employees and supervisors of permanent staff. First-line managers direct those whom they supervise and serve as a conduit for two-way communication with library administration. They must also work with their peers and their own supervisors. Normally, supervisors of student employees do not supervise other supervisors.

The organization of the academic library determines, to a large degree, how the supervisor of student employees manages and is managed.

HIERARCHICAL LIBRARY ORGANIZATION

Most academic libraries are organized in hierarchies with a dean or director, associate or assistant deans or directors for public and technical services, department heads within each division, and unit heads within departments. There are formal lines of communication and specialization of worker function within each department. Normally an administrative group composed of the dean or director and the assistants, with selected others is the decision-making body of the organization. Department heads are consulted by the assistant deans or directors and the department heads in turn consult with unit heads or their staff. Control, authority, communication, and interaction among employees are vertical in the traditional hierarchic structure. Decisions are made by the administration and communicated down the hierarchy.

Some academic libraries are transforming their organizations in an attempt to more effectively address today's problems of shrinking budgets, increased materials costs, new technologies, and increased demands for services. One of the approaches being used is team management.

TEAM MANAGEMENT

While a hierarchy stresses control, team management stresses cooperative facilitation. Responsibility for performance falls to the group in a team management situation. Team members are involved in solving problems and do not rely solely on decisions from the administration. Another major difference is that team members must communicate directly with their colleagues both within and without the team rather than relying on management as the sole source of information. Katherine W. Hawkins, has described how a library can implement a team management approach, emphasizing that commitment must exist for both workers and management in order for it to succeed.[1]

Humanistic Management by Teamwork (HMBT)

The University of New Mexico General Library implemented a team management approach in September 1986, called Humanistic Management by Teamwork (HMBT). General Library Dean Robert L. Migneault has described the approach in *Library Administration and Management*.[2]

The associate deans for technical services, collection development, and public services were eliminated, and a library administrative team composed of the Dean, Associate Dean, and all directors and department heads was formed. Each of the twenty members of the Library Management Team has all of the information needed to run the General Library, including the entire operating budget and departmental reports. The team has responsibility for establishing programs, determining priorities, assigning responsibilities, and allocating resources. The Dean's primary responsibilities are to provide leadership, represent the Library Management Team to university administration, serve as convener of the team, and facilitate discussion. Team members report directly to the Dean, but, in the practical everyday operation of the General Library, team members work with, not for, the Dean.

The benefits of the Humanistic Management by Teamwork approach at the University of New Mexico:

1. Two associate dean positions have been eliminated.

2. The split between public and technical services has been eliminated.

3. Bureaucracy was reduced by eliminating four administrative groups.

4. Quicker decision-making has been facilitated.

5. The quality of decisions has improved.

6. Change throughout the organization has been effected by the Team collectively.

7. High morale, self-esteem, and pride in the organization are evident throughout the Library.

The success of HMBT at the University of New Mexico General Library can be attributed to the leadership of the Dean and the commitment of the library faculty and staff to team management. An important aspect of management by teamwork is participative decision making.

Participative Management

Participative management encourages participation of employees in making decisions about library operations. True participative management encourages employees to express their thinking and opinions of the organization and the work and how it should be. Participative management as practiced in the library:

1. Gives all employees the opportunity to be creative members of a cooperating group. Staff members, regardless of status, can serve together on numerous committees.

2. Leads to new relationships being formed between employee and supervisor and between an employee and other employees, and encourages horizontal communication among departments of the library.

3. Spurs less skilled employees to greater effort, and encourages them to accept responsibility. The attitude of cooperation, like its opposite, among library employees is contagious.

4. Usually results in more job satisfaction and improved job performance when employees have a say in how their work should be done, output increases. Morale in the library is higher when employees have a stake in the organization.

5. Raises interest in what other people are doing and enhances the personal dignity of each individual.

6. Enables change to be accepted much more easily, particularly when those affected by it have participated in deciding what, when, and how it should be implemented.

Whether called team management or participative management, this approach will involve the entire library staff in the operation of the library. Student employees working in this environment are expected to contribute not only their time and best effort on the job, but will also be called upon to participate fully as members of their teams.

Regardless of the library's organizational structure, the supervisor performs five basic management functions.

FIVE FUNCTIONS OF MANAGEMENT

The traditional functions of management are the basis of every supervisor's job. The set of activities carried out by managers are: planning; organizing; staffing; leading and motivating; and controlling.

1. The planning function includes determining the mission, goals and objectives, and direction of a unit, and developing strategies for achieving them.

2. Organizing involves creating a structure for accomplishing tasks, including assigning work.

3. Staffing is the process of selecting, training, evaluating, disciplining, and rewarding staff.

4. Leading and motivating include creating a climate in which employees want to accomplish their work with pride.

5. Controlling involves determining if and how well the unit is accomplishing its goals.

Seldom will you find a supervisor who can name the five functions of management, let alone describe the activities or techniques utilized to perform each of the five functions, but good supervisors do perform these five functions constantly. In order for student employees to be successful, their supervisor must bear in mind that supervision is more than scheduling and assigning work to students. Supervisors perform all five functions of management, often without realizing it. A review of the principles and techniques of management will help you assess your own abilities.

AUTHORITY

Authority is handed down from the top, beginning with the highest levels. Those who appoint the governing body of the institution give them authority. Authority for the operation of the institution is delegated by the governing body to the university president, who, in turn, delegates authority to the vice president(s), who delegate authority to the dean or director of the library, and so on, to the supervisors of student employees. As authority is passed down the line, the delegated authority becomes more specific. While the dean or director has the authority to manage the personnel budget and a large staff, the student employee supervisor has the authority needed to supervise a group of student employees with specific jobs and work to perform.

Authority is the power you need to carry out your responsibilities. A student employee supervisor who, in the opinion of the employees, exceeds that supervisory authority will find that employees will question or even resist that authority. Student employee supervisors must remember that their authority is retained only so long as its use is approved by the organization and accepted by the majority of employees supervised.

According to *Webster's New World Dictionary of American English*, the definition of authority is: "1. the power or right to give commands, enforce obedience, take action, or make final decisions; jurisdiction... 2. this power as delegated to another; authorization... [as, he has my authority to do it] 3. power or influence resulting from knowledge, prestige, etc...."[3]

Authority is much misused and misunderstood in business and industry: supervisors often fail to use their authority when it should be used while other supervisors try to use authority when it does not belong to them, and some others may even use it to try to dominate other people. It is extremely important to understand that authority carries with it the responsibility to use it correctly. Supervisors of student employees must respect the problems and needs of their employees in the same way as the student employees must respect the authority of their supervisor.

New supervisors and experienced ones who have been assigned special projects often misuse their authority. Persons unaccustomed to directing or coordinating the efforts of others must be careful not to let the newly acquired authority affect how they treat people. Overuse of authority almost always causes employees to become less cooperative.

Exerting Authority

Every supervisor wants to know how to exercise authority well and feel comfortable doing it. It is not easy for those who are given authority for the first time, but who are accustomed to following orders, to use that authority. Some advice may be in order from supervisors who have experience:

1. Be certain you know what authority you have and don't have. Clarify this beforehand with your supervisor.

2. Be careful that authority does not go to your head.

3. Do not flaunt your position.

4. Delegate authority to get the job done, not to show who is boss.

5. Be considerate of others.

6. Try to promote team spirit through the careful exertion of your authority.

7. Use persuasion when you can instead of exerting your authority.

In addition to the authority given you by the organization, you will find that you can be more successful and may reinforce your authority or power with one or more of the following:

1. Your job knowledge (What do you know?)

2. Your personal influence in the organization (Who do you know?)

3. Your personal charm (Do you have it?)

4. Your abilities (How good are you at your job?)

5. Your ability to persuade (How well can you communicate?)

Delegating Authority

Generally, organizations have three levels of authority based on how supervisors make decisions:

1. Complete authority: may take action without consulting your supervisor.

2. Limited authority: may take action but your supervisor must be informed of your actions.

3. No authority: may not take action without checking with your supervisor.

In order to accomplish your department's objectives, it will be necessary to delegate responsibility and authority to subordinates. Remember that the two go together. In delegating, you must make it clear what authority is being delegated and at what level. Of course, there are responsibilities and authorities which cannot be delegated to student employees, discipline for example.

Authority is an essential part of a supervisor's job. Always be sure to find out what authority you have and set about exerting it wisely and carefully. Your success as a supervisor may well depend on it.

RESPONSIBILITY

There is an important difference between the positions of worker and supervisor: by accepting a supervisory position, one accepts the attendant responsibilities of the position.

According to *Webster's New World Dictionary of American English*, the definition of responsibility is: "1. condition, quality, fact, or instance of being responsible; obligation... 2. a thing or person that one is responsible for."[4]

Responsibility and authority go hand in hand, but are quite different. Responsibilities are those things for which you are held accountable by your supervisor and library management. Authority is the power you need to carry out your responsibilities as student employee supervisor.

It is important for you, as a student supervisor, to determine with your supervisor what your responsibilities are. If asked, your supervisor may simply reply, "You are responsible for the students in this department." Your next question should be, "Do I also have the authority to take necessary actions without consulting you or do you want me to check with you first?" Your supervisor may reply, "Just do what you think is right but keep me informed." In this brief conversation, you have determined that you are entirely responsible for planning, organizing, staffing, leading and motivating, and controlling all aspects of student employment in your department and that your supervisor has given you limited authority: you may take action but your supervisor must be informed.

In addition, there are obvious legal responsibilities which apply to supervisor and employee alike: (1) the responsibility to perform the work for which hired; and, (2) the responsibility to follow organizational policies, procedures, and rules.

MAKING DECISIONS

Without question, being decisive is a valuable attribute for a supervisor. When making decisions, the supervisor exhibits leadership skills and provides assurance to employees that everything is under control. The skills of making decisions under pressure must be developed in order to be effective.

To be decisive you must want to solve problems and have the confidence to do so. A good decision-maker must know how and when to make decisions and be aware of the factors which influence decisions. Most importantly, you must have information with which to make good decisions. Successful decision-makers don't decide without the facts. Find out what you need to know. Who is involved? What has been the past practice? When must the decision be made?

The good supervisor is not reluctant to make decisions. You can and should learn to be decisive. The following suggestions will help you develop a pattern of decision-making which works.

1. Dispose of minor decisions quickly: by making these decisions promptly, you will have more time to devote to important matters.

2. Be firm in making a decision: don't leave any doubt about what you have decided.

3. Don't waste time thinking about what you could have done.

4. Dispel any thoughts that you might make a mistake.

5. Carry out your decisions promptly.

Making Good Decisions

You can make good decisions if you do not act hastily, get the facts, and take time to think. It is not necessary to have experience with similar problems to make good decisions. There are four basic steps:

1. Be sure you understand the problem. If you are able to clearly state the problem, you are well on the way to resolving it. Writing it down often helps you define it.

2. Get as much information as possible. Look for alternative answers.

3. Examine the good and bad points of each alternative. Will each actually solve the problem? What are the risks of each? What is wrong with what appears to be the first choice?

4. Select the best alternative as your decision. Take action and monitor the results.

Even though it is your responsibility to make decisions, there are occasions when the best decision is to take no action at all. How can a supervisor determine when a decision must be made or when to leave a condition well enough alone? Experienced supervisors have learned to distinguish real problems from conditions or situations which are merely irritating.

Supervisors are usually required to make a number of decisions each day. At times you may question whether a specific decision is really yours to make or whether it should be made at a higher level. Common sense dictates that decisions should be made at the lowest level of the organization, consistent with the functions of each supervisory position. If the problem requiring a decision fits into the normal duties and responsibilities of your position, the decision should rightly be made by you. If the decision will affect more than your unit's staff, procedures, or services, or if it is in conflict with existing policy, the decision should be made at a higher level.

There is much more to making a decision than just deciding. You need to consider the feelings of the people affected by your decision: by having others participate in making the decision you will have much greater acceptance. Timing must also be considered: carefully pick the time and place for announcing a decision. Be certain that you feel good about it before making an important decision.

No One Is Perfect — Bad Decisions

Eventually you will make a bad decision—probably more than one. The most experienced and successful supervisors make mistakes. When a bad decision is made, you must do what you can to correct it. Be sure to make the extra effort and devote the time needed when reconsidering your decision. If you plan to reverse a decision, be sure to seek advice in order to avoid making another bad decision when correcting the first one.

One approach to developing decision-making skills is to examine the causes of poor decisions:

1. Insufficient or inaccurate information. Lack of information can lead to false conclusions, and therefore poor decisions.

2. Insufficient time to decide. By taking the time to gather information, you increase your chance of making a good decision.

3. Fear of making a bad decision. If you lack confidence in your abilities, the quality of your decisions may be affected.

4. Overcaution. If you are overly concerned about the risks involved, you may be too cautious.

5. Not enough authority. If you have responsibility without the authority, your decisions will be unenforceable.

6. Underestimated importance. If you misjudge the seriousness or importance of the situation, you may not give it enough attention or ignore it all together.

7. Emotion. Poor decisions result when emotion rather than reason is used in making decisions.

If Your Decisions Are Challenged

Not all of your decisions will be readily accepted. People have their own opinions, may think differently than you, or have more information than you have. In most cases, a decision is challenged because people do not understand it or why you made it. If you have made a good decision, you should have no trouble explaining it. Persons who have valid and logical arguments may still disagree. When questioned, calmly say that you would be glad to discuss their opinions. Listen to their points of view and, if you discover that you have made a bad decision, be willing to admit it and correct it. Listening is without question, one of the most important skills in supervision.

COMMUNICATION

The term "communication" is defined as the process in human relations of passing information and understanding from one person to another. Communication between supervisor and employees is extremely important as are communication among supervisors and between supervisor and boss. Human communications suffer the same problems as mechanical or electronic communications: poor reception, interference, or being tuned to the wrong channel.

Communicating with Individuals

For a supervisor, nothing is better than face-to-face communication with employees. Being able to see how your words are affecting the person to whom you are talking is valuable. Your haste, tone, mood, gestures, or facial expression may affect how the individual reacts. The opportunity for two-way communication is extremely important. A disadvantage is that it takes time. At the end of the day you may feel that you have done nothing but talk.

Communication with individuals may take the form of informal talks, planned appointments, or telephone calls. Face-to-face communication should always be used when the subject is of personal importance to either person. Written communication may take the form of memos, letters, or reports. The advantage of written communication is that all recipients are given exactly the same information. It is needed for messages that are intended to be formal or official, or to have long-term effects. The use of memos should not be overdone: they should be used as seldom as possible. Face-to-face communication is much preferred.

Communicating with Groups

Effective communication with groups requires special skills. The best way of developing group cohesiveness is the use of regular, informal staff meetings, supplemented with individual face-to-face communication. Scheduling a time when all of the student employees in your unit can meet is always a problem. It is important, however, to recognize the need to schedule such meetings if at all possible. Written communication for groups normally takes the form of bulletin board notices or a "must read" notebook. The notebook is an effective way to make certain that all written information is seen by all student employees in your unit.

Encouraging Employees to Communicate with You

In the long run, people will not listen to you if you will not listen to them. Employees will learn to talk to you if you will demonstrate that you listen. How can you improve your listening skills?

1. Don't assume or anticipate anything. Allow the employee to tell you what is wanted.

2. Don't interrupt. Wait for the employee to finish speaking. Don't give anyone the impression that you do not have the time to listen.

3. Try to understand the need. Look for the reason the employee wants your attention. Often what the employee says is wanted is not the real thing. Student employees are typically more straightforward and able to express themselves better than many employee groups.

4. Don't react too quickly. Try to understand the other person's viewpoint. Be patient and do not jump to conclusions.

Communicating with Student Employees

Listening cannot be overemphasized. When an employee comes to you with a problem and the solution is very clear, offer it, but if it is possible, help student employees develop their own solutions.

What is the best form of communication? For a supervisor, nothing can beat face-to-face communication. In a participative management environment, student employees are involved in the discussions and decisions on procedure and policy. Good communication is critical to your success as a supervisor.

GROUP EFFORT

Organizations depend on the effectiveness of group effort. The success of any supervisor depends on how well the employees in the group perform their work. The individuals assembled to perform work comprise the work group. In the library, student employees work varied schedules, often spread throughout an eighty to one hundred hour workweek. When a supervisor needs a minimum of three student workers on duty all of the hours the library is open, it is not unusual for two students in the same department to never work at the same time. Turnover in the student work force and changes in class schedules also contribute to changes in the group. At any given time the supervisor is supervising different combinations of student workers in an ever-changing work group.

What groups do best is solve problems. Get group support for problem solving by encouraging participation. Get individuals to work together to attain common goals, by getting the individuals in groups to work with you. By sharing knowledge and information, decision-making, and credit with the group, you can assure that the group will work most effectively.

GIVING DIRECTIONS

The successful supervisor is able to be the boss without being obvious about it. It used to be assumed that all a supervisor had to do was order an employee to do something and the employee would do it. Today's employees deserve more consideration. If employees feel they are offered some say in decisions that affect them, they will work harder. Student employees do not need to be ordered: generally speaking, a request carries the same weight as an order and implies that the employee has some choice in the matter.

Guidelines for Giving Directions

1. Avoid an "I'll show you who's boss" attitude when giving direction. You should project the idea that there is a situation that requires the employee's attention, and that it is based on more than your whim.

2. Be firm when giving direction. If delivered in an offhand manner, the request may not be taken seriously.

3. Watch what you say when giving direction. Be specific so there is no misunderstanding about what you want done.

4. Don't assume the employee understands. Give the student employees a chance to ask questions or to complain about the assignment if they wish. It is better to clear up any questions or concerns right away.

5. Don't overdo it. Be selective in issuing instructions and avoid giving too many orders. Don't give complex instructions when brief ones will do. Think about what information the person you are talking to really needs.

6. Avoid conflicting instructions. Make certain that you are telling your student employees the same thing as supervisors in similar departments are telling theirs.

7. Don't overwork the cooperative employee. Some people are more cooperative than others. Be sure you do not give directions only to those you know will cooperate without complaint.

8. Distribute the unpleasant tasks fairly. Resist the temptation to punish certain employees by assigning the difficult or unpleasant jobs to them only.

9. Don't flaunt your authority. You don't have to crack the whip to gain student employees' cooperation and respect.

Getting Cooperation

Good supervision is the art of getting others to do what you want, when you want it, and how you want it. In order to succeed as a supervisor, you must get others to cooperate with you. You have to develop good relations with those you supervise and earn their cooperation. Here are eight ways to promote cooperation:

1. Stress team effort whenever possible. Use the word "we" when talking with employees.

2. Reward people who do more than you ask of them.

3. Set realistic goals with the help of your employees.

4. Praise your employees. Never criticize an employee in front of others.

5. Supervise with persuasion, not force or pressure.

6. Help your employees when they need and request it.

7. Be honest about problems and issues with your employees.

8. Involve your employees in problem-solving and decision-making.

MOTIVATION

All supervisors want motivated employees. There will always be highly motivated individuals and self-starters who wish to work in the library, and some of them may work for you. However, many employees are unmotivated, often resulting from and causing low morale, absenteeism, and high turnover. Employee motivation can be defined as those techniques used to influence an individual to integrate personal needs and goals with those of the organization.

The individual's motivational drives and societal attitudes toward work affect employee motivation. The supervisor can inhibit or contribute to an individual's motivation but it is primarily self directed. Employee motivation is an important aspect of any supervisor's job and one which seems quite difficult on the surface.

Job satisfaction and motivation are closely tied. To help you understand how your employees can become motivated from the job itself, think about the worst and best jobs you've ever had. When you consider the worst jobs, more than likely what will come to mind are things that made it unbearable: long hours, bad weather, dirty, boring, bad boss, no chance for advancement, etc. Those things which made the job bad were mainly bad environment, rather than the nature of the job itself.

When you consider the best job you've had, you may think about how hard you worked, the long hours, how you couldn't wait to get to work, and couldn't believe how fast the time went. The best job probably provided challenge, responsibility, variety, recognition, and meaning. The good job has some of the same characteristics as the bad—long hours, poor working conditions, not enough money. In addition, however, the good job carries with it responsibility, challenge, recognition, and meaning.

If your student employees' job carry some responsibility and provide challenge, recognition, and meaning, does it not make sense that the job itself can be a motivator to employees? Examine your students' jobs and determine how you can add some of these elements. Motivation can also be accomplished through coaching.

Coaching

Coaching can be considered continuous training. Just as an athletic coach provides the knowledge and skill training for athletic competition, the manager is charged with the responsibility of not only initial training but also keeping up the employees' skills and knowledge.

As employees' basic skills begin to slip away, coaching is needed. There are many possible reasons for this deterioration in a person's skills. Boredom with routine tasks causes many employees to look for shortcuts which, taken over time, diminish the employees' ability to remember exactly what the tasks were originally. The shortcuts or changes in the job are attempts to add variety to the job. This deterioration of skills is called "professional degeneration." Another reason for skills deterioration is that employees want independence and will want to try things their own way. While employees often bring fresh ideas about how the job should be done, they need to be kept on the right track so that the job is done correctly and efficiently. Regular coaching is one of the best ways of keeping employees on the right track.

Certain employee behaviors can be changed by holding group meetings, but individual coaching is usually the most effective means of coaching. It is not uncommon, however, for supervisors to hold group training sessions to correct the behavior of one individual. Individual performance causes group performance: for the group to succeed, each individual must succeed. Coaching one-on-one is usually the most effective means for changing individual behavior.

The Coaching Process

You first must identify the behavior that needs to be changed and know what behavior you want to substitute. How do you change it? Saying to the employee, "Look, Mary, I've shown you twice how to do that. If you don't do it right, your replacement will do it right," is counterproductive. Coaching is teaching, not scolding. Here is a logical step-by-step process:

1. Observe the present behavior, compare it to the total behavior, and identify what must be changed.

2. Discuss the needed changes with the employee. Does the student employee know the present behavior is wrong? Does the employee know the correct behavior?

3. Get the employee to talk about ideas for improving the task.

4. Demonstrate the desired behavior until the employee can do it correctly and can explain the reason for doing it that way.

5. Praise the employee for correct behavior.

A good supervisor coaches student employees in much the same manner as a football coach coaches a team: corrective measures are taken when a change is needed in an observable behavior. Coaching is an excellent way to alter behavior, making a good employee an excellent employee. It is a continual process which is an extension of training.

COUNSELING

Counseling has a more personal aspect to it than coaching. While coaching is intended to improve a person's skills, counseling is a private discussion of problems, other than personal ones, which have a bearing on job performance. When there is something which is worrying the employee, the supervisor must discover and correct it if possible.

You will encounter two types of counseling sessions: those you initiate and those initiated by the student employee. Neither is more important than the other and you must be available whether the purpose is to discuss a personal problem or to allow the employee to "blow off steam."

You may need to speak with a student employee if you have heard or observed that things were not going well for the student. The employee has exhibited behavior which tells you something is wrong and you feel that a counseling session is needed.

Counseling Sessions You Call

The following is a step-by-step procedure will help you improve the counseling sessions you call:

1. Determine why the student employee is exhibiting the wrong behavior. The reasons may be revealed by observing the employee or talking privately with the employee's co-workers. These conversations should take place only with those you trust to maintain confidentiality. Be sensitive to privacy considerations. Try to determine the cause before you talk to the affected employee.

2. Plan ahead for the counseling session. Carefully think through what you want to discuss.

3. Notify the employee that you want to meet a day or two in advance of the meeting. Never call a counseling session on the spur of the moment unless it is an emergency.

4. Meet privately. If you can't stop the phone calls and interruptions, hold the meeting away from your office.

5. Put the employee at ease. Discuss anything except the topic at hand for a few minutes. If the purpose is to discuss poor performance, stress first the positive aspects of the employee's abilities.

6. State that the discussion will be kept confidential.

7. Get to the point of the session. Encourage the employee to talk while you listen.

8. Help the student employee save face by letting the employee know that you or others have faced similar situations.

9. Come to an agreement about what needs to be done.

10. Offer your assistance if possible and set a time to discuss what has been done.

11. If job-related, make a written note of the discussion for the file which includes date, time, location, subject, and outcome. File the note for future reference if needed.

12. Keep your promise to maintain confidentiality.

Counseling Sessions the Employee Requests

When you call the meeting, you have the advantage of being able to plan for it, but the situation is quite different when the employee asks to talk to you. It often starts with the employee appearing at your office door and saying, "Do you have a minute, Steve? I need to talk to you," or "Mary, when could I see you for thirty minutes?" A good practice is not to jump into a counseling session unless it is an emergency. Ascertain, if you can, what the subject of the meeting is beforehand and then set a time later in the day or the next day if possible. It is entirely possible, however, that you will not know the subject of the meeting until it takes place. The procedure for a meeting initiated by an employee is similar to the one called by a supervisor, but with a few differences:

1. You may only be needed as a sounding board for the employee, i.e., someone to talk to about a personal problem.

2. Know your limitations. Psychologists and psychiatrists have the proper training to counsel students with emotional problems. Your advice or answers may do more to complicate the problem than solve it for the student employee.

3. Be careful to avoid becoming involved in a student's emotional problems and be sensitive to privacy considerations.

4. After the student employee has vented the problem, ask the employee to offer possible solutions.

5. After possible solutions have been discussed, offer encouragement and ask if the employee would like to schedule a future meeting to discuss the situation.

6. What the two of you have discussed is confidential. Keep it that way.

The supervisor of student employees should be familiar with all of the counseling services available on campus and be prepared to describe them. Remember that you are not alone. Seek the advice of your supervisor or fellow student employee supervisors, making sure to maintain confidentiality. Be aware, however, that no one may have had precisely the same problem with the same circumstances.

Not All Counseling Is Negative

It must be noted that not all counseling sessions are negative. The student employee may be interested in discussing prospects for advancement on the job or seeking your advice. A good supervisor makes it a habit to counsel employees on a regular basis. Most of us do not consider this to be counseling, but it is good practice to give student employees regular opportunities to discuss the job or anything they wish to talk about.

Counseling can be used to resolve employee problems or to give them opportunities to discuss anything on their minds. It lets them know you are interested in them as employees and individuals.

SUPERVISORY PRINCIPLES

A quotation from Benjamin Spock's *Baby and Child Care* seems quite appropriate here: "Trust yourself. You know more than you think you do." Many of the principles which are the basis of supervision are plain, old-fashioned common sense. It is important that you develop a foundation of knowledge in supervision but, when in doubt, use your common sense.

The next chapter describes how to resolve problems common to student employee supervision.

NOTES

[1]Katherine W. Hawkins, "Implementing Team Management in the Modern Library," *Library Administration and Management*, (Winter 1989): 11-15.

[2]Robert LaLiberte Migneault, "Humanistic Management by Teamwork in Academic Libraries," *Library Administration and Management*, (June 1988): 132-36.

[3]*Webster's New World Dictionary of American English*, 3rd College edition (Cleveland, OH: Webster's New World, 1988), 92.

[4]Ibid, 1144.

BIBLIOGRAPHY

Advances in Library Administration and Organization. Greenwich, CT: JAI Press, 1982- (annual).

Armstrong, Michael. *A Handbook of Management Techniques*. New York: Nichols, 1986.

Armstrong, Michael. *How to Be an Even Better Manager*. New York: Nichols, 1988.

Beach, Dale S. *Personnel: The Management of People at Work*. 5th ed. New York: Macmillan, 1985.

Belker, Loren B. *The First-time Manager: A Practical Guide to the Management of People*. New York: AMACOM, 1978.

Bird, Malcolm. *There Is a Better Way to Manage*. New York: Nichols, 1985.

Bittel, Lester R. *What Every Supervisor Should Know*. New York: McGraw-Hill, 1980.

Bommer, M. R. W., and R. W. Chorba. *Decision Making for Library Management*. White Plains, NY: Knowledge Industry Publications, 1982.

Bottomley, Michael H. *Personnel Management*. Plymouth, England: MacDonald and Evans, 1983.

Boyatzis, Richard E. *The Competent Manager: A Model for Effective Performance*. San Francisco: Jossey-Bass, 1987.

Bradford, David L., and Allen R. Cohen. *Managing for Excellence*. New York: Wiley, 1984.

Broadwell, Martin M. *Moving up to Supervision*, 2d edition. New York: Wiley, 1986.

Broadwell, Martin M., and Ruth Sizemore House. *Supervising Technical and Professional People*. New York: Wiley, 1986.

Broadwell, Martin M. *Supervising Today: A Guide for Positive Leadership*, 2d edition. New York: Wiley, 1986.

Brown, Nancy A. "Academic Libraries: An Operational Model for Participation." *Canadian Library Journal* 36 (August 1979): 201-7.

Brown, Nancy A. "Managing the Coexistence of Hierarchical and Collegial Governance Structures." *College & Research Libraries* 46 (November 1985): 478-82.

Burckel, Nicholas C. "Participatory Management in Academic Libraries: A Review." *College & Research Libraries* 45 (January 1984): 25-34.

Cowen, John. *The Self-Reliant Manager*. New York: AMACOM, 1977.

Daughtrey, Anne Scott, and Betty Roper Ricks. *Contemporary Supervision: Managing People and Technology*. New York: McGraw-Hill, 1988.

Dickinson, D. W. "Some Reflections on Participative Management in Libraries." *College & Research Libraries* 39 (July 1978): 253-62.

Drucker, Peter F. *Management: Tasks, Responsibilities, Practices*. New York: Harper and Row, 1974.

Dutton, B. G. "Staff Management and Staff Participation." In *A Reader in Library Management*, edited by Ross Shimmon, 129-45. London: Bingley, 1976.

Engel, Herbert M. *How to Delegate: A Guide to Getting Things Done*. Houston: Gulf Press, 1983.

Evans, G. Edward. *Management Techniques for Librarians*. 2d ed. New York: Academic Press, 1983.

Evered, James F. *Shirt-Sleeves Management*. New York: AMACOM, 1981.

Fallon, William K., ed. *Leadership on the Job: Guides to Good Supervision*. New York: AMACOM, 1981.

Franklin, W. H. "Why You Can't Motivate Everyone." *Supervisory Management* 25 (April 1980): 21-8.

Fuller, Robert M., and Stephen G. Franklin. *Supervision: Principles of Professional Management*. New York: Macmillan, 1982.

Gardner, James E. *Training the New Supervisor*. New York: AMACOM, 1980.

Grant, P. C. "Why Employee Motivation Has Declined in America." *Personnel Journal* 61 (December 1982): 905-9.

Hawkins, Katherine W. "Implementing Team Management in the Modern Library." *Library Administration and Management* (Winter 1989): 11-15.

Hodgetts, Richard M. *Effective Supervision: A Practical Approach*. New York: McGraw-Hill, 1987.

Howard, Helen. "Personnel Administration in Libraries." *Argus* 11, nos. 3/4 (May-August 1982): 85-90.

Imundo, Louis V. *The Effective Supervisor's Handbook*. New York: AMACOM, 1980.

Kaplan, Louis. "The Literature of Participation: From Optimism to Realism." *College & Research Libraries* 36 (November 1975): 473-79.

Kaplan, Louis. "On the Road to Participative Management: The American Academic Library, 1934-1970." *Libri* 38, no. 4 (1988): 314-20.

Kirkpatrick, Donald L. *How to Improve Performance through Appraisal and Coaching*. New York: AMACOM, 1982.

Kleingartner, Archie, and Carolyn S. Anderson. *Human Resource Management in High Technology Firms*. Lexington, MA: Lexington Books, 1987.

Koontz, Harold, and Heinz Weihrich. *Management*. 9th ed. New York: McGraw-Hill, 1988.

Lieberman, Ernest D. *Unfit to Manage!* New York: McGraw-Hill, 1988.

Lynch, Beverly P. "Participative Management in Relation to Library Effectiveness." *College & Research Libraries* 33 (September 1972): 382-90.

MacCrimmon, Kenneth R., and Donald A. Ehrenburg, with W. T. Stanbury. *Taking Risks: The Management of Uncertainty*. New York: Free Press, 1986.

Maher, John R. *New Perspectives in Job Enrichment*. New York: Van Nostrand Reinhold, 1971.

Maidment, Robert. *Robert's Rules of Disorder: A Guide to Mismanagement*. Gretna, LA: Pelican, 1976.

Marchant, Maurice P. "Participative Management, Job Satisfaction, and Service." *Library Journal* 107 (15 April 1982): 782-84.

Marchant, Maurice P. *Participatory Management in Libraries*. Westport, CT: Greenwood Press, 1977.

Martin, Murray S. *Personnel Management in Academic Libraries*. Greenwich, CT: JAI Press, 1981.

Matthieson, E., and J. Hollwitz. "Giving Instructions That Get Followed." *Supervisory Management* 28 (May 1983): 20-4.

Migneault, Robert LaLiberte. "Humanistic Management by Teamwork in Academic Libraries." *Library Administration and Management* (June 1988): 132-36.

Miles, Raymond E. *Theories of Management Implications for Organizational Behavior and Development*. New York: McGraw-Hill, 1975.

Morgan, Gareth. *Images of Organizations*. Beverly Hills, CA: Sage, 1986.

Myers, Donald W. *Human Resources Management: Principles and Practice*. Chicago: Commerce Clearinghouse, 1986.

Peters, Thomas. *Thriving on Chaos: Handbook for a Management Revolution*. New York: Knopf, 1988.

Porter, Jack Nusan, and Ruth Taplin. *Conflict and Conflict Resolution: A Sociological Introduction with Updated Bibliography and Theory Section*. Lanham, MD: University Press of America, 1987.

Preston, Paul, and Thomas Zimmerer. *Management for Supervisors*. 2d ed. Englewood Cliffs, NJ: Prentice-Hall, 1983.

Reinharth, Leon, et al. *The Practice of Planning: Strategic, Administrative and Operational*. New York: Van Nostrand Reinhold, 1981.

Reitz, H. Joseph. *Behavior in Organizations*. 3d ed. Homewood, IL: Dow Jones-Irwin, 1987.

Rizzo, John R. *Management for Librarians: Fundamentals and Issues*. Westport, CT: Greenwood Press, 1980.

Rooks, Dana C. *Motivating Today's Library Staff: A Management Guide*. Phoenix, AZ: Oryx, 1988.

Rosenbaum, B. L. "Understanding and Using Motivation." *Supervisory Management* 24 (January 1979): 9-13.

Sager, Donald J. *Participatory Management in Libraries*. Metuchen, NJ: Scarecrow Press, 1982.

Sashkin, Marshall, and William C. Morris. *Experiencing Management*. Reading, MA: Addison-Wesley, 1987.

Savall, Henri. *Work and People: An Economic Evaluation of Job Enrichment*. New York: Oxford University Press, 1981.

Scarpello, Vida Gulbinas, and James Ledvinka. *Personnel/Human Resource Management*. Boston: PWS-Kent, 1988.

Schuster, Frederick E. *Human Resource Management: Concepts, Cases and Readings*. 2d ed. Reston, VA: Reston Publishing Company, 1985.

Siegel, Laurence, and Lane, Irving M. *Personnel and Organizational Psychology*. 2d ed. Homewood, IL: Richard D. Irwin, 1987.

Simon, Herbert A. *Administrative Behavior: A Study of the Decision-Making Processes in Administrative Organization*. 3d ed. New York: Free Press, 1976.

Smith, Kenwyn, and David N. Berg. *Paradoxes of Group Life: Understanding Conflict, Paralysis and Movement in Group Dynamics*. San Francisco: Jossey-Bass, 1987.

Steinmetz, Lawrence L. *The Art and Skill of Delegation*. Reading, MA: Addison-Wesley, 1976.

Stevens, Norman D. *Communication throughout Libraries*. Metuchen, NJ: Scarecrow Press, 1983.

Stewart, Henry. "Staff Participation in the Management of Libraries and Its Relationship to Library Performance Characteristics." Ph.D. diss., Indiana University, 1972.

Stueart, Robert D., and Barbara B. Moran. *Library Management*. 3d ed. Littleton, CO: Libraries Unlimited, 1987.

Taylor, Harold L. *Delegate: The Key to Successful Management*. New York: Beaufort Books, 1984.

Vroom, Victor H., and Edward L. Deci, eds. *Management and Motivation: Selected Readings*. Harmondsworth, England: Penguin, 1970.

Webb, Gisela M. "Implementing Team Management at the Texas Tech University Libraries." *Library Personnel News* 1, no. 4 (1987): 39-40.

Weiss, W. H. *Supervisor's Standard Reference Handbook*. 2d ed. Englewood Cliffs, NJ: Prentice-Hall, 1988.

White, Herbert S. *Library Personnel Management*. White Plains, NY: Knowledge Industry Publications, 1985.

Resolving Problems with Student Employees

It is not the same to talk about bulls as it is to be in the bull ring.
— Spanish Proverb

STUDENT EMPLOYEE PROBLEMS

This chapter includes some of the most common problems in supervising student employees in academic libraries. The suggestions offered are certainly not absolute answers since situations, circumstances, and the people involved differ from one time to another. You, the supervisor, will have to evaluate individually each problem you face and decide what course of action would be the most appropriate for the student employee and the library.

After reading this chapter, you will find that many problems can be resolved by talking to or counseling student employees, but be careful to avoid becoming involved in a student's emotional problems. Know your own limitations: your advice or answers can do more to complicate the problem than solve it for the student employee. Only psychologists and psychiatrists have the proper training to counsel students with emotional problems.

Before labeling a student employee a problem, consider the possibility that the cause may be poor management. One study found that about half of the employees labeled problems by supervisors were victims of poor supervision.[1] These employees had not been adequately trained, had not been given counseling when needed, or had not received written warnings when required. Supervisors who do not have the patience nor the ability to help employees change their behavior should resolve to improve their own behavior or seriously consider getting out of supervision.

Remember that you are not alone. Seek the advice of your supervisor or fellow student employee supervisors, although no one may have had precisely the same problem with precisely the same circumstances. There are also numerous books on supervision which can be consulted. Mix all you learn from colleagues and books with a large dose of common sense and humanity and you will do well.

THE STUDENT EMPLOYEE WHO COMPLAINS

Student employees who complain are a constant source of frustration to supervisors. Chronic complainers often do a poor job or avoid work, as a poor attitude, exhibited by complaining, manifests itself in poor work performance and unhappiness. Supervisors need to take action when complaining affects the amount of work being accomplished or is unsettling to others in the department.

The first step is to talk privately to the student. Remember that a complaint is always justified from the point of view of the complainer and the complaint (or the complainer) must be dealt with promptly. Explain that you understand that the employee is unhappy with the work and has complaints about the library. Investigate the nature of the complaint with questions such as, "What's wrong?" or "What happened?" Listen carefully. Empathize with the complainer and show your concern.

Poor communications are behind many complaints. Providing a clear explanation may resolve the complaint. Other complaints result from the transfer of anger: something has happened which put the employee in a poor frame of mind. A few questions about how things are going in general may reveal the situation.

Handling a complaint or complainer is one of the most difficult parts of a supervisor's job. Put yourself in the complainer's position and try to understand how the complainer feels.

THE UNMOTIVATED STUDENT EMPLOYEE

The unmotivated student employee is a constant concern to supervisors. Whether the person does not like the work, appears to be lazy, dawdles on the job, is bored, or feels unappreciated, the result is usually that the employee and the employer both are dissatisfied.

Motivation is a severe problem for many student employees since their primary focus is on their education. They work in the library because they need the money and probably are not interested in working in the library for longer than is necessary to reach their own goals.

The unmotivated employee can be a poor influence on fellow workers and the problem must be addressed. The first step is to talk with the employee and determine the cause.

If the student does not like the work, there may be something else in the department or the library more suited to the employee's interests and abilities. If not, the student employee should be referred to the student employment office for reassignment.

If the student appears to be lazy or dawdles on the job, calling the student employee's attention to it may help the individual make adjustments, even if only temporarily. If the student employee continues to exhibit the same behavior, make it clear in a private conversation that, unless there is a change in behavior, both the employee and the department would be better served if the student worked somewhere else.

If the student employee is bored, an effort should be made to enrich the job by adding other duties. Just calling attention to the obvious boredom may help the employee make adjustments, but if the student employee continues to exhibit the same behavior, inform the employee that termination may result and suggest that the employee might be more suited to other work.

If the student feels unappreciated, the supervisor must take steps to address the problem. Inform the employee that you and the library appreciate and depend on the student employee's contribution. Give your full attention and show interest when the employee communicates with you. Compliment the employee in the presence of others. Impart to the student employee that you are interested.

In dealing with the unmotivated employee, supervisors must be alert to the need to make *all* employees feel a part of the department's team. Just being a member of a group is important for job satisfaction and good productivity and compatibility among workers promotes good performance.

Chapter 8 contains more suggestions on motivating employees.

THE STUDENT EMPLOYEE WITH LOW MORALE

Closely related to employee motivational problems, low morale can disrupt the workplace. Low morale is exhibited most often by student employee complaints about wages and working conditions, but it can be caused by a number of things including low pay, difficult work, schedules, lack of advancement, and quality of working conditions.

To understand the causes of low morale, supervisors must know that all humans share five basic needs. These needs, which govern behavior, vary in intensity for different people, but must be satisfied in order from outer needs to inner needs: physical needs; security needs; need to belong; ego needs; and achievement needs.

Physical needs are the basic animal needs for food and shelter. Until these needs are satisfied, the others are unimportant, but once satisfied, other needs emerge. The needs to be protected from bodily harm, for a job, and for financial security are the security needs. Once an individual feels secure, the need to belong, to be accepted by others, to have friends, and to identify with others must be satisfied. This is the human herd instinct. After the need to belong is satisfied, ego needs become important, including the need to be recognized and well thought of, to be independent and avoid embarrassment, to have a good self-image, and to be in control of situations. When ego needs have been essentially met, the achievement needs become important. Achievement or self-fulfillment needs result in the drive to be the best and to advance on the job.

The physical and security needs and the need to belong are, for the most part satisfied, in most student employees, as are the ego and achievement needs. Those student employees with low morale most often complain about wages (security need) and lack of advancement (achievement need).

Efforts must be made to be certain that student employees are paid for work performed. Find out whether the student is being paid fairly in relation to other student employees performing duties at the same level and, if you find that the student is paid fairly, explain explicitly how wages are determined. If the student is in a position of needing more pay to meet financial obligations, refer the employee to the employment office to see if placement in another position in the library or on campus is possible. If there are other duties which can be assigned which would result in a higher wage and if it is within the supervisor's authority to do so, the student's security and achievement can be satisfied and the problem of low morale resolved. The student should be made to feel that both the student personally and the student's work are essential to the successful operation of the department.

THE DISLOYAL STUDENT EMPLOYEE

Unfortunately, not all employees are loyal to the organization for which they work. If there are student employees who are disloyal to the library, so what? The student employees are paid to work and nothing else aren't they? What possible harm could there be in having student employees who are not loyal? In fact, disloyalty can have serious consequences. They show their disloyalty to the library, both on- and off-the-job, and their statements and actions or inactions hurt both the library and themselves. Disloyalty is shown by employees who speak badly of the library, fail to keep promises, take advantage of the library in work procedures, or threaten to leave. Loyal student employees, on the other hand, are concerned about the library, its success, and its future. Supervisors must be alert to signs of disloyalty among student employees and act when they see or hear indications of it.

Employees often withhold loyalty until the supervisor and the library have earned it. You cannot buy or win loyalty with favors: it must be built by making employees feel that they belong and are part of the library. Student employees must be made to feel that the success of the library depends on each of them doing their share and cooperating with co-workers and supervisors.

Student employees' value to the library depends not only on their talents and abilities but also on their willingness to use those abilities and talents to help the library. When they do not use those talents and abilities for the good of the library, employees are hurting themselves and their reputations, as well as their employer and co-workers.

Supervisors need to determine to what extent their student employees are involved in planning for the department. When employees, student or permanent full-time, are involved in planning, they feel a commitment to helping carry out the plans they helped formulate. Even the student employee who is involved in planning and is an important member of the team may fail, however, to perform as expected, or may be absent too often. It is important to talk to such students, making sure the importance of everyone's contribution to the accomplishment of departmental objectives is understood. If the student fails again, inform the employee of the consequences of this action and follow through with disciplinary action at the next offense.

The student employee who criticizes the library can also have a negative effect on other employees and on library users, thus seriously harming the library's reputation and programs. If you were to ask a student employee how loyal the student was to the library, your sanity might be questioned since most employees tend to think about a library's loyalty to the employees rather than the opposite. They think only of the benefits, such as job security, etc., offered by the library which help employees meet personal needs.

The supervisor must determine the cause of the criticism. Has the library in some way mistreated the student? Can the student employee give you examples of how the library has treated the student or other employees unfairly? When you have learned the reasons for this attitude, you can either prove to the student employee that it is the wrong attitude or correct the problem.

THE STUDENT EMPLOYEE WHO VIOLATES LIBRARY RULES

Violation of company rules has always plagued business and industry. In order to avoid such problems, companies provide employees with handbooks of regulations and procedures. A handbook, however, is a poor substitute for personal training because the handbooks are seldom read or understood in toto. Supervisors should inform new student employees about library rules and regulations as soon as possible after they are hired.

When a rule is broken, the supervisor must determine first whether or not the student worker was aware of the rule and understood the reason for it. The supervisor is responsible for disciplining chronic rule breakers: by overlooking a violation or saying nothing, you are condoning the action and making that particular rule completely unenforceable. Supervisors must speak and act with authority. Appearing unsure only causes confusion, anxiety and worry for everyone.

Remember that the purpose of discipline is corrective, not punitive. Avoid using sarcasm or threats, and never penalize anyone without an explanation. Spend time discussing the rule and explain concisely what you expect of the employee in the future.

The library's policies should clearly spell out personnel rules and regulations and must be communicated to student workers. A student handbook, although it may not be read or understood, is essential. The orientation of new employees should stress the importance of reading the handbook and accepting responsibility for abiding by the policies therein.

THE STUDENT WORKER WITH ABSENTEEISM PROBLEMS

Probably the most frequent problem with student employees is their inability to work all of the hours scheduled. Whether they are scheduled to work at the circulation desk or to search new book orders, student workers are expected to perform those duties on a scheduled basis. The library must maintain a certain level of staffing, especially for night and weekend service hours. Students are required, however, to meet specific requirements for courses, e.g., field trips, special lectures or performances, extra classes, tests, etc. Students are not immune to illnesses or family crises which require their absence from work. The obvious solution is for the library to employ sufficient permanent staff so as not to rely on student workers, but in the real world of academic libraries, funds are not available to hire all the staff members needed. Student employees, therefore, are crucial in the daily operation of libraries. Student employee absences must be accepted and taken into account. Policies must exist to regularize the library's response to absences including how much notice must be given of schedule changes, how the work or hours will be covered, and whether or not the hours missed can be made up either in advance of or after the absence. Once established, these policies must be communicated to student workers and adhered to by all supervisors.

An absence policy should answer the following questions:

1. What constitutes an unexcused absence?

2. How many unexcused absences are allowed before disciplinary action is required?

3. What disciplinary action is to be taken?

4. What constitutes an excused absence?

5. How is an anticipated absence to be reported?

6. What notice is required?

7. Will someone have to take the absent student's place during the hours missed?

8. Whose responsibility is it to find a replacement?

9. Can students switch hours with one another?

10. How is a switch to be communicated to supervisors?

11. Is there a limit to the number of excused absences allowed?

An unexcused absence occurs when the employee does not come to work for the scheduled hours and fails to notify the supervisor. Many libraries require that, after one unexcused absence, the student employee be given a warning in writing that a second unexcused absence will result in termination.

An excused absence occurs when the employee makes prior arrangements to be absent during specified scheduled hours, or calls in prior to the scheduled hours to report a reasonable inability to come to work. When replacements must be found, the amount of advance notice is critical.

You must make a judgement as to whether absences interfere with the department's ability to meet its objectives. Is the morale of the department affected by this employee's absences? Are you being fair in your treatment of all employees? When talking with a student worker about excessive absences, make it clear that presence on the job is important and how absences affect the entire department. If the student employee cannot assure you that the number of absences will be reduced, you should consider reassigning the student to other duties or asking that the employee be reassigned to another department or on-campus job.

Counseling will probably help those student employees whose pressures off the job affect their commitment to work, those for whom work appears dissatisfying, those who have unpleasant relationships with co-workers, and those for whom a straightforward word to the wise would help. Counseling would probably not be successful for those student employees for whom the pay or the job have no attraction, those for whom off the job activities have much greater appeal than the job, and those for whom the sole purpose of their being absent is to inconvenience, punish, or disrupt the department. For this latter group, termination may be the only recourse.

TIME, TELEPHONE, AND DRESS POLICIES

Rules regarding arriving and leaving on time should be included in the student employee's handbook. The supervisor must ascertain the reasons, if any, for arriving late or leaving early. Perhaps the schedule can be adjusted to allow for a student to arrive early and leave early, or arrive late and leave late, as long as the student is present during the number of hours to be worked. Disciplinary actions should include warnings and termination of habitual rule breakers.

Another common library rule relates to the use of telephones for personal calls. Common business practice is to permit staff use of the telephone as long as it is not abused and does not interfere with the work. The individual supervisor will have to determine and consistently enforce what constitutes abuse.

Library rules regarding dress in public universities have become passé. A good rule of thumb can be found at the entrances to many places of business: NO SHIRT, NO SHOES, NO SERVICE. Supervisors are within their rights to require shirt, shoes, and decency, but should go no farther. Some private institutions have enforceable dress codes. In matters of personal hygiene, the supervisor may privately suggest to a student that cleanliness is a concern.

THE STUDENT WHO IS DISHONEST

A problem which fortunately occurs rarely but is, nonetheless, a concern is dishonesty, often commonly observed as cheating on time sheets. It is the supervisor's responsibility to review and verify reports of time worked. By signing a time sheet, the supervisor verifies that the student worker is entitled to be paid for the hours reported. The student who arrives late, leaves early, or does not work scheduled hours and signs a time sheet that certifies that all of the scheduled hours have been worked has cheated and been dishonest.

Falsifying a time sheet is a serious offense. The supervisor who knows that hours are incorrectly reported—and it *is* your responsibility to know—should first talk with the student. Point out the errors on the time sheet and allow the employee to correct them. Make certain the employee understands the importance of correctly reporting time worked and the consequences of falsifying time reports. The student employee who purposely falsifies a time sheet should be warned, if there is any doubt, and terminated if it can be proven. Time sheets should never be completed by student employees in advance of time worked unless directed by their supervisors to do so. Never sign a time sheet you believe is incorrect.

Procedures should be established which call for auditing cash receipts and balancing the cash box or register on a regular basis. Establish procedures which will protect student workers who work with cash from suspicion if shortages occur. Such procedures should require that someone other than the persons taking in or passing out cash perform the count and do the balancing. The location of Lost and Found can also be a problem. If items are turned in at Circulation, they should be claimed in the Library Office in order that the circulation staff not be placed in the position of being accused of stealing those items.

The student employee suspected of theft (cash, personal items, library materials/supplies) should be warned if there is any doubt, and terminated if it can be proven. Involvement of campus or local police is a local issue which should be addressed by university policy. Always be careful, however, to protect your employee's rights.

THE STUDENT EMPLOYEE WHO VIOLATES UNIVERSITY RULES

Normally, the student government association governs the behavior of students. University rules relating to academic honesty and classroom behavior are enforced by the student government, the faculty, and the university administration, and it is the duty of library employee supervisors to cooperate with those bodies. A student who is expelled from an institution—for whatever reason—is normally ineligible for employment by the library (especially those students who receive College Work-Study or other university financial awards).

THE STUDENT EMPLOYEE WITH PERSONALITY PROBLEMS

Do not label anyone as having personality problems just because you do not like them. You cannot solve real personality problems, nor should anyone expect you to solve those problems. Extreme cases must be left to psychiatrists and psychologists. Student services on university campuses are available to students and you should know about those services and how to refer students to them.

Persons with personality problems (for the purposes of this discussion) are defined as those whose work habits, attitudes, and outlook on life are difficult to understand, and those who are prone to public displays of emotion and tend to affect the morale and productivity of their co-workers. Types of personality problems may include frequent anger, oversensitivity, eccentric and unpredictable behavior, negativity and pessimism, and excessive talking. You are probably not a trained psychologist or psychiatrist, but you may help some student employees by communicating with them, understanding them, and treating them the same way you treat all student employees. This common sense advice is applicable to all workers.

Persons who frequently "fly off the handle" or lose their tempers are difficult to work with and are not to be tolerated. Talking constructively to an angry person is difficult: avoid, if possible, talking to anyone while they are angry. Set up another time to talk and, if the student becomes angry again, listen and don't talk. When you are able to talk, inform the individual that the behavior is unacceptable and that it interferes with the employee's work and the work of others. Disciplinary action may not change these individuals but will let them know that the library will not tolerate the behavior. Warn that if the problem is not corrected on the job, the employee will be terminated. If you do give a warning, be sure you are prepared to follow through.

Persons who are very sensitive to criticism and are easily hurt can also be a problem. When a student employee who needs constructive criticism reacts by bursting into tears, the first inclination is to never criticize. Instead, when criticism must be given, it should be offered with kid gloves. If possible, use the words, "we" and "our" when referring to the work and how it is to be done. Avoid anything which will undermine this person's self-confidence. Praise for work well done and appreciation expressed to these persons will help them gain confidence and improve their ability to accept direction.

The eccentric or unpredictable student employee is not uncommon in university libraries because a university is often the place where young people test their ideas and investigate alternative life-styles. It is not unusual for a student to change during the college years and during employment in the library. Should you accept this behavior or try to change the person? It is unlikely that you or anybody else can change this individual, or the way the job is handled. You must, however, expect the eccentric student employee to perform the assigned duties in the same manner as other student employees. This employee is to be held to the same level of accountability as others. If the creative approach to the job does not result in acceptable performance or interferes with the work of others, this behavior needs to be addressed privately.

The negative or pessimistic student employee can be a disruption in a work group. The common sense advice for dealing with this student is to accentuate the positive. Be sure you are always positive when talking with the employee and assign tasks at which you know the employee can excel. The secret of getting people to think positively is to convince them that positive thinking is good for them. When the supervisor conveys a positive attitude to workers, they feel better and want to do a good job.

The employee who talks excessively is usually not productive and wastes the time of others. Excessive talking on the telephone should be addressed by pointing out the library's policy on telephone use. If the employee persists in wasting time and distracting others, speak to the employee privately. Inform the employee that the issue is time, not personality; point out that excessive talking wastes time and interferes with the work to be done. Tell the employee that too many people (including yourself?) have the same problem on the job. If the problem persists, inform the employee that if the problem is not corrected, you will need to take disciplinary action.

Remember that you cannot and should not attempt to solve severe personality problems. You should be aware of student services offices on campus which are set up to assist students and, if a student comes to you for help, do not hesitate to suggest an appropriate office.

THE STUDENT EMPLOYEE WITH PERSONAL PROBLEMS

All of us have personal problems of one type or another: family, financial, relationship, etc. Student employees may have academic problems in addition. To some extent, you can help some student employees by communicating with them, understanding them, and treating them the same way you treat all student employees.

Family problems may require that the student be absent for a period of time. The student employee is usually concerned about having a job upon return. Arrangements can usually be made to hold the position for the employee. When dealing with financial and relationship problems, the inclination is to give students advice you would give your children. Whether or not you give advice, however, depends on your confidence in counseling young people and it is often advisable not to get involved. Academic problems may require that the student reduce the number of hours worked. Whether this can be permitted or the student must resign depends entirely on your staffing situation, but remember that tutoring help for students is available on most campuses.

If a student employee voluntarily brings a problem to you, you can be most helpful by listening without interruptions, advice, prescriptions, solutions, pontifications, or preaching and then, recognizing your own limits in dealing with situations like this.

DEALING WITH RUMORS IN THE WORK PLACE

Few organizations can claim that their people don't start or spread rumors. One of the primary responsibilities of supervisors is to keep staff informed, and, therefore, rumors must not be ignored. The most effective way to dispel a rumor is to determine whether there is any truth to it and to inform your staff about what you learn. If there is no truth to a rumor, tell your staff but, if you have no information, tell them that. If the supervisor keeps staff informed, there will be no need for rumors (but this does not mean rumors will not continue to appear).

It is important to let your staff know that they can come to you to check out rumors, and they should be encouraged not to repeat a rumor. It is especially important to keep student workers informed because they work different schedules. A library newsletter distributed to all staff and routed to student workers is a good way to keep students informed of library activities.

THE STUDENT EMPLOYEE WHO PROCRASTINATES

People procrastinate most often when faced with unpleasant or difficult jobs to do. It is one of the biggest barriers to getting work done. Student employees are as susceptible to this behavior as any other employee. Since everyone procrastinates to one degree or another, it is important to be able to overcome it in yourself and to help others do the same.

You will not procrastinate nearly as often if you develop a positive attitude about work. Nothing is as difficult as it seems; once you have completed a job you have dreaded doing, the satisfaction derived is that much greater.

Student employees who procrastinate need to learn to overcome it. If you want to help someone who is procrastinating, you must learn why the person is putting off doing something that should be done. If the tasks students avoid are either difficult or boring, sharing the load among several student workers may lessen the tendency to procrastinate.

If your boss is procrastinating on something important to you or your staff, you may be able to help. By subtly applying pressure, by persuasion, and by offering to assist with the job, you may provide the incentive which is needed. Of course, you must be very diplomatic in what you say or do. You do not want to be judgemental or be seen as a nag. If the boss offers an excuse for not doing something, drop it. Your help is not wanted.

THE STUDENT WORKER WHO RESISTS CHANGE

In academic libraries today, there are changes in procedures, policies, staffing, and job duties at a greater rate than ever before. Major changes have been made and continue to be made because of the automation of technical and public services functions.

Changes which affect the duties of student workers will sometimes require that their jobs be reclassified. Most student employees like change and accept it graciously; they are probably the most adaptable of all library staff. While change is inevitable on the job, however, some people will resist it. Supervisors must do all they can to help employees expect, understand, and accept change. If you do this, resistance will be greatly reduced.

One of the most effective ways to overcome resistance is to involve student workers in planning for change. Change is more acceptable if it is kept simple and done without a lot of fanfare. You need to give people time to adjust to change and you must recognize that some resistance may never be completely overcome.

DEALING WITH STRESS

Stress can develop on any job and in any employee. It is true however, that stress usually does not occur in employees who adjust easily to change or to persons in good mental and physical condition and who have a positive attitude. All stress is not bad, but stress which causes fear, anger, or frustration can be harmful. Employees who fear making mistakes or losing their jobs waste energy in combating those fears. Stress which challenges, encourages initiative, and raises competitive feelings can be positive.

In many cases, a heavy work load is the cause of stress. Reducing that work load may not reduce the level of stress, however, because an individual's personality often determines the amount of stress the employee perceives. Student employees are likely to be under greater stress during mid-term or final examinations than at other times of the year. Probably as much or more than other groups of employees, student workers are likely to bring stress to the job because of their coursework.

There is not a lot that can be done for the student worker who is affected by academic stress. You may grant requests for time off, and some libraries do permit students to study at work for limited periods of time during final examinations. For more information on stress, see chapter 3.

DEALING WITH INSUBORDINATION

Insubordination can take one of two forms: (1) an employee may willfully refuse or refrain from carrying out a direct order, or (2) an employee may direct threats, abusive language, or physical violence at a supervisor.

If a worker refuses to carry out a direct order, the supervisor must first mentally reconstruct the conversation to be certain an order was given. Once certain, the supervisor should try to determine whether the employee was unable to do what was requested, or the employee felt that the order was irrational. Talk with the employee and ask for an explanation; explain the consequences of insubordination in the library: normally, immediate termination. If it is determined by the supervisor that the order given was reasonable and within the capabilities of the student employee, the supervisor can warn or terminate the employee.

Insubordination that takes the form of physical violence toward the supervisor is not so easily handled. The policy in most libraries is that physical violence or the threat of physical violence in the presence of others is grounds for immediate termination. No counseling or conversation is required or expected when the supervisor's personal safety or that of other workers is threatened.

DEALING WITH OLDER STUDENT EMPLOYEES

The average age of students enrolled in colleges and universities is becoming steadily higher. Returning students, called nontraditional students, are becoming more and more common on today's campuses. Nontraditional students can be real assets to the library but supervisors must be careful to treat the older student in the same way as all other students.

RESOLVING PROBLEMS

Please remember that the suggestions offered are not absolute answers. The situations, circumstances, and the people involved differ from one problem to another. You will have to evaluate each instance individually and decide what course of action would be the most appropriate.

Know your limitations. Your advice or answers may do more to complicate the problem than solve it for the student employee. Remember that you are not alone. Seek the advice of your supervisor or fellow student employee supervisors. Be aware that no one may have had precisely the same problem with the same circumstances. Mix all you learn with a large dose of common sense.

NOTES

[1]Clayton V. Sherman, *From Losers to Winners: How to Manage Problem Employees ... and What to Do If You Can't*. (New York: AMACOM, 1987): 14.

BIBLIOGRAPHY

Allerton Park Institute. *Supervision of Employees in Libraries*. Edited by R. E. Stevens. Champaign, IL: University of Illinois Press, 1979.

Bittel, Lester R. *What Every Supervisor Should Know*. New York: McGraw-Hill, 1980.

Chapman, Elwood N. *Supervisor's Survival Kit: A Mid-Management Primer*. 2d ed. Chicago: Science Research Associates, 1975.

Collins, Eliza G. C., ed. *The Executive Dilemma: Handling People Problems at Work*. New York: Wiley, 1984.

Flynn, W. R., and W. E. Stratton. "Managing Problem Employees." *Human Resources Management* 20 (Summer 1981): 28-32.

Herzberg, Frederick. *The Managerial Choice: To Be Efficient and to Be Human*. Homewood, IL: Dow Jones-Irwin, 1976.

Hunt, John W. *Managing People at Work*. 2d ed. New York: McGraw-Hill, 1988.

Imundo, Louis V. *The Effective Supervisor's Handbook*. New York: AMACOM, 1980.

Imundo, Louis V. *Employee Discipline: How to Do It Right*. Belmont, CA: Wadsworth, 1985.

Levinson, Harry. "Emotional Health in the World of Work." In *Management by Guilt and Other Uncensored Tactics*, edited by Nicholas V. Iuppa, 267-91. New York: Harper and Row, 1964.

Library Administration and Management Association. *Problem Employees: Improving Their Performance*. LAMA Program, Dallas ALA Conference, 1979. Chicago: ALA, 1984.

Nierenberg, Gerald I. *The Art of Negotiating*. New York: Pocket Books, 1984.

Odiorne, George S. *How Managers Make Things Happen*. 2d ed. Englewood Cliffs, NJ: Prentice-Hall, 1982.

O'Reilly, C. A., and B. A. Weitz. "Managing Marginal Employees: The Use of Warnings and Dismissals." *Administrative Science Quarterly* 25 (September 1980): 467-84.

Roseman, Edward. *Managing the Problem Employee*. New York: AMACOM, 1982.

Shapero, Albert. *Managing Professional People: Understanding Creative Performance*. New York: Free Press, 1985.

Trotta, Maurice S. *Supervisor's Handbook on Insubordination*. Washington, DC: Bureau of National Affairs, 1967.

Van Fleet, James K. *The 22 Biggest Mistakes Managers Make and How to Correct Them*. West Nyack, NY: Parker Publishing Company, 1973.

Walton, Richard E. *Managing Conflict: Interpersonal Dialogue and Third Party Roles*. 2d ed. Reading, MA: Addison-Wesley, 1987.

Weiss, W. H. *The Supervisor's Problem Solver*. New York: AMACOM, 1982.

Weiss, W. H. *Supervisor's Standard Reference Handbook*. 2d ed. Englewood Cliffs, NJ: Prentice-Hall, 1988.

White, R. N. "Documenting Employee Problems." *Supervisory Management* 27 (August 1982): 38-42.

Wishnie, H. A., and J. Nevis-Oleson. *Working with the Impulsive Person*. New York: Plenum, 1979.

Wylie, Peter, and Mardy Grothe. *Problem Employees: How to Improve Their Performance*. Belmont, CA: Pitman Management and Training, 1981.

10

Performance Appraisal

If you can talk about and do it, then, buddy, you ain't braggin'!
—Jay Hanna ("Dizzy") Dean

HOW AM I DOING?

Everyone wants to know, "How am I doing?" Performance appraisals provide one opportunity to tell student employees how they are doing. Although it should not be the only time workers are told how they are doing, a performance evaluation system guarantees that they are given an assessment at least that once or twice each year, depending on the schedule.

Appraising the performance of employees is a basic task of managers. It is impossible to make intelligent managerial decisions about employees without measuring their performance in some manner.

Formal performance appraisal is as old as the concept of management and informal appraisal is as old as human history. All employees want and deserve to know not only how they are doing, but also what's being done well, what can be done better, and how their performance can be improved.

"PRAISES AND RAISES"

Student employees, like all employees, want "praises and raises." Performance appraisals offer the opportunity for supervisors to formally document and communicate their employees' performances and provide the evidence for "praises" and, if applicable, "raises."

Supervisors are cautioned that performance appraisals, if done poorly, can be debilitating for student employees. Anyone who has received a poor evaluation from a supervisor—deserved or not—knows that criticism is difficult to accept and (no matter how tough-skinned a person is, or thinks they are) that the experience can be devastating. Performance appraisals do not always result in "praises or raises," but they can and should always be constructive and positive experiences for you and your student employees.

Job Evaluation Versus Performance Appraisal

Job evaluation is an evaluation of the duties and responsibilities of a specific job or group of jobs. Performance appraisal is a measurement of how well an employee is doing that job. Performance appraisal or performance evaluation is sometimes called a merit rating. Essentially, job evaluation is a technique for evaluating a job; the other evaluates an individual.

Purposes of Performance Appraisal in Industry

Performance appraisals have two basic purposes: employee evaluation and employee development. For most companies, evaluation has been the most common use of the process; appraisals of employee performance provided the basis for administrative decisions about promotions, demotions, terminations, transfers, and rewards. The development purpose has generally been secondary but is becoming more common in industry. Table 10.1 shows how companies utilized performance evaluations in 1984 and indicates a shift to a more balanced approach.[1]

Table 10.1.

Purposes of the Performance Appraisal Process

PURPOSE OF APPRAISAL	PERCENTAGE OF RESPONDENTS
compensation	85.6
counseling	65.1
training and development	64.3
promotion	45.3
manpower planning	43.1
retention/discharge	30.3
validation of selection technique	17.2

Purposes of Performance Appraisal in Libraries

Academic institutions view performance appraisal from both viewpoints. There are three basic reasons for performance appraisal for library student employees:

1. To encourage good performance and to correct or discourage substandard performance. Good performers expect a reward, even if it is only praise. Those employees who perform below standard should be made aware that continued poor performance will, at the very least, stand in the way of advancement, while at worst, poor performance may lead to termination.

2. To satisfy the student employees' curiosity about how well they are doing. It is a fundamental drive in human nature for individuals to want to know how well they fit into the organizations for which they work. While a student may dislike being judged, the need to know is very strong.

3. To provide a foundation for later judgements concerning employees: pay increases, promotions, transfers, or termination. Supervisors are to be cautioned not to stress pay raises as part of the appraisal process. It is natural for student employees whose performance is rated good to expect a pay raise to follow. If your institution or library's compensation plan doesn't work that way, don't mislead student employees by telling them that their good work will result in a promotion or pay increase. Tell students just how the appraisal will be used.

HOW FORMAL SHOULD THE PERFORMANCE APPRAISAL BE?

The formality or informality of the process may vary greatly. Some libraries have detailed evaluation procedures, while others leave it up to the supervisors. The perceived relative value of student employees to the library is often reflected in its student employee evaluation process. Many formal programs are dictated by the university's student employment office, but others have been carefully developed by the libraries. If given the choice of evaluating or not evaluating, you should do it. If you don't presently have a formal procedure, you should propose one. Examples from evaluations used by libraries are included in this chapter.

Peer Evaluation

The evaluation of student employees is a managerial and supervisory responsibility which is not easily shared with others and should not be delegated. Peer evaluation, however, is one technique which can be used to gain input for the appraisal. Because co-workers have more continuous contact with each other and more opportunities to observe each other's performance, peer ratings can be quite valid measurements. Peers judge performance from a perspective which is different from the supervisor's, and, although subject to influence by friendships, peer comments are often very perceptive.

Peer evaluation deserves consideration by student employee supervisors in organizations which have developed a climate of interpersonal trust among co-workers and have non-competitive reward systems. It can be an effective tool for libraries utilizing team management. Student employee supervisors are cautioned that, unless peer evaluation is an established part of your library's appraisal program, it should be avoided. Improper use of peer evaluation can cause enormous problems. It is often helpful, nonetheless, to gather input from persons the employee comes in contact with and to discuss your opinions with your supervisor as you prepare student employee evaluations.

More Than the Supervisor's Opinion

A good performance appraisal includes facts as well as the supervisor's opinion. Included in the information gathered for an appraisal are facts on quantity of work, quality of work, dependability, and records of work incidents, good and bad. These facts comprise the objective factors of the evaluation. Subjective factors are opinions about attitude, personality, and adaptability, which may or may not be substantiated by data.

QUESTIONS TO BE ANSWERED IN AN APPRAISAL

Although the questions which are answered in student employee evaluations vary from one appraisal plan to another, there are some basics:

1. What has the individual done since the last evaluation?

2. How well has it been done?

3. How much better could it be done?

4. Have the strengths and weaknesses in the student employee's approach to the job affected performance? How?

5. Can the weaknesses be corrected?

6. What is the student employee's potential?

7. How well could this person do if given a chance?

HOW OFTEN SHOULD STUDENT EMPLOYEE APPRAISALS BE DONE?

If student employees are evaluated too often, those evaluations are likely to be affected too much by day-to-day occurrences. If done too infrequently, the supervisor is likely to forget incidents which need to be included in an appraisal. If annual evaluations are required, it is a good idea to do an informal, unwritten appraisal more often. Twice-a-year performance appraisals, one formal and one informal, would serve to keep the student employees informed of their performance and should not create undue hardships for supervisors.

SEQUENCE OF ACTIVITIES IN PERFORMANCE APPRAISAL

Performance appraisal follows an established sequence of activities. This sequence is: (1) set performance standards; (2) communicate those standards; (3) observe employees doing their work; (4) collect data; (5) have employees perform self-appraisals; (6) do a supervisor's appraisal; and (7) present the appraisal and receive a response.

Set Performance Standards

What are the expectations for the student employees? Performance standards are those benchmarks against which the student worker's performance is measured. In some libraries, those standards are based on historical data and the same form is used for all student employees. An example of the standards (rated on a scale of "exceeds objective," "meets objective," or "does not meet objective") found on one library's student employee performance evaluation forms is the following:[2]

1. Quantity of Work: Maintains a pace adequate to accomplish all assigned tasks within work period; is able to accommodate normal work flow.

2. Quality of Work: Performs tasks with precision and neatness; meets all responsibilities; all facets of job are executed correctly and in the appropriate sequence.

3. Reliability: Punctual; able to work without direct supervision when necessary; conduct is appropriate for work environment.

4. Initiative: Commences necessary actions without direction; exercises independent judgement in problem situations; devises and applies appropriate solutions to work-related problems.

5. Staff Relationships: Works harmoniously with staff members at all levels.

Communicate Standards

Student employees should know from the beginning what is expected of them and what the basis of their evaluations will be, i.e., what constitutes good, acceptable, marginal, and unacceptable performance. The evaluation form in use by the library should be shown to student employees as part of their orientation. Make sure there is no question about what will be evaluated and how it will be done.

Observing Employees As They Work

Employees should be observed during the appraisal period as they perform their daily tasks, and information regarding their performance should be noted. Do not observe them only in the last minutes or days before the evaluation.

Collect Data

Data for the performance evaluation should be collected throughout the appraisal period, not only prior to the evaluation. Supervisors of student employees should record both positive and negative incidents, quality and quantity of work, contributions to meetings, etc. These reports become part of the employee's file of information and should be referred to when evaluating performance. In addition, records of attendance, etc., should be checked. Accurate, current information is critical in making objective judgements of worker performance. Unfair, inequitable, or unsupportable decisions are often made because of incomplete data.

Employees' Self-Appraisal Process

Student employees may be asked to complete an appraisal of their own performance. The following procedure should be followed:

1. Discuss the purpose of self-appraisal with the student employee.

2. Review the format and clarify what the employee should do.

3. Provide the student employee with the form at least a week before it is to be completed and returned.

4. Set a specific time for the self-appraisal to be completed.

5. Stress the importance of the self-appraisal to the total performance appraisal process.

Utilizing the Information Gathered

The information gained from observation, data collection, and the self-appraisal will be useful to the supervisor in completing the student employee performance appraisal. The information may be used in five primary ways:

1. To make administrative decisions, such as promotion, suspension, demotion, transfer, or termination.

2. To make decisions on who should receive merit increases.

3. To identify training needs, such as what kind of training is needed and who can benefit from it.

4. To motivate and provide feedback by letting student employees know how they are doing, what their strengths are, and what improvements are needed.

5. To validate the selection process by comparing worker performance to desired performance. If a significant percentage of the workers are performing below expected levels, the selection criteria should be examined to determine if the requirements for the job are accurate and what qualities should be sought in students to be hired in the future.

Evaluating the Employee

Plan a time when you will not be disturbed so that you can concentrate on writing performance evaluations. Develop a procedure which you will follow for each student employee. Gather all of the performance data and review all of the data on each employee before writing that employee's evaluation. Write a draft copy and set it aside for at least an hour; then go back to the draft and try to read it as if someone else had written it. Rewrite the evaluation as necessary. Remember to evaluate the employee on performance, not personal traits or characteristics.

In writing the evaluation, remember that performance has at least two major elements: motivation and ability. If performance is poor, a common supervisor error is to assume that there is a motivation problem. While this may be true, there are many times when the employee cannot do the work because of lack of ability or lack of proper training. Corrective strategies for "won't and can't" are quite different and it is very important to recognize the difference.

APPRAISAL AND RESPONSE

Complete the performance appraisal by providing a copy of the written appraisal and by holding a meeting to discuss the evaluation. Policies on conducting a meeting with the student employee vary: usually an invitation to the employee to schedule a meeting with the supervisor to discuss the appraisal is part of the process, but some institutions require a meeting.

Most supervisors do not like to conduct performance appraisal meetings because they often make both supervisors and employees nervous and uncertain. The first meetings are always the most difficult, but careful planning can make them less stressful. The purposes of the performance appraisal meeting between the supervisor and the student employee are:

1. To be sure there are no misunderstandings about the performance appraisal ratings.

2. To allow employees to share their feelings about their performance.

3. To provide an opportunity for a straightforward and honest discussion.

4. To build a better relationship between supervisors and student employees.

Preparing for an Appraisal Meeting

The meeting between supervisor and student employee is an opportunity for the supervisor to inform, encourage, and give recognition to the employee. The following checklist provides guidelines for preparation by supervisors for this meeting.

1. Schedule the meeting far enough in advance.

2. Deliver a copy of the written appraisal to the student and ask that it be read prior to the meeting.

3. Ask the employee to come prepared to discuss the self-appraisal.

4. Make it clear that the purpose of the meeting is to discuss performance on the job.

5. Find a comfortable setting for the meeting.

6. Review the employee's job description, performance standards, and the appraisal.

7. List specific good things which you can compliment.

8. List the bad things and plan to discuss them.

9. Note what reactions you think the employee might have and plan to handle them.

10. Keep a detailed list of facts supporting your appraisal.

11. Make a list of corrective actions if needed.

12. Plan how to present and gain acceptance of corrective actions.

13. Note follow-up activities which may be needed.

Conducting an Appraisal Meeting

Conducting appraisal meetings requires planning and, if you are well prepared for the performance appraisal meetings and are comfortable with your appraisals of the student employees, the stress of conducting such meetings will largely disappear. Review what you will say to the employees, define the order in which you will discuss the evaluations, and make the performance appraisal meetings productive experiences for the employees and you. Here are suggestions on how to make each experience a positive one:

1. State the purpose and create a positive attitude: put the employees at ease.

2. Ask how they see their job and working conditions.

3. Ask if there are problems which need discussion.

4. Give your view of their performance, avoiding comparisons to other employees.

5. Mention desirable behavior you would like to see continue.

6. Capitalize on their strengths.

7. Identify opportunities for self-improvement.

8. Prepare employee improvement plans which are theirs, not yours.

9. Review future opportunities for advancement, pay increases.

10. Warn poor performers, if necessary.

11. Ask if there are questions.

12. End the meetings with constructive, encouraging comments.

Discussing Poor Performance

Many supervisors find it easy, and even enjoyable, to give employees good evaluations. Often, however, you must also be prepared to give student employees unfavorable comments on their performance. The following are suggestions for handling the performance appraisal meetings with poor performers:

1. Don't be too harsh.

2. Be firm, be specific, and don't rub it in. Nothing is to be gained by being soft on student employees: if their performance has been bad, tell them that performance has been bad and be specific.

3. You can be firm and direct without being cruel. Leave the student employees with their self-respect. One useful technique is the "sandwich" technique described in the next section.

4. Summarize what you have found to be satisfactory as well as things that are unsatisfactory.

5. Always end your appraisal meetings with positive, encouraging comments.

Supervisors dislike giving "bad news" almost as much as employees dislike getting it. By giving a negative appraisal, you are trying to correct something in an employee's behavior. When the discussion gets started, however, these overall objectives can get lost. When a performance discussion starts to get rough, the tendency is for the participants to begin digging out all the ammunition they have. If the employee gets defensive and brings up side-issues, don't retaliate even though you may feel backed against the wall. Don't allow side-issues to dilute your original objectives: explain that those issues will be discussed at a later meeting if desired. The best strategy is to have resolved the minor issues and gripes as they arise and not let them accumulate until the appraisal dialogue.

The "Sandwich" Technique

A technique for discussing performance which needs improvement is the "sandwich" technique. Very simply, this is done by starting the discussion with a compliment, then discuss the performance which must be improved upon, and finish with something good about the employee's work. For example, "I'm very pleased with your handling of reserve check-outs. Your accuracy, however, must be improved. You have got to remember to follow all of the steps in order for the transaction to be properly recorded. I'm sure you will be able to do that because your other work is very good." This technique can be used throughout the appraisal meeting. No matter how bad an evaluation, you should be able to stress the good things and to make the discussion a positive one.

Allowing the Employee to Save Face

When discussing poor performance with student employees, be sure to give them every opportunity to explain why performance is substandard. They will, if given the chance to explain, tell you what obstacles stand in the way of their doing well. Don't interrupt their explanations or say, "That's just an excuse." Be patient and let student employees talk. If you listen carefully, the employees will tell you the real reasons for their poor performance. Don't get into an argument and don't show your anger, even if the student employee gets angry.

Handling Charges of Favoritism

Unfavorable criticism can hurt an employee so much that the employee may charge you with favoritism. Your denial will likely fall on deaf ears, so instead of just denying it, try to determine why the employee feels that way.

Supervisor: Judy, why do you think I might be favoring Sheila?

Employee: Because you give Sheila the easy jobs all the time, and you never let me do them.

Supervisor: That may be true. I just find it easier to ask Sheila to do things. You seem hesitant to accept additional work because you just don't act like you want to be here.

Employee: Well, I do. I don't think I'm appreciated.

Supervisor: If you can assure me that you are willing to take on extra tasks, I will ask you more often. If I've been favoring Sheila, I will consciously make an effort to treat you more equally.

Denial is a natural reaction to criticism on both the employee's part and yours: don't let a charge of favoritism divert your attention from the original point. Make sure you cover all of the items you originally planned to discuss in the appraisal meeting.

Appraisal Errors

Some of the more common errors which must be guarded against when conducting performance appraisals of workers are:

1. Personal bias: unfairly judging members of different races, religion, sex, or national origin.

2. The halo effect: letting your appraisal of one factor affect your appraisal of all other factors.

3. Central tendency: judging most workers as average, thus making no distinction between good and poor performers.

4. Harshness: judging everyone at the low end of the scale.

5. Leniency: judging everyone at the high end of the scale.

6. Similarity: judging people who are like you higher than people who are different from you.

7. Recency of events: allowing what happened recently to affect your judgement of the person's performance over the entire evaluation period.

8. Seniority: unfairly judging workers on how long they have been on the job.

9. Acquaintanceship: letting how well you know workers affect your appraisal.

Validity and Reliability

Good performance appraisals measure what they should (have validity), and the measures are consistent (have reliability). When a performance appraisal is valid, it measures the things the supervisor wants it to measure. Performance evaluations are not valid if they fail to measure performance-related behaviors or if the measures are not relevant to the job. When a supervisor allows a worker's hair length, style of clothing, or political beliefs to influence an evaluation, it is invalid. These are not performance-related behaviors and have no value in a performance appraisal.

When a performance appraisal is reliable, it provides a consistent measure of work performance. Supervisors must strive for consistency in evaluating every employee. The most common types of reliability problems in appraisal are constant errors and random errors. Constant errors occur when all evaluations are in error to the same degree and in the same direction. A supervisor who rates all employees one point higher than their true rating, for example, is making a constant error. A random error occurs whenever a rating is unpredictably higher or lower than the individual should receive.

One way to deal with reliability errors is to have multiple observations. If one of the criteria to be evaluated is job speed, then there should be two or more questions on the rating form which relate to job speed. If the rating on one shows that the worker is very slow, then the answers to the other questions relating to speed should match. If they do not, there is an inconsistency. Multiple observations help supervisors correct erroneous evaluation responses and attain consistency.

Making Nondiscriminatory Appraisals

We are living in a litigious society. More and more employers are being sued by employees and former employees, and, therefore, it is important to be aware of what is legal and permissible in appraising employee performance. The keys to making nondiscriminatory appraisals are quite simple — evaluate all employees on the basis of job performance only, and without regard to their age, race, sex, religion, or national origin, be consistent in your application, and apply criteria objectively to all employees. Evaluating employees on the basis of job performance means judging them only on the way they do their jobs and putting aside any personal likes or dislikes.

Confidentiality of Appraisals

The entire appraisal process should be confidential. The appraisal of one student employee should never be discussed with other student employees. You cannot control what student employees discuss with one another, but the supervisor should never be the source of information for those discussions. Avoid comparisons of student employees when conducting your appraisal meetings. Make it clear that each student knows that you treat each rating and each appraisal as confidential.

GOOD EVALUATIONS DO NOT ALWAYS RESULT IN ADVANCEMENT

The student employee who consistently gets very good appraisals may find it hard to accept the fact that it is not possible to move up in a seniority-based system until the person ahead gets promoted or quits.

> *Employee*: Every time, you tell me I'm doing a good job but it hasn't gotten me a better job. I know John is not doing as well but he still makes more money—just because he's been here longer. All the appraisal does for me is to rub salt in the wound.

Handle this complaint by admitting that the situation exists. Even though the employee's claim about a co-worker may be true, don't discuss relative worth of any other student employee. Tell the student that one of the purposes of appraisals is to evaluate performance and that without them, performance can slip. Make certain the student understands that the seniority system applies to everyone: there may be a time when some less senior student employees will register a similar complaint about the student being evaluated, who will have become the most senior member.

GOOD EVALUATIONS DO NOT ALWAYS RESULT IN MORE MONEY

If your compensation system is not tied directly to your appraisal system, tell your student employees. If merit increases are possible, describe the process to your employees, but if longevity is the deciding factor in raises, tell them so. Make it clear to student employees why the appraisal process is followed. Misconceptions about how the performance appraisals are used must be cleared up so everyone has a common understanding of the process.

APPRAISAL FORMATS

The library probably has an evaluation form developed internally or by the student employment office. There are three basic types of performance appraisal forms: comparative, absolute, and outcome-based.

If a comparative format is used, the supervisor evaluates employees in relation to each other. Comparative methods include ranking, paired comparisons, and forced choice. When absolute formats, the most common ones, are used, the supervisor evaluates each employee's performance without comparing employees to each other. Absolute methods include narrative, critical incidents, graphic rating scales, weighted checklists, and behaviorally anchored rating scales (BARS). If an outcome-based format is used, supervisors evaluate employees on the basis of performance outcomes. Common forms of outcome-based formats are standards of performance and management by objectives (MBO).

If you are involved in the development of an evaluation instrument, bear in mind that the form is a device to be used by human beings. Ratings on the forms will be the result of complex human processes including interpersonal perception, memory, evaluation, and decision-making. Persons using the form will typically have many other responsibilities besides supervision. Develop a form which is usable.

Comparative Appraisal Formats

Employee performances are compared to one another in comparative appraisal forms. The ranking method requires the supervisor to rate each employee on an overall basis and then list all employees in ascending (lowest to highest) or descending (highest to lowest) order, usually by identifying the best performer, the worst performer, the next best, the next worst, and so on until all employees have been listed. Ranking is the simplest comparative evaluation.

Supervisors using the paired comparison method must compare each employee to every other employee being appraised. Employee A is compared to Employee B and given a "1" or "2," and then compared to every other employee in the same manner. The total number of points given to each results in a numerical ranking for all employees being appraised.

The forced choice method requires that a percentage of employees be forced into certain groups, for example:

excellent	10%
above average	20%
satisfactory	40%
below average	20%
unsatisfactory	10%

Comparative formats are fairly simple to use but do not provide any measure of the differences between the rankings. An employee ranked fourth in a group of eight may be considerably better than the person ranked fifth. The employee receives a ranking which provides little information and the system provides no basis for employee development. Comparative formats are seldom used in academic settings.

Absolute Appraisal Formats

Absolute appraisal forms do not require comparison to other employees. The narrative form requires the supervisor to write a description of an employee's performance which outlines the worker's strengths, weaknesses, and potential. Obviously much depends on the supervisor's writing ability. To reduce this difference, a standardized form may be used to provide some uniformity to the information to be recorded. The narrative form is more commonly used for faculty and staff evaluations than for student employees.

On critical incidents forms supervisors list both the good and the bad things that employees do in performing their jobs. As with narrative forms, the critical incidents form may be dependent upon supervisor writing skills.

Graphic rating scales are the oldest absolute appraisal method and the most common type of evaluation used by libraries for student employees. The scale contains a number of traits or behaviors which relate to job performance, for example, "Dependability," and the evaluator checks where the employee fits on the continuum, for example, a scale of 1 to 5. The graphic rating scale is criticized because "dependability" has different meanings to different evaluators. To be used effectively, graphic rating scales must include a brief description of the behavior and a definition of what is needed to earn a "1," "2," etc.

On weighted checklists a value is assigned to each of the traits or job behaviors, according to the perceived importance of the item. For example, "quality of work" may be more important than "quantity of work" and count more (20 points) than quantity (15 points).

Behaviorally Anchored Rating Scales (BARS) concentrate on job behaviors, not personal characteristics. A committee determines a set of "behavioral anchors," or statements which describe desired behaviors; the employees are evaluated on the basis of those statements.

Outcome-Based Appraisal Formats

The best known forms of outcome-based methods are standards of performance and management by objectives (MBO). Standards of performance involves comparing performance to a list of standards established through negotiation between each worker and the supervisor. The list of standards are conditions which must be met if the job is considered to have been done well.

MBO is a method of evaluation which focuses on specific objectives or goals established by negotiation between each employee and the supervisor. The employee is judged on how well those objectives are met.

WHAT HAPPENS TO THE APPRAISAL FORMS?

Be sure that student employees know what will happen to the appraisal forms and how they may be used. Who has access to them? A written library policy is needed. Does the library give references for former student employees and are the appraisal forms used? The confidentiality of the forms should be covered by the library's written policy. Appraisal forms should become part of the confidential personnel files of the library.

AFTER THE APPRAISAL

The appraisal is done, the meeting has been held, and the forms have been filed. Is that all there is? No, appraisal is not something that is done today and forgotten tomorrow. To be of value, you should follow up the appraisal meeting by:

1. Keeping your promises. If you have agreed to do something during the appraisal meeting, do it. If, for example, you've said that you will show the employee data you've referred to in the meeting, be sure to follow through.

2. Implementing employee development plan. If you said the employee needs training in an area, make arrangements to provide that training. Locate courses, workshops, or seminars which will provide the needed training, or talk to the individual who will train the employee. Communicate those arrangements to the employee.

3. Keep in touch. Continue to show interest in the development of the student employee. Monitor the employees performance and give credit for improvement and point out deficiencies if you're not satisfied.

DO NOT WAIT FOR THE ANNUAL REVIEW

Frequently, supervisors and student employees assume too much: supervisors that student employees know exactly what is expected of them and that they know how well they are doing, and student employees that the work is being performed to their supervisor's satisfaction. The "no news is good news" syndrome operates in many libraries until—in extreme cases—tempers flare, feelings are hurt, and productivity declines. Annual or semi-annual performance appraisals are certainly useful, but performance appraisal should be an on-going activity. There will be no surprises at appraisal time if you talk regularly with your student employees and discuss informally their work. The performance appraisal itself ceases to be a confrontational or traumatic experience for you or the employees if you have shown your interest and concern on a regular basis.

POSITIVE APPROACH TO PERFORMANCE APPRAISAL

Supervisors usually take one of two stands on performance appraisal: (1) they see the value in the process and turn performance appraisal into a positive tool; or (2) they see no purpose and fight it all the way. Supervisors who approach appraisal in a positive manner will discover that their employees will benefit from the evaluation. Those who fight the process will find that their employees mirror their feelings. Here are suggestions on how to make it a positive experience:

1. Accept the fact of performance appraisal. Of course you should make suggestions on how it can be improved, but accept the system and make it work for you.

2. Turn the appraisal meetings into profitable counseling sessions. They may be the only regularly scheduled face-to-face meetings you have with your student employees.

3. Don't take the easy way out. Be honest in your appraisals. Remember that you are evaluating performance, not personality.

4. Discuss the evaluation with the employee, don't just deliver it.

5. Don't hurry the evaluation, either its preparation or the appraisal meeting.

6. Make the appraisal a positive tool. Remember that the appraisal is not a tool used to embarrass, intimidate, or harass the employee.

7. Be careful with promises. Don't make promises to the employees you cannot keep.

8. Follow up. A good follow-up is essential to the success of the system.

The resources provided in the following bibliography provide additional information on performance appraisal.

NOTES

[1]Evelyn Eichel and Henry E. Bender. *Performance Appraisal: A Study of Current Techniques*. (New York: American Management Association, 1984): 7.

[2]University of Rochester River Campus Libraries. "Student Performance Evaluation." *Student Assistants in ARL Libraries, SPEC Kit 91*. (Washington, DC: Association of Research Libraries, 1983): 96.

BIBLIOGRAPHY

Alexander Hamilton Institute. "Will Your Next Performance Appraisal Land You In Court?" *Management Studies* 31, no. 7 (July 1986): 5-9.

Allan, Ann, and Kathy J. Reynolds. "Performance Problems: A Model for Analysis and Resolution." *Journal of Academic Librarianship* 9 (May 1983): 83-89.

American Library Association, Office for Personnel Resources. *Managing Employee Performance*. Chicago: ALA, 1988.

Association of Research Libraries, Office of Management Studies. *Performance Appraisal in Research Libraries*. Washington, DC: ARL, 1988.

Association of Research Libraries, Office of Management Studies. *Performance Appraisal in Reference Services*. Washington, DC: ARL, 1987.

Berkner, Dimity S. "Library Staff Development through Performance Appraisal." *College & Research Libraries* 40 (July 1979): 335-44.

Cascio, Wayne F., and H. John Bernardin. "Implications of Performance Appraisal Litigation for Personnel Decisions." *Personnel Psychology* 34 (1981): 211-26.

Creth, Sheila. *Performance Evaluation: A Goals-Based Approach*. Chicago: ACRL, 1984.

DeProspo, Ernest R. "Personnel Evaluation As an Impetus to Growth." *Library Trends* 20 (July 1971): 60-70.

Fear, Richard A. *The Evaluation Interview*. 3d ed. New York: McGraw-Hill, 1973.

Gibbs, Sally E. "Staff Appraisal." In *Handbook of Library Training Practice*, edited by Ray Prytherch, 61-81. Brookfield, VT: Gower, 1986.

Hilton, R. C. "Performance Evaluation of Library Personnel." *Special Libraries* 69 (November 1978): 429-34.

Hodge, Stanley P. "Performance Appraisals: Developing a Sound Legal and Managerial System." *College & Research Libraries* 44 (July 1983): 235-44.

Irish, Richard K. *If Things Don't Improve Soon I May Ask You to Fire Me*. Garden City, NY: Anchor, 1975.

Johnson, Robert G. *The Appraisal Interview Guide*. New York: AMACOM, 1979.

Kikoski, J. F., and J. A. Litterer. "Effective Communication in the Performance Appraisal Interview." *Public Personnel Management* 12 (Spring 1983): 33-42.

King, Patricia. *Performance Planning and Appraisal: A How-To Book for Managers*. New York: McGraw-Hill, 1984.

Kroll, H. R. "Beyond Evaluation: Performance Appraisal As a Planning and Motivational Tool in Libraries." *Journal of Academic Librarianship* 9 (March 1983): 27-32.

Levinson, Harry. "Appraisal of What Performance?" *Harvard Business Review* 54 (July-August 1976): 30-36.

Library Administration and Management Association, Personnel Administration Section, Staff Development Committee. *Personnel Performance Appraisal: A Guide for Libraries*. Chicago: LAMA, 1979.

Lindsey, Jonathan A. "The Human Dimension in Performance Appraisal." *North Carolina Libraries* 42, no. 1 (Spring 1984): 5-7.

Lindsey, Jonathan A. *Performance Evaluation: A Management Basic for Librarians*. Phoenix, AZ: Oryx, 1987.

Lubans, John. "Performance Evaluation: Worth the Cost?" *North Carolina Libraries* 42, no. 1 (Spring 1984): 15-17.

Mager, Robert F., and Peter Pipe. *Analyzing Performance Problems, or: You Really Oughta Wanna*. 2d ed. Belmont, CA: Wadsworth, 1987.

Maier, Norman R. F. *The Appraisal Interview*. Revised. San Diego, CA: University Associates, 1976.

McGregor, Douglas. "An Uneasy Look at Performance Appraisal." *Harvard Business Review* 35 (May-June 1957): 89-94.

Neal, James E., Jr. *Effective Phrases for Performance Appraisals*. 5th ed. Perrysburg, OH: Neal Publications, 1988.

Patten, Thomas H. *A Manager's Guide to Performance Appraisal*. New York: Free Press, 1982.

Performance Appraisal. Chicago: ACRL, 1980.

Pinzelik, Barbara P. "A Library Middle Manager Looks at Performance Appraisal." In *Energies for Transition, Proceedings of the Fourth National Conference of the ACRL*, edited by Danuta A. Nitecki, 141-45. Chicago: ACRL, 1986.

Reneker, Maxine H. "Performance Appraisal in Libraries: Purpose and Techniques." In *Personnel Administration in Libraries*, edited by Sheila Creth and Frederick Duda, 227-89. New York: Neal-Schuman, 1981.

Rice, B. "Performance Appraisal: The Job Nobody Likes." *Psychology Today* 19 (September 1985): 30-36.

Vincelette, J. P. "Improving Performance Appraisal in Libraries." *Library and Information Science Research* 6 (April 1984): 191-203.

Wylie, Peter, and Mardy Grothe. *Problem Employees: How to Improve Their Performance*. Belmont, CA: Pitman Management and Training, 1981.

Yarbrough, Larry N. "Performance Appraisal in Academic and Research Libraries." *ARL Management Supplement* 3 (May 1975): 1-6.

Employee and Employer
Rights and Responsibilities

Trust everybody — but cut the cards.
— Finley Peter Dunne (1867-1936)

EMPLOYEE AND EMPLOYER RIGHTS

It is not uncommon to hear the following: "You can't do that — I know my rights!" It may often seem that rights are a one-way proposition, but in fact, both employees and employers have rights. Supervisors of student employees must understand employee rights and clearly communicate them to the employees.

Employee's right can be granted by law or by the library or university. There are some general rights that come with employment.

LEGAL RIGHTS

Employees are protected by certain inalienable rights. Among others, these include the right to a safe work environment and a workplace free of discrimination or harassment. Employees also have termination rights, privacy rights, and where applicable, the right to participate in unions.

The Right to a Safe Work Environment

In the Occupational Safety and Health Act of 1970 (OSHA), the federal government guarantees employees a safe work environment. Under the terms of the law, all employees have the right to request a Department of Labor inspection of any perceived safety or health problem. The request must identify specific violations and be sent to the Department of Labor with a copy to the employer. The employee requesting an inspection must sign the Department of Labor request but need not sign the employer copy. Employees may refuse to work or perform a task if the work itself or the work environment is felt to be unsafe. The following conditions must be met before an employee can refuse to work:

157

1. Normal procedures to resolve the problem, e.g., notification of the appropriate management officials, etc., have not been successful.

2. The worker's fears of unsafe conditions are supported by evidence and the worker believes that conditions are unsafe.

3. Documentation needs to be provided on the conditions and steps taken.

The Right to a Nondiscriminatory Workplace

As a supervisor, it is your responsibility to assure that discrimination does not occur in hiring, promotion, transfer, or termination of student employees. It is also your responsibility to report any instances of discrimination to the appropriate person. Even the perception of discrimination based on race, creed, sex, age, sexual preference, national origin, or handicap in the library must be avoided. Laws governing equal employment opportunity are:

1. Title VII of the 1964 Civil Rights Act, as amended, protects against discrimination in employment decisions based on race, color, religion, sex, and national origin.

2. The Equal Pay Act of 1963 makes it unlawful to pay females less than males who do similar work.

3. The Age Discrimination in Employment Act of 1967, as amended, protects all persons over the age of 40 against discrimination on the basis of age.

4. The Rehabilitation Act of 1973, enforced by the Americans with Disabilities Act of 1990, prohibits discrimination in employment on the basis of a mental or physical handicap.

5. The Vietnam Era Veterans' Readjustment Assistance Act of 1974 requires federal contractors and subcontractors to take affirmative action to employ or advance in employment, qualified disabled veterans and veterans of the Vietnam era.

6. The Pregnancy Discrimination Act of 1978 protects against discrimination in employment because of pregnancy. Pregnancy should be treated as any other temporary disability and an employer may not refuse to hire a qualified female because she is pregnant.

7. The Immigration Reform and Control Act of 1986 (IRCA) makes it illegal to recruit, hire, refer for hire any unauthorized alien; requires documentation of identity and eligibility of worker to work in the United States; and prohibits discrimination on the basis of national origin or citizenship status.

Employees who believe that they are victims of employment discrimination have the right to avail themselves of the library's grievance process. The grievant may also file a complaint with the local or regional office of the Equal Employment Opportunity Commission. If you are named in a discrimination grievance, be prepared to present documentary evidence that will clearly show nondiscriminatory intent or action. The grievance procedure will be discussed later on in this chapter.

The Right to a Workplace Free of Harassment

Harassment can be verbal abuse, subtle pressure for sexual activity, or physical aggressiveness. Verbal abuse may also be discrimination in the form of ethnic, racial, or sex-related jokes, slurs, or name-calling. Employees have a right to expect their supervisors to put an end to this form of harassment. Victims of verbal abuse which is discriminatory may file a grievance or a complaint with the Equal Employment Opportunity Commission.

While sexual harassment most often takes place when there is a power differential between the persons involved, sexual harassment may also occur between persons of the same status: between student and student, librarian and librarian, or staff member and staff member. It may take place between two males or two females and is not restricted to male-female or female-male incidents. While the vast majority of victims are female and the vast majority of offenders are male, the prohibition of sexual harassment applies regardless of the genders of the parties.

Unwanted verbal or physical sexual conduct is considered sexual harassment in the following instances:

1. Submission to the conduct is an explicit or implicit condition of an individual's employment.

2. Submission to or rejection of such conduct by an individual is used as the basis for employment decisions affecting the individual.

3. Such conduct has the purpose or effect of interfering with an individual's work performance or creating an intimidating, hostile, or offensive work environment.

As a supervisor, it is extremely important that you know that the employer is liable for sexual harassment charges if the supervisor is aware of—or should have known about—such activity taking place. The supervisor must put an immediate end to any activity which even hints at sexual harassment. It is essential that you, the supervisor, be familiar with your library and your university's policy on sexual harassment.

Termination Rights

Student employees have certain rights relating to the termination of their employment with the library. Legally, an employee's termination may be declared invalid if an employee is:

1. Discharged for a reason specifically prohibited by federal or state standards. Termination which is in direct violation of Title VII of the Civil Rights Act of 1964 or the Occupational Safety and Health Act, for example, is illegal.

2. Discharged for complying with a statutory duty. Termination for performing jury duty, for example, is illegal.

3. Discharged in violation of implied promises made at employment. For example, if your handbook says employees may be terminated only for unsatisfactory performance, what happens if the student employee is caught stealing the overdue fine money?

4. Discharged without having received due process. The employee has the right to be guaranteed that certain procedural steps will be followed, and the right to know the reason for termination (except, perhaps, during a probationary period).

5. Discharged through malice or retaliation may be ruled to be invalid.

There is a right way and a wrong way to terminate student employees. Your library's policies should be clear on how termination is to be handled. For additional suggestions on how to handle termination of student employees, review chapter 12.

Privacy Rights

Employees have the right to keep personal information from those who have no need to know. This privacy includes employment references, personnel files, and protection from unreasonable searches.

The best practice to follow when prospective employers contact you for employment references for current student employees is to provide only the most basic employment information: confirmation of employment, dates of employment, and the specific position held. Many libraries have policies forbidding supervisors from giving employment references for their staff or student employees except that an employer is ethically bound to pass on negative information about the moral character of a former student employee, if relevant. For example, if a student employee discharged for stealing has applied for a position with a financial institution, the prospective employer has a right to know.

Student employees have a right to expect that the information contained in their personnel files is confidential and also have the right to see most of the information in their own files. Management has the right to withhold some information from the employee, for example, a confidential memorandum discussing a promotion which was not given. Information that is irrelevant to the employees' jobs or performance should be regularly purged from all personnel files. Supervisors tend to keep their own personnel files, duplicating the centralized files. If those files contain information not relevant to jobs or performance, remove and destroy it.

Constitutional protection against unreasonable searches is provided by the Fourth Amendment. It appears that the focus is on searches by government officials and not by private employers and, therefore, that private employers can conduct searches without fear of constitutional violation. Nonetheless, employers considering establishing a search policy must make sure that it includes providing adequate advance notice to employees. The best policy is to seek advance consent before any search of employees' lockers, desks, etc. The following guidelines apply:

1. The search policy must be based on legitimate employer interest. The prevention of theft, drinking, or the use or possession of drugs are legitimate employer interests.

2. The policy must include all types of searches, including searches of the person, lockers, and personal possessions.

3. The policy must advise employees that lockers are library property, and that lockers may be routinely searched.

4. The search procedure must be applicable to all employees.

5. A statement should be included that a request to undergo a search does not imply an accusation.

6. The search policy must be communicated to all employees. It should be included in handbooks, and employees should be asked to sign a consent statement at the time of employment.

7. Those responsible for conducting searches should be given explicit instructions regarding search procedure.

8. The search should be conducted in a dignified and reasonable manner. Never conduct a search of one employee's person in the presence of other employees.

Those libraries which have access to the services of institutional legal counsel or a campus police department should seek their advice and assistance in all matters regarding employee searches. Remember, employees have a right to expect that *unreasonable* searches will not be conducted.

Union Participation Rights

Although this does not apply to the majority of libraries, it should be noted that both union and nonunion employees have the right to participate in organizing and maintaining membership in a union. This right is guaranteed by the National Labor Relations Act (Wagner Act). See the following list of general guidelines for supervisors who may have to relate to union organizing in the workplace.[1]

- YOU MAY tell employees about current wages and benefits and how they compare to other jobs.

- YOU MAY tell employees you will use all legal means to oppose unionization.

- YOU MAY tell employees the disadvantages of having a union (especially the cost of dues, assessments, and requirements of membership).

- YOU MAY show employees articles about unions and negative experiences others have had elsewhere.

- YOU MAY accurately explain the unionization process to your employees.

- YOU MAY forbid distribution of union literature during work hours in work areas.

- YOU MAY enforce disciplinary policies and rules in a fair manner.

- YOU MAY NOT promise employees pay increases or promotions if they vote against the union.

- YOU MAY NOT threaten employees with termination or discriminate when disciplining employees.

- YOU MAY NOT spy on or have someone spy on union meetings.

- YOU MAY NOT make a speech to employees or groups at work within 24 hours of the election.

- YOU MAY NOT ask employees how they plan to vote or if they have signed authorization cards.

- YOU MAY NOT urge employees to persuade others to vote against the union (such a vote must be initiated solely by the employee).

RIGHTS GRANTED BY THE EMPLOYING INSTITUTION

In addition to those rights guaranteed by law, employees also have rights which are granted by the employing institutions. Rights granted by universities usually include the right to an appeal and grievance process and the right to equitable compensation.

The Right to an Appeal and Grievance Process

Universities, and in turn their libraries, grant to all employees the right to a grievance and appeal process. Some universities grant the same rights to student employees and permanent staff while other universities provide slightly different processes to the two groups. Normally the difference concerns the extent of the grievance or appeal: temporary employees and probationary employees are often given access to only the first step of the process. Student employees may be considered as temporary employees in some libraries.

The primary purpose of an appeal and grievance procedure is to provide a means by which employees can express complaints about their work or working conditions without jeopardizing their jobs and can obtain a fair hearing through progressively higher levels of management. Complaints charging discrimination based on race, creed, sex, age, sexual preference, national origin, or handicap may be handled by the regular grievance procedure or be dealt with by the university's affirmative action office. The appeal and grievance procedure serves to avoid the high costs, in terms of both dollars and morale, of court action.

The Two-Step Grievance Procedure. A two-step grievance and appeal process is common in university libraries. The time limits included in the process may vary considerably. In step one, a grievance is filed in writing by the employee within five working days following the act or discovery of the condition which gave rise to the grievance. Normally, the written grievance is submitted to a university personnel office. A personnel officer conducts a preliminary investigation of the grievance and attempts to mediate the dispute. If the grievance is resolved to the satisfaction of both parties, the officer prepares a report of the resolution, provides copies to both sides, and closes the grievance record. If the grievance is not resolved through mediation, a report to that effect is prepared and provided to both parties and step two of the procedure may be invoked by the appealant.

The employee appeal to step two must be filed in writing within five working days from receipt of the step one report. Failure to file within the specified period constitutes forfeiture of the right to appeal, and the grievance may be considered closed. The appeal is heard by a "Grievance Review Committee" which may be composed in many different ways: in one institution it is the Director of Personnel, the Dean of the library, and one other uninvolved employee selected by the aggrieved employee. The written decision of the Grievance Review Committee, including a statement of the case and the rationale for the decision, is provided to the employee and employer, usually within fifteen working days of the hearing. There is no further right to appeal in the two-step procedure and any further action by the employee must be taken in civil court.

Mediation and Arbitration. In the previously described two-step grievance procedure, both mediation and arbitration are utilized: mediation by the personnel office and arbitration by the review committee.

Mediation occurs when an impartial third party helps the employee and the employer to reach a voluntary agreement to settle a grievance. The mediator often makes suggestions or recommendations and attempts to reduce the emotions and tensions which prevent resolution of the complaint. In order to be successful, the mediator must have the trust and respect of both parties.

During arbitration, a neutral third party, in this case the Grievance Review Committee, studies the grievance, listens to the arguments on both sides, and makes recommendations which may or may not be binding on both.

Common Types of Grievances. The grievance is a formal charge made by a student employee that the employee has been adversely affected by a violation of rights or university or library policies. Grievances always allege that there has been a violation. Often the situation has started as a gripe by the employee, but when it is not handled by the supervisor to the employee's satisfaction, a grievance is filed. Some of the most common types of grievances deal with the following situations:

1. Discipline or termination for absenteeism, insubordination, misconduct, or substandard work.

2. Promotion or transfer of student employees.

3. Complaints charging discrimination based on race, creed, sex, age, sexual preference, national origin, or handicap.

If a Grievance Is Filed Against You. Library management hopes that student employees will never need to file grievances, yet few libraries are able to completely avoid them. That is not to say that libraries in which no grievances have been filed have student employees who are completely happy with their jobs and their supervisors. It is better to have problems openly discussed than to have a staff who do not express their feelings and, if complaints and employee concerns are addressed by the supervisor, grievances should not occur. When there are a lot of grievances, management must look at its supervisors.

Supervisors must know how to handle a complaint before it becomes a grievance, but, if a grievance is filed, it is important that the supervisor not consider it an attack on the supervisor, but only a situation that has not been resolved to the employee's satisfaction. Remember that employees have the right to file grievances without jeopardizing their jobs.

If you can determine the nature of the grievance, you have taken the first step to successfully handling it. Determine if the stated complaint is the problem or if it is only a symptom of the real problem. Investigate the grievance objectively and thoroughly. One of the biggest mistakes supervisors make is to make light of complaints. If the employee files a grievance, it is important and the employee will not be satisfied until the grievance is resolved. The supervisor must be willing to work with the mediator in a grievance, and if you've made a mistake, admit it. When the grievance is resolved, regardless of the outcome, you may not punish the grievant nor allow this to affect the grievant's employment circumstances. The employee has exercised a *right* given by the university.

The Right to Equitable Compensation

In addition to the right to an appeal and grievance process, employees have a right to fair and equitable compensation for the work they perform. Student employees should be made aware of the pay schedule for different jobs in the library and are entitled to pay equity. All student employees should be rewarded fairly in relation to what other student employees are paid for the work they perform. Pay rates for student employees are discussed in chapter 4.

EMPLOYEE RESPONSIBILITIES

Employees must recognize that they have responsibilities, as well as rights. The legal responsibilities of employees are to perform the work for which they were hired and to follow the library's policies, procedures and rules.

Employees also have a responsibility to contribute positively to the library's image. In the eyes of many people, student employees are the library and their image of the library is often formed by their view of the student employees. Loyalty to the library is an ethical responsibility of student employees. Given the opportunity, student employees should speak positively about the library and, if employees have gripes, they should be taken to their supervisors, not to persons outside.

Other specific moral and ethical actions for which student employees should be held responsible include:

1. To come to work for all scheduled hours, unless excused.

2. To comply with instructions issued by the supervisor.

3. To complete assigned work.

4. To be safety conscious.

5. To take care of library materials and property.

6. To be honest in dealings with both the public and the library staff.

7. To avoid abusive, threatening, coercive, indecent, or discourteous language and behavior.

8. To be sober and drugfree on library time, library property, or while conducting library business.

9. To keep accurate records and to avoid any hint of intentional falsification of time reports.

10. To cooperate with co-workers.

ETHICS FOR SUPERVISORS

Student employees and the public make few distinctions between lower- and upper-level management of the library. To most of the university community, all supervisors are part of library management and you can be expected to be praised or tarred with the same brush as your supervisor and the dean or director. As a result, you must be concerned with managerial ethics.

Ethics is concerned with what a person does which is right or wrong according to what the individual, friends, co-workers, and society think is right or wrong. There is a fine line between acceptable and unacceptable behavior in organizational life. The following situations present ethical problems: it is a rare individual who would not bend one of these ethical standards.

Answer the following questions as truthfully as you can. Only you can judge their significance or the correct answers.

- Would you ask a maintenance person employed by the university to do a small repair job at work on your own kitchen appliance?

- Would you go on a free vacation sponsored by the company that sells supplies to the library? Would you do so if your supervisor has said it is okay?

- Would you approve a promotion for a family member who was less qualified than other candidates?

- Would you take home for your personal use office supplies such as pencils or scratch pads?

- Would you use the library's telephone to conduct a private business of your own?

- Would you use the library's telephone to make long-distance personal calls at university expense?

- Would you work on a personal, nonjob-related project on library time?

- Would you dismiss a particularly troublesome employee on a technicality, even though, in this instance, the employee was blameless?

Library Ethics

The concern for ethics must be addressed by both the individual and the organization. Supervisors of student employees must adhere to the same ethical standards as their supervisors and the librarians in the organization. The American Library Association has had a Code of Ethics since 1939.[2]

AMERICAN LIBRARY ASSOCIATION STATEMENT ON PROFESSIONAL ETHICS, 1981

Since 1939, the American Library Association has recognized the importance of codifying and making known to the public and the profession the principles which guide librarians in action. This latest revision of the CODE OF ETHICS reflects changes in the nature of the profession and its social and institutional environment. It should be revised and augmented as necessary.

Librarians significantly influence or control the selection, organization, preservation, and dissemination of information. In a political system grounded in an informed citizenry, librarians are members of a profession explicitly committed to intellectual freedom and the freedom of access to information. We have a special obligation to ensure the free flow of information and ideas to present and future generations.

Librarians are dependent upon one another for the bibliographical resources that enable us to provide information services, and have obligations for maintaining the highest level of personal integrity and competence.

CODE OF ETHICS

I. Librarians must provide the highest level of service through appropriate and usefully organized collections, fair and equitable circulation and service policies, and skillful, accurate, unbiased, and courteous responses to all requests for assistance.

II. Librarians must resist all efforts by groups or individuals to censor library materials.

III. Librarians must protect each user's right to privacy with respect to information sought or received, and materials consulted, borrowed, or acquired.

IV. Librarians must adhere to the principles of due process and equality of opportunity in peer relationships and personnel actions.

V. Librarians must distinguish clearly in their actions and statements between their personal philosophies and attitudes and those of an institution or professional body.

VI. Librarians must avoid situations in which personal interests might be served or financial benefits gained at the expense of library users, colleagues, or the employing institution.

Managerial Ethics

While the American Library Association Code of Ethics may guide you in certain situations, a different code of ethics relates directly to managers and supervisors.[3]

CODE OF ETHICS FOR MEMBERS OF THE INSTITUTE OF CERTIFIED PROFESSIONAL MANAGERS

I will recognize that management is a call to service with responsibilities to my subordinates, associates and supervisors, employer, community, nation, and world.

I will be guided in all my activities by truth, accuracy, fair dealings, and good taste.

I will earn and carefully guard my reputation for good moral character and citizenship.

I will recognize that, as a leader, my own pattern of work and life will exert more influence on my subordinates than what I say or write.

I will give the same consideration to the rights and interests of others that I ask for myself.

I will maintain a broad and balanced outlook and will look for value in the ideas and opinions of others.

I will regard my role as a manager as an obligation to help subordinates and associates achieve personal and professional fulfillment.

I will keep informed on the latest developments in the techniques, equipment, and processes associated with the practice of management and the industry in which I am employed.

I will search for, recommend, and initiate methods to increase productivity and efficiency.

I will respect the professional competence of my colleagues in the ICPM and will work with them to support and promote the goals and programs of the institute.

I will support efforts to strengthen professional management through example, education, training, and a lifelong pursuit of excellence.

The bibliography contains resources for information on employee/employer rights and responsibilities.

RIGHTS AND RESPONSIBILITIES

Employees and employers have certain inalienable rights in the workplace. The supervisor must know employee rights granted by law and by the university and make sure those rights are communicated to student employees. Employee rights should be detailed in the university's personnel and student employee handbooks. In addition to rights, you and your employees have legal and ethical responsibilities to your employer. A summary of rights and responsibilities follows:

Rights

1. Right to a safe work environment

2. Right to a nondiscriminatory workplace

3. Right to a workplace free of harassment

4. Termination rights

5. Privacy rights

6. Union participation rights

7. Right to an appeal and grievance process

8. Right to equitable compensation

Responsibilities

1. Perform work for which hired

2. Follow policies, procedures, and rules

3. Adhere to ethical standards

4. Maintain high level of personal integrity

NOTES

[1]Adapted from Robert L. Mathis and John H. Jackson, *Personnel*, 4th ed. (St. Paul: West Publishing, 1985), 576.

[2]American Library Association, *Statement on Professional Ethics* (Chicago: ALA, 1981).

[3]Institute of Certified Professional Managers, *Code of Ethics* (Dayton, OH: ICPM, 1980).

BIBLIOGRAPHY

American Bar Association. *Law in the Workplace*. Chicago: ABA, 1987.

Baer, Walter E. *Grievance Handling: 101 Guides for Supervisors*. New York: American Management Association, 1970.

Bittel, Lester R. *What Every Supervisor Should Know*. New York: McGraw-Hill, 1980.

Black, James Menzies. *The Basics of Supervisory Management*. New York: McGraw-Hill, 1975.

Bowers, Mollie H. "Grievance Mediation: Another Route to Resolution." *Personnel Journal* 59 (February 1981): 132-36.

Chapman, J. Brad. "Constructive Grievance Handling." In *Supervisory Management Tools and Techniques*, edited by M. Gene Newport. St. Paul: West Publishing, 1976.

Cihon, Patrick J., and James O. Castagnera. *Labor and Employment Law*. Belmont, CA: PWS-Kent, 1988.

Curley, Arthur. "Library Personnel Administration: The Legal Framework." In *Personnel Administration in Libraries*, edited by Sheila Creth and Frederick Duda, 1-31. New York: Neal-Schuman, 1981.

Daughtrey, Anne Scott, and Betty Roper Ricks. *Contemporary Supervision: Managing People and Technology*. New York: McGraw-Hill, 1988.

Eisemann, Charles, and Stuart L. Lourie. "Grievance Handling: How to Carry the Ball." *Supervisory Management* (November 1983): 556-89.

Evered, James F. *Shirt-Sleeves Management*. New York: AMACOM, 1981.

Fallon, William K., ed. *Leadership on the Job: Guides to Good Supervision*. New York: AMACOM, 1981.

Flippo, Edwin B. *Principles of Personnel Management*. 4th ed. New York: McGraw-Hill, 1976.

Gasaway, Laura N., and Barbara B. Moran. "The Legal Environment of Personnel Administration." In *Personnel Administration in Libraries*, edited by Sheila Creth and Frederick Duda, 1-31. New York: Neal-Schuman, 1981.

Guy, Jeniece. "Equal Employment Opportunity and the College Library Administrator." In *College Librarianship*, edited by William Miller and D. Stephen Rockwood, 87-96. Metuchen, NJ: Scarecrow Press, 1981.

Hall, Francine S., and Maryann H. Albrecht. *The Management of Affirmative Action*. Santa Monica, CA: Goodyear, 1979.

Hite, Frederic C. *Aliens in the Workplace: An Employer's Guide to Immigration*. Boston: Immigration Information Center, 1988.

Hodgetts, Richard M. *Effective Supervision: A Practical Approach*. New York: McGraw-Hill, 1987.

Imundo, Louis V. *The Effective Supervisor's Handbook*. New York: AMACOM, 1980.

Kahn, Steven C., et al. *Personnel Director's Legal Guide*. Boston: Warren, Gorham, and Lamont, 1984.

Kelly, John G. *Equal Opportunity Management: Understanding Affirmative Action and Employment Equity*. Don Mills, Ontario: CCH Canadian, Ltd., 1986.

Kusack, James M. *Unions for Academic Library Support Staff*. New York: Greenwood Press, 1986.

Lewin, David, and Richard B. Peterson. *The Modern Grievance Procedure in the United States*. New York: Quorum Books, 1988.

Lieberman, Ernest D. *Unfit to Manage! How Mis-Management Endangers America and What Working People Can Do about It*. New York: McGraw-Hill, 1988.

Mika, Joseph J., and Bruce A. Shuman. "Legal Issues Affecting Libraries and Librarians." *American Libraries* 19, no. 2 (February 1988): 108-12.

Mosher, Lanning. "Grievance Procedures." *Supervisory Management* (August 1976): 20-26.

Nelson, Mary Ann. "Emerging Legal Issues for Library Administrators: Preparing for the 1990's—A Bibliographic Essay." *Library Administration and Management* 2, no. 4 (September 1988): 188-90.

O'Reilly, Robert C., and Marjorie I. O'Reilly. *Librarians and Labor Relations: Employment under Union Contracts*. Westport, CT: Greenwood Press, 1981.

Potter, Edward E., ed. *Employee Selection: Legal and Practical Alternatives to Compliance and Litigation*. Washington, DC: Equal Employment Advisory Council, 1983.

Preston, Paul, and Thomas Zimmerer. *Management for Supervisors*. 2d ed. Englewood Cliffs, NJ: Prentice-Hall, 1983.

Price, Janet R., Alan H. Levine, and Eve Cary. *The Rights of Students: The Basic ACLU Guide to a Student's Rights*. 3d ed. Carbondale, IL: Southern Illinois University Press, 1988.

Schuster, Frederick E. *Human Resource Management: Concepts, Cases and Readings*. 2d ed. Reston, VA: Reston Publishing, 1985.

Siegel, Laurence, and Irving M. Lane. *Personnel and Organizational Psychology*. 2d ed. Homewood, IL: Richard D. Irwin, 1987.

Smith, Robert Ellis. *Workrights*. New York: E. P. Dutton, 1983.

Sovereign, Kenneth L. *Personnel Law*. Englewood Cliffs, NJ: Prentice-Hall, 1984.

Trotta, Maurice S. *Handling Grievances: A Guide for Management and Labor*. Washington, DC: Bureau of National Affairs, 1976.

Weiss, W. H. *Supervisor's Standard Reference Handbook*. 2d ed. Englewood Cliffs, NJ: Prentice-Hall, 1988.

Progressive Discipline and Termination Procedures

It is too late to pull the rein when the horse has gained the brink of the precipice.

—Chinese Proverb

DISCIPLINE AND DISCHARGE

Two of the most unpleasant responsibilities of your job as supervisor are disciplining and terminating student employees. The most emotionally difficult is having to fire an employee. Termination is very difficult for the supervisor, for the person being fired, and for the other people in the department. Any supervisor who has fired a student employee realizes the importance of hiring the right people and training them well in order to reduce the possibility that an employee will have to be involuntarily terminated.

Disciplining and discharging student employees requires that specific procedures be followed. Those procedures should be spelled out in each university's or library's personnel or student handbooks. The following are suggestions on handling discipline and discharge. Readers are cautioned, however, to pay close attention to their own library or university policies and to seek the advice of their supervisors and campus legal counsel as needed.

TERMINATION OF EMPLOYMENT

As surely as student employees are hired, they will also terminate their employment in the library. The very nature of student employment involves frequent turnover in student employees: after all, they are students first, and it is our hope and theirs that they will graduate. Termination of employment, as used here, is the process by which student employees end their employment in the library, whether voluntary (resigned) or involuntary (fired).

Terminations of employment may be categorized as one of the following:

1. Resignation: termination at the employee's request (VOLUNTARY).

2. Release: termination when a temporary job is completed (INVOLUNTARY, but usually known beforehand).

3. Being relieved: termination during a probationary period (INVOLUNTARY).

4. Layoff: termination because of a reduction in force or lack of work (INVOLUNTARY).

5. Discharge: termination for cause (INVOLUNTARY).

Resignation. Most student employees leave the library through resignation. While not usually specifically required, student employees are often asked to give two weeks notice of resignation in order to allow supervisors to seek replacements. In some organizations, employees are considered to have resigned if they walk off the job, fail to report to work on three consecutive work days without permission to be absent, or fail to return to work within a prescribed period of time following a leave of absence.

Release. In some libraries, student employees are considered temporary employees and as such, they are automatically terminated at the end of each semester, academic year, or summer session and must be rehired in order to continue working during the next employment period. This process allows the student employment office to clear its files for a new allocation period.

Being Relieved. A probationary period of three to six months is utilized by many libraries for all new student employees. The student employees are being trained and it is important for the supervisor to make an assessment of progress during this period. If a student employee appears to be ill-suited for the job, cannot perform the work, or will not work out for whatever reason, this is the time to terminate the employee. In most cases, probationary employees may be terminated any time prior to the completion of the probationary period without recourse to the grievance and appeal process.

Layoff. Student employees may be terminated because of a reduction in force due to lack of funds, lack of work, or other compelling reasons. Selection of student employees for layoff should be made on the basis of qualifications and performance, but may be made on the basis of seniority if all are substantially equal.

Discharge. Sometimes referred to as "termination," "firing," "let go," "dismissal," or even "derecruitment," this is the last resort for supervisors who have exhausted all available remedies in a situation. Whatever it is called, it is an unpleasant event for both parties—the supervisor and the employee. A student employee should be discharged only when the seriousness of some matter is such that the student employee cannot be permitted to remain on the library's payroll.

Before resorting to the termination process, the supervisor should provide the student employee with an opportunity to become aware of and correct the misconduct or substandard performance. This "last-chance" may make it possible for the employee to resume work as a productive member of the group and represents fairness on the supervisor's part.

REASONS FOR TERMINATION

Termination, as used here, is the process by which a student employee ceases working for the library, whether it be voluntary (resigned) or involuntary (released, relieved, laid off, or discharged). The following list of reasons for termination are taken from a form which supervisors are required to complete for the Personnel Office at the University of New Mexico:

LACK OF WORK

- Reduction in force
- Job eliminated
- Reorganization
- End of temporary employment
- End of seasonal employment
- Project completed
- Partially unemployed reduced hours
- Temporary

QUIT

- Reason unknown
- Abandoned job
- Walked off job
- Did not return from leave
- Did not return from layoff
- Personal — not job related
- Returned to school
- Marriage
- Relocated
- Family obligations
- Unable to obtain babysitter
- Transportation
- Accepted another job
- Go into business
- Illness
- Maternity

- Enter military
- Dissatisfaction — work hours
- Dissatisfaction — salary
- Dissatisfaction — working conditions
- Dissatisfaction — performance review
- Dissatisfaction — supervisor
- Dissatisfaction — policies

DISCHARGE
- Insubordination
- Violation of rules or policies
- Violation of safety rules
- Reported under influence of alcohol
- Reported under influence of drugs
- Destruction of property — willful
- Destruction of property — carelessness
- Fighting
- Leaving work station
- Falsification of employment application
- Dishonesty — falsified records
- Dishonesty — unauthorized removal of property
- Dishonesty — monetary theft
- Dishonesty — other
- Absenteeism — unreported
- Absenteeism — excessive and/or unauthorized
- Tardiness — frequent
- Excessive garnishments
- Quality of work
- Quantity of work
- Poor performance
- Probationary — not qualified for job
- Poor judgement — no misconduct
- Lack of technical knowledge
- Inability to work — illness

MISCELLANEOUS

- No information whatsoever
- Refusal to work
- Disciplinary suspension
- Death

LIMITING THE NUMBER OF PROBLEM EMPLOYEES

It is not possible to entirely avoid having problem employees who must be disciplined or discharged, but there are ways to reduce their number:

1. Don't hire persons who provide clues during the interview that there may be problems.

2. Train new employees thoroughly.

3. Make sure new employees understand organizational rules and policies and the consequences of breaking those rules or violating library or university policies.

4. Take advantage of the probationary period. Don't hesitate to let a student employee go before or at the end of a probationary period if they are not performing satisfactorily. Terminating an employee during a probationary period is much easier than doing it later.

5. Review employee performance at regular intervals and deal with problems as they occur.

6. Don't pawn off your problem employees on another student employee supervisor. Deal with your own problems.

7. Before you discharge an employee, be certain that progressive discipline will not solve the problem.

PROGRESSIVE DISCIPLINE

Progressive discipline, also called corrective discipline, is designed to make employees aware of misconduct or poor performance and to give them the chance to correct it. The first step in progressive discipline is to give the student employee a verbal warning for minor infractions or to correct poor performance. A written warning addressed to the employee is utilized if the infraction or deficiency is of a more serious nature or may follow the verbal warning if there is no improvement. An employee may be suspended without pay for serious offenses or for continued poor performance or misconduct after previous attempts to correct have failed. Discharge is not a progressive discipline step but may be the result if the previous steps of progressive discipline have failed.

It is not necessary that the steps be followed in order. Each situation must be judged independently. A particular situation may require, as a first step, a written warning, a suspension, or even a discharge, depending on the seriousness of the situation. The following examples are provided as instances when certain steps are called for:

1. Verbal warning: substandard work performance, unexcused absences, or tardiness.

2. Written warning: continued substandard work performance, unexcused absences or tardiness.

3. Suspension: continuation of above examples, insubordination, drinking or intoxication, gambling, fighting, or sleeping on the job.

4. Discharge: all previously listed examples if continued after attempts to correct, and theft or dishonesty, conviction of a felony, willful damage to university property, assault, deliberate falsification of employee applications, time cards, or other university records, and possession of or working under the influence of illegal drugs.

Before taking progressive discipline steps, supervisors are advised to discuss any action with the appropriate authorities in the library and the university.

Steps to Take before Discharging Any Employee

The first rule in any disciplinary situation is document, document, document, but this cannot be emphasized enough in cases of involuntary termination. Recognizing that the discharge of an employee is a last resort in all cases except those requiring immediate discharge, the following steps are suggested:

1. Implement the appropriate progressive discipline steps.

2. Get all the facts including any remarks the employee might add.

3. Determine whether there is a policy which calls for dismissal in this instance and be prepared to cite it.

4. Determine whether the employee was aware of the policy.

5. Determine whether there have been any previous exceptions made to the policy calling for discharge and whether this situation is similar.

6. Be sure that discrimination is not involved, especially if the employee is a member of a minority group or some other class of protected persons.

7. Determine whether this discharge will make the employee a "martyr," and if so, prepare to deal with those co-workers and staff who remain.

8. Make sure the employee's file has proper documentation to support discharge.

9. At the time of discharge, arrange to have another managerial employee present.

10. Make sure that the procedures used in the discharge are the same as those used in previous discharges.

HOW TO DISCHARGE EMPLOYEES

There are four basic considerations which need attention when discharging an employee:

1. Documentation. There must be written documentation which defines and supports the discharge.

2. Communication. What can and must be said to other employees in the department and to others?

3. Legalities. An employee's termination may be declared invalid if any of the following conditions exist: discharge for a reason specifically prohibited by law; discharge for complying with a statutory duty; discharge in violation of actual or implied promises made at employment; discharge without due process; or discharge which is motivated by malice or retaliation.

4. Discharge interview. The who, where, when, why, and what of the termination.

The Discharge Interview

When planning the discharge interview, first review the employee's file and the reasons for discharge. To lessen the impact, avoid termination on the individual's birthday or anniversary date. Consider what the employee's medical and emotional state is. Does the individual anticipate termination? How much of a shock or surprise will it be to the employee?

Who should discharge the student employee? The responsible supervisor must be the one who gives the message, but you may wish to have another person present as a witness or for support.

Where should the discharge interview be held? It is best to hold the interview in an empty office or conference room. When you are through, you can leave. It is difficult to walk out of your office and it may be difficult to get the employee to leave.

When to terminate should be carefully planned. Friday or the day before a holiday are the worst days to terminate employees. Plan to hold the termination interview early in the week.

Why is the employee to be terminated? You and the individual may discuss resignation instead of termination. What will persons who inquire for references be told? What will co-workers be told? A formal discharge interview is not required for employees discharged for severe infractions which require immediate dismissal, although a witness to the discharge is desirable.

What should the student employee be told in the interview? The termination message should be clear and irrevocable. Avoid debates and rehashes of the past. Make it clear that the decision has been made and that it is final. Be empathetic but uncompromising. Know ahead of time what you plan to say and don't be sidetracked.

The termination of student employees for poor performance should never come as a surprise to them. Through proper training, coaching, and if needed, progressive discipline, poor performers should always know where they stand with you. While discharge is an unavoidable part of the supervisor's job, it shouldn't have to be done often. When involuntary termination is required, however, it must be done correctly.

Mistakes Made in Discharges

The following pitfalls may lead to charges of discrimination or unfair treatment by persons who are discharged:

1. The wrong person was chosen to handle the discharge.

2. The reasons for discharge were not made clear and unequivocal.

3. Possible severe emotional reactions were not anticipated.

4. Lawsuits were not anticipated.

5. Documentation was lacking.

6. The effects on remaining employees are not anticipated.

7. The employee had not been given sufficient help to correct substandard performance.

8. The employee had not been given a definite set of performance standards.

9. Performance evaluations were poorly done or not done at all.

10. The employee was unaware of the policy or that discharge could result.

11. The employee was given too many "second chances."

12. The employee was given regular salary increases and thought they were because of merit. In some cases, even merit increases may have been given.

13. The employee was treated differently than others in similar jobs.

THE PSYCHOLOGICAL IMPACTS OF TERMINATION

Voluntary terminations or separations are often accompanied by friendly good-byes, staff get-togethers, and sometimes farewell parties. Each spring, library staff members say good-bye to graduating student employees and undergraduate student employees for the summer months. Involuntary terminations, on the other hand, are seldom occasions for celebration for anyone. In nearly every involuntary termination, the organization and the individuals involved are negatively impacted.

The greatest impact, of course, is felt by the individual being discharged. Studies have shown that the level of emotional stress resulting from being terminated can equal the stress of being told that one is dying of an incurable disease. The individual first experiences shock and anger, followed by the conviction that there has been a mistake. After a series of mood swings, the terminated individual may experience a period of depression and, finally, renewed self-confidence. Of course, the severity of these experiences differs according to the individual, the individual's perception of the job, length of time on the job, and many other factors. Suffice it to say that the terminated individual will be greatly impacted by this action.

Co-workers of the terminated individual may also experience shock and excitement over the news, relief that it hadn't happened to them, possible fear that it might happen to them next, compassion for the terminated individual, and possibly anger at the supervisor or relief that it has finally happened. These reactions will be affected by how well the employee was liked, their perceptions of the terminated individual, and their opinions of their supervisor.

The supervisor of the terminated employee may feel guilt and self-pity for having to take the action, while feeling compassion for the individual. Once the decision to terminate has been made, however, the supervisor should have already done everything possible to avoid the action. After the termination, supervisors must be able to show compassion and empathy for the individual while believing firmly in the justification for the action and having confidence in the decision and the correctness of the procedure. The terminated employee is not to be viewed as a criminal and should be given whatever help possible in finding another suitable position if asked.

Every termination is an individual case with differing circumstances and resulting impacts. The supervisor must be able to deal with the emotions as the terminator, of the individual being terminated, and of the co-workers, all while objectively following procedures. A termination is successful when it is done objectively, humanely, and cleanly. It was a good termination when it can honestly be said that it was the best thing for all involved.

The bibliography that follows provides sources with additional suggestions on how to handle discipline and discharge.

BIBLIOGRAPHY

Coulson, Robert. *The Termination Handbook*. New York: The Free Press, 1981.

Daughtrey, Anne Scott, and Betty Roper Ricks. *Contemporary Supervision: Managing People and Technology*. New York: McGraw-Hill, 1988.

Evered, James F. *Shirt-Sleeves Management*. New York: AMACOM, 1981.

Fallon, William K., ed. *Leadership on the Job: Guides to Good Supervision*. New York: AMACOM, 1981.

Flippo, Edwin B. *Principles of Personnel Management*. 4th ed. New York: McGraw-Hill, 1976.

Hodgetts, Richard M. *Effective Supervision: A Practical Approach*. New York: McGraw-Hill, 1987.

Imundo, Louis V. *The Effective Supervisor's Handbook*. New York: AMACOM, 1980.

Kingsley, Daniel T. *How to Fire an Employee*. New York: Facts on File, 1984.

Mika, Joseph J., and Bruce A. Shuman. "Legal Issues Affecting Libraries and Librarians." *American Libraries* 19, no. 2 (February 1988): 108-12.

Preston, Paul, and Thomas Zimmerer. *Management for Supervisors*. 2d ed. Englewood Cliffs, NJ: Prentice-Hall, 1983.

Schuster, Frederick E. *Human Resource Management: Concepts, Cases and Readings*. 2d ed. Reston, VA: Reston Publishing, 1985.

Sweet, Donald H. *A Manager's Guide to Conducting Terminations*. Lexington, MA: Lexington Books, 1989.

Weiss, W. H. *Supervisor's Standard Reference Handbook*. 2d ed. Englewood Cliffs, NJ: Prentice-Hall, 1988.

Questions Asked by New Supervisors

Should you wish to know the road through the mountains, ask those who have already trodden it.

— Chinese Proverb

Any Questions? How is this book different from all of the other employee supervision handbooks?

1. This book is not designed for the first line supervisor in a manufacturing plant, or for the meat department manager at your local supermarket.

2. It is written for the librarian or staff member who has responsibility for the supervision of student employees.

3. It is written by a librarian with more than twenty years of experience in managing programs, staff, and student employees.

4. It contains information basic to an understanding of supervision, student employment, and libraries and offers advice on translating management and supervision literature into usable information for library staff.

If you have read sections of this book, you will have noticed that the author has injected suggestions, opinions, and bits of advice throughout. In this concluding chapter, the reader will find the author's answers to a sampling of questions asked by new supervisors. The bibliography contains resources dealing with the future of libraries and library administration and management.

Will I Have to Change to Become a Supervisor? Yes and no. You may have to change some of your behaviors when you become a supervisor but you will not change your basic personality. As a supervisor, you will be the same person you were before, but, while you should continue to be friendly, you may become less intimate with your employees. You should continue to be relaxed, but you should also be conscious of the need to set a good example for your employees. You should continue to be supportive of library goals and policies, but, if you have complaints or challenges to library policy, you will take them up with your colleagues or management, not with your employees. You will know that you have made the change from employee to supervisor when you start referring to library management as "we," not "they."

Why Do Beginning Supervisors Feel Underpaid? Many new supervisors feel that their new responsibilities are so great that the difference between a worker's salary and a supervisor's salary is not worth it. The change in responsibilities sometimes does seem overwhelming at first, but, given time, the new supervisor will gain control. It may be that the salary difference is indeed not enough for the work involved, but it is a price one pays to reach higher levels and salaries later. The new supervisor must take the long view.

How Much Should I Depend on Other Supervisors? How much you can depend on other supervisors for help and advice depends on the kind of supervisors they are. In most cases, you find that other supervisors can be of tremendous help. A good rule to follow is to seek and accept help or advice from other supervisors based on your knowledge of their skills. You are better off following your own instincts than poor advice from another supervisor. Your own supervisor can be an excellent source of help but, if you disagree with him or her, tactfully explain why. Ask the same question of several supervisors. You will soon learn who you can go to for help.

Where Else Can I Turn for Help? Don't forget that you work in an ideal setting when it comes to information. There are many excellent books on supervision, many of which are listed in the bibliography of this and other chapters of this book. Examine the supervision books and find one that best matches your supervisory style. You will also find information on supervision in the periodical literature. Four of the best periodicals containing articles for the practitioner are *Personnel* (American Management Association; monthly), *Personnel Journal: Magazine for Industrial Relations and Personnel Management* (A. C. Croft; monthly), *Supervision: The Magazine of Industrial Relations and Operating Management* (National Research Bureau; monthly), and *Supervisory Management* (American Management Association; monthly).

How Important Is Education to Advancement? Formal education is the best route to advancement, so take advantage of the opportunities provided by working for a university. Watch for workshops and training sessions offered through the university which will improve your skills. Experience combined with strong motivation also helps you advance. Demonstrating that you have the skills for supervision will go a long ways toward helping you succeed.

How Do I Cope with Too Much Work? There are countless demands on your time, many beyond your control. Your primary responsibility is to react calmly and keep your unit functioning while trying to squeeze in time for planning. Do your planning at home if you have to in order to get control. That planning will eventually help you react better to all of the demands placed on you. Many supervisors of student employees also perform other job responsibilities such as cataloging, reference, selection, and instruction. Supervision may only be a portion of your job but it can consume a seemingly disproportionate number of hours. Review the section on time management in this book and find a way to control your time.

How Can I Get Everything Done? Planning is the key. Your job probably contains a combination of many rather routine tasks with all of the unplanned-for events in a supervisor's workday. Complete first those routine tasks that you must perform in order to free yourself for more creative work and delegate, delegate, delegate. You may find it difficult at first to let go of the responsibilities you had as a worker, some of which you may really enjoy, but let them go you must. Do not allow yourself to get bogged down with routine tasks, even though they may be what you want to do. If they can be delegated, do so.

What Should I Do When I Get Discouraged? If you get so discouraged with your supervisory role that you feel you should resign, go to your supervisor or someone else you trust and then discuss the problem openly and honestly. It is not unusual for the new supervisor to become discouraged. It happens to nearly everyone because the adjustment is more difficult than you think. Talking things over occasionally will help you survive until you get things under control and become accustomed to the supervisory role. Resigning without talking things over with someone would be foolhardy. Remember that you are not alone. All veteran supervisors have experienced many of the same feelings you have when they were just beginning to supervise.

How Can I Be Sure I Want to Be a Supervisor? To be fair to yourself, plan to spend at least a year before making a firm commitment or asking to be relieved. Whether or not you should continue as a supervisor you need to feel that you are performing close to your potential in the supervisory role and that you are able to cope with your multiple responsibilities. It may take longer than a year to know whether or not supervisory responsibilities satisfy your needs for a fulfilling, stimulating work experience.

Where Will I Be in Five Years? As soon as you have become a capable supervisor, you will be able to do some career planning. As a supervisor, you have more freedom to establish and reach career goals than if you were an employee. Set realistic goals and don't become frustrated if you don't advance as quickly as you hoped. Much will depend on circumstances and events beyond your control, but all libraries need good supervisors at all levels. Your success in the supervision of student employees will translate very well to the supervision of other staff.

How Do I Know When I Have Developed a Leadership Style? It may take a few years to develop a leadership style that works as well as you would like. You will know when you have developed a style when you feel comfortable with yourself and when those you supervise feel comfortable with you. Your department or unit will function efficiently and without turmoil. Your reputation will grow as a good supervisor, but, even then, don't become complacent: there will always be room for improvement.

In a Few Words, What Is the Best Advice for Supervisors? As a new supervisor of student employees, you should ask questions, seek advice, never stop learning, and, the best advice (as Dr. Benjamin Spock says to new parents), "trust yourself, you know more than you think."

BIBLIOGRAPHY

The Future of Libraries

Ackerman, Page. "Governance and Academic Libraries." *Library Research* 2, no. 1 (Spring 1980/81): 3-28.

Bezold, Clement, et al. *The Future of Work and Health*. Dover, MA: Auburn House, 1986.

Boyd, Craig. *Technostress: The Human Cost of the Computer Revolution*. Reading, MA: Addison-Wesley, 1984.

Cline, Hugh F., and Loraine T. Sinnott. *The Electronic Library*. Lexington, MA: Lexington Books, 1983.

Cordell, Arthur J. "Work in the Information Age." *Futurist* 19, no. 6 (December 1985): 12-14.

De Gennaro, Richard. *Libraries, Technology, and the Information Marketplace*. Boston: G. K. Hall, 1987.

Deken, Joseph. *The Electronic Cottage*. New York: Bantam, 1981.

Drucker, Peter F. "The Coming of the New Organization." *Harvard Business Review* 66, no. 1 (January/February 1988): 45-53.

Evans, G. Edward. "Research Libraries in 2010." In *Research Libraries: The Past 25 Years, the Next 25 Years*, edited by Taylor E. Hubbard, 77-94. Boulder, CO: Colorado Associated University Press, 1986.

Garson, Barbara. *The Electronic Sweatshop: How Computers Are Transforming the Office of the Future into the Factory of the Past*. New York: Simon and Schuster, 1988.

Gould, Leroy C., et al. *Perceptions of Technological Risks and Benefits*. New York: Russell Sage Foundation, 1988.

Howard, Robert. *Brave New Workplace*. New York: Viking Press, 1985.

Johnston, William B., and Arnold E. Packer. *Workforce 2000: Work and Workers for the 21st Century*. Indianapolis, IN: Hudson Institute, 1987.

Leontief, Wassily, and Faye Duchin. *The Future Impact of Automation on Workers*. London: Oxford University Press, 1986.

Lynch, Beverly P., ed. *The Academic Library in Transition: Planning for the 1990's*. New York: Neal-Schuman, 1989.

Mason, Marilyn Gell. "Trends Challenging the Library: Technological, Economic, Social, Political." *The ALA Yearbook of Library and Information Services* 11 (1986): 1-6.

Provenzo, Eugene F., Jr. *Beyond the Gutenberg Galaxy*. New York: Teachers College Press, 1986.

Riggs, Donald E., and Gordon A. Sabine. *Libraries in the '90's: What the Leaders Expect*. Phoenix, AZ: Oryx, 1988.

Shaiken, Harley. *Work Transformed: Automation and Labor in the Computer Age*. New York: Holt, Rinehart and Winston, 1985.

Library Administration and Management

Anderson, A. J. *Problems in Library Management*. Littleton, CO: Libraries Unlimited, 1981.

Boaz, Martha, ed. *Current Concepts in Library Management*. Littleton, CO: Libraries Unlimited, 1979.

Dougherty, Richard M. "Personnel Needs for Librarianship's Uncertain Future." In *Academic Libraries by the Year 2000: Essays Honoring Jerrold Orne*, edited by Herbert Poole, 107-18. New York: Bowker, 1977.

Dougherty, Richard M., et al. *Scientific Management of Library Operations*. 2d ed. Metuchen, NJ: Scarecrow Press, 1982.

Durrey, Peter. *Staff Management in University and College Libraries*. Oxford, England: Pergamon Press, 1976.

Evans, G. Edward. *Management Techniques for Librarians*. 2d ed. New York: Academic Press, 1983.

Galvin, Thomas J., and Beverly P. Lynch, eds. *Priorities for Academic Libraries*. San Francisco: Jossey-Bass, 1987.

Georgi, Charlotte, and Robert Bellanti, eds. *Excellence in Library Management*. New York: Haworth, 1985.

Gore, Daniel. "Things Your Boss Never Told You about Library Management." *Library Journal* 102 (1 April 1977): 765-70.

Harvey, John F., and Peter Spyers-Duran. *Austerity Management in Academic Libraries*. Metuchen, NJ: Scarecrow Press, 1984.

Holley, Edward G. "Defining the Academic Librarian." *College & Research Libraries* 46 (November 1985): 462-68.

Hyatt, James A., and Aurora A. Santiago. *University Libraries in Transition*. Washington, DC: National Association of College and University Business Officers, 1987.

Jones, Ken. *Conflict and Change in Library Organizations: People, Power and Service*. London: Bingley, 1984.

Ladd, Dwight R. "Myths and Realities of University Governance." *College & Research Libraries* 36, no. 2 (March 1975): 97-105.

Line, Maurice B. *Academic Library Management*. London: Library Association, 1990.

Lomas, Tim. *Management Issues in Academic Libraries*. London: Rossendale, 1986.

Lyle, Guy R. *The Administration of the College Library*. 4th ed. New York: H. W. Wilson, 1974.

Lynch, Beverly P. "Libraries as Bureaucracies." *Library Trends* 27 (Winter 1979): 259-67.

MacCrimmon, Kenneth R., and Donald A. Ehrenburg, with W. T. Stanbury. *Taking Risks: The Management of Uncertainty*. New York: Free Press, 1988.

McElroy, A. Rennie. *College Librarianship*. Phoenix, AZ: Oryx, 1984.

Moran, Barbara B. *Academic Libraries: The Changing Knowledge Centers of Colleges and Universities*. Washington, DC: Association for Study of Higher Education, 1984.

Munn, Robert F. "The Bottomless Pit, or the Academic Library as Viewed from the Administration Building." *College & Research Libraries* 29 (January 1968): 51-54.

O'Neil, Robert M. "The University Administrator's View of the University Library." In *Priorities for Academic Libraries*, edited by Thomas J. Galvin and Beverly Lynch, 5-12. San Francisco: Jossey-Bass, 1982.

Rizzo, John R. *Management for Librarians: Fundamentals and Issues*. Westport, CT: Greenwood Press, 1980.

Rogers, Rutherford D., and David C. Weber. *University Library Administration*. New York: H. W. Wilson, 1971.

Shaughnessy, Thomas W. "Technology and the Structure of Libraries." *Libri* 32, no. 2 (1982): 144-55.

Stueart, Robert D., ed. *Academic Librarianship: Yesterday, Today, Tomorrow*. New York: Neal-Schuman, 1982.

Stueart, Robert D., and Barbara B. Moran. *Library Management*. 3d ed. Littleton, CO: Libraries Unlimited, 1987.

Thompson, James, and Reg Carr. *An Introduction to University Library Administration*. 4th ed. London: Bingley, 1987.

Veaner, Allen B. *Academic Librarianship in a Transformational Age: Program, Politics, and Personnel*. Boston: G. K. Hall, 1990.

Vosper, Robert. "Library Administration on the Threshold of Change." In *Issues in Library Administration*, edited by Warren M. Tsuneishi, et al., 37-51. New York: Columbia University Press, 1974.

Wasserman, Paul, and Mary Lee Bundy, eds. *Reader in Library Administration*. Washington, DC: Microcard Editions, 1968.

Weisbord, Marvin R. *Productive Workplaces: Organizing and Managing for Dignity, Meaning, and Community*. San Francisco: Jossey-Bass, 1987.

Willard, D. D. "Seven Realities of Library Administration." *Library Journal* 101 (15 January 1976): 311-17.

Zaltman, Gerald, ed. *Management Principles for Nonprofit Agencies and Organizations*. New York: AMACOM, 1979.

Absenteeism, of student employees, 130-31
Accountability, measuring, 33-34
Active learning, versus passive learning, 99
Age Discrimination in Employment Act of 1967, 72, 158
American Library Association
  Statement on Professional Ethics of 1981, 166-67
Americans with Disabilities Act of 1990, 72, 158
Application for employment, 61-62
Appraisal. *See* Performance appraisal
ARL. *See* Association of Research Libraries
Association of Research Libraries (ARL), statistics
  on student employees, 5
  on staffing, 6-7
  on supervisors, 10
Attitudes, 18
  measures of, 19
Authority, 108
  defined, 32
  delegating, 110
  exerting, 109
  and responsibility, 32
Automation, changes in libraries, 1

Behaviorally anchored rating scales, 151

Change
  managing, 34
  overcoming resistance to, 34
Civil Rights Act of 1964, Title VII, 72, 158, 160
Coaching, 117
  process, 117-18
Code of Ethics for Members of the Institute of Certified Professional Managers, 167-68
College Work-Study Program (CWS), 8, 84
  during nonenrollment periods, 86
  eligibility, 60
  employment conditions and limitations, 85-86
  job description characteristics, 84-85
  pay rates, 86
  student employee allotments, 58-59

Communication
  encouraging, 114
  generally, 113
  with groups, 113
  with individuals, 113
  with student employees, 114
  supervisor's role in, 10
Controlling, supervisor's role in, 11
Cooperation, 116
Cottam, Keith M., 4
Counseling, 118-20
  employee-requested, 119
  supervisor-initiated, 118-19
CWS. *See* College Work-Study Program

Decision making
  bad decisions, 112
  challenged, 113
  generally, 111
  good decisions, 111
Dependability, 18
Development, versus training, 94
Development training. *See* Training—developmental
Differentiated pay, 56
Discharge. *See also* Discipline; Termination
  errors in, 179
  how to do it, 178
  interviews, 178-79
Discipline. *See also* Discharge; Termination
  generally, 172
  progressive, 176-77
Downey, Mary Elizabeth, 3-4

Employee Polygraph Protection Act of 1988, 72
Employee rights. *See also* Employee responsibilities
  to appeal and grievance process, 163-64
  to equitable compensation, 164
  to harassment-free workplace, 159
  institutional, 162
  to nondiscriminatory workplace, 158-59
  to privacy, 160-61
  regarding termination, 159-60
  to safe workplace, 157-58
  to union participation, 161-62

Employee responsibilities, 165
Employment discrimination, hiring and, 72-73
Equal Employment Opportunity Commission, 159
Equal employment opportunity laws, 71-72, 158
Equal Pay Act of 1963, 72, 158
Ethics
    American Library Association statement on, 166-67
    for supervisors, 165-68
Evaluation, by peers, 141. *See also* Performance
    appraisal—evaluating employees
Expectations, for student employees, 9-10

Family contribution, 79, 84
Federal student financial aid. *See* Student financial
    aid—federal programs
Financial need
    citizenship, 81
    cost of attendance, 79
    eligibility, 81-82
    family contribution, 79, 84
    "independent student," 80

Goals, of supervisors, 20
Graphic rating scales, 151
Grievance process, 163-64
Group effort, in problem solving, 114
Guaranteed Student Loan Program. *See* Stafford Loan
    Program

Higher Education Act of 1965, Title IV, 78, 83-84
Higher Education Amendments of 1980, 78, 83
Higher Education Amendments of 1986, 78-80, 83
Hiring
    interviews, 68-73
    legal implications, 71-72
    notifying candidates, 74
    recruitment, 67
    reference checks, 73-74
    screening, 67-68
    supervisors and, 66-75
Humanistic Management by Teamwork, 106-7

Immigration Reform and Control Act of 1986, 72, 158
"Independent student," defined, 80
Initiative, 18

Interviews
    conducting, 69
    directed, 68
    nondirected, 68
    nondiscriminatory, 73
    preparing for, 68
    questions to avoid, 71
    sample questions, 70-71
    stress, 68
Job analysis, 47
Job descriptions
    characteristics of, 49
    group I, 50
    group II, 50, 56
    group III, 53
    guidelines for preparing, 48
    for libraries, 50
    purposes of, 48
    samples of, 51-52, 54-55
    uses of, 49
Job design, 47
Job evaluation, versus performance appraisal, 140
Job Instruction Training, 96-97
Job matching, 61

Koopman, Harry Lyman, 3

Leadership
    kinds of, 30
    potential for, 30-32
    qualities of, 29-30
    supervisor's role in, 10-11
    as supervisory quality, 17, 29-32
Librarian's Conference (1853), 3
Library organization, 105-6
Library policies, regarding student employees, 131
Library rules, student employee violations of, 129-30

Management. *See also* Authority; Responsibility;
    Supervision
    of change, 34
    functions of, 10-11, 107-8
    generally, 105
    organizing function of, 46
    participative, 107
    team, 106
    of time, 34

Management by objectives, 151
Mediation and arbitration, 163
Melnyk, Andrew, 5
Morale, low level of, in student employees, 128
Motivation, 116-17
    coaching, 117-18
    and job satisfaction, 116
    lack of, in student employees, 127

National Direct Student Loan Program. *See* Perkins
    Loan Program
1988-89 Congressional Methodology, 79

Occupational Safety and Health Act of 1970, 157, 160
Organizing
    creating structure, 46
    job analysis, 47
    and job description, 48
    job design, 47
    student employees, 63
    supervisor's role in, 10
    system for positions, 46-47
Orientation
    checklist, 93-94
    reasons for, 91
    of student employees, 92-94
    student handbook in, 92-93
OSFA. *See* U.S. Department of Education—Office
    of Student Financial Assistance

Parent Loans to Undergraduate Students Program,
    78, 83
Participative management. *See* Management—
    participative
Passive learning, versus active learning, 99
Pay rates, 56-57
    College Work-Study Program, 86
Pell Grant Formula 1988-89, The, 79
Pell Grant Program, 78-79
    student aid index, 79, 83
"People" skills, 18
Performance appraisal
    absolute, 152
    appraisal meeting, 145-47
    collecting data, 143-44
    communicating standards, 143

    comparative, 151
    confidentiality, 150
    consequences of, 150
    discussing poor performance, 147
    errors in, 148
    evaluating employees, 145
    favoritism charges, 148
    formats, 150-51
    frequency of, 142
    generally, 139
    in industry, 140
    in libraries, 140-41
    nondiscriminatory, 149-50
    observation of employees, 143
    outcome-based, 152
    peer evaluation, 141
    post-appraisal actions, 153
    questions, 142
    "sandwich" technique, 147-48
    self-appraisal, 144
    setting performance standards, 143
    student employee response to, 148
    supervisors' attitudes toward, 153-54
    supervisor's opinion in, 142
    using data, 144
    validity and reliability of, 149
    versus job evaluation, 140
Perkins Loan Program, 78, 84, 86-87
Planning
    to become a supervisor, 26
    supervisor's role in, 10
PLUS. *See* Parent Loans to Undergraduate Students
    Program
Potential for supervisory position, 38-39
Pregnancy Discrimination Act of 1978, 72, 158
Problems. *See* Student employee problems
Public services
    circulation, 2
    equipment maintenance, 2
    patron assistance, 2
    periodical management, 2
    reference, 2
    security, 3
    shelving, 2

Reference checks, 73-74
Rehabilitation Act of 1973, 72, 158
Reports, 41-42

Responsibility, 110. *See also* Authority; Management; Supervision
   and authority, 32
   measuring, 33-34
Robert C. Byrd Honors Scholarship Program, 87
Rumors, dealing with, 134

Scheduling, work-study student hours, 58-59
SEOG. *See* Supplemental Educational Opportunity Grants
Skill development, 42
SLS. *See* Supplemental Loans to Students Program
SSIG. *See* State Student Incentive Grant Program
Staffing
   statistics on, 6-7
   supervisor's role in, 10
Stafford Loan Program, 78, 83
Standards of performance, 151
State Student Incentive Grant Program, 87
Stress. *See also* Interviews—stress; Student employee problems—stress
Student aid index, 79, 83
"Student Aides in Our Library (Blessings and Headaches)," 5
Student employee problems. *See also* Student employee roles; Student employees
   absenteeism, 130-31
   complaints, 126-27
   dishonesty, 131-32
   disloyalty, 128-29
   generally, 126
   insubordination, 136
   lack of motivation, 127
   low morale, 128
   personal, 134
   personality, 132-33
   procrastination, 134-35
   resistance to change, 135
   resolving, 136
   rule breaking
      of library rules, 129-30
      of university rules, 132
   stress, 135
Student employee roles
   in public services, 2-3
   in technical services, 3
Student employee supervisors. *See* Supervisors

Student employee work force
   size of, 5
   and staff, 5, 8
Student employees. *See also* Employee responsibilities; Employee rights; Student employee problems; Student employee roles; Student employment
   assistants, 53
   college work-study allotments, 58-59
   differences between supervisors and, 20
   eligibility for college work-study program, 60
   expectations from library employment, 10, 19
   hiring, 66-75
   job descriptions, 50, 51-52(samples), 53, 54-55(samples)
   libraries' expectations for, 9-10
   motivations, 8-9
   in 1930s, 3
   older, 136
   organizing, 63
   orientation, 91-94
   pay rates, 56-57, 86
   as percent of library work force, 2, 5
   and performance appraisal, 139-54
   as potential librarians, 4
   problems with, 8, 126-36
   recruiting, 67
   referral to library, 66-67
   relationship with supervisors, 10
   responsibilities of, 48
   screening, 67-68
   and staff, 5, 8
   status of, 4
   and technological changes, 1
   training, 91-102
Student employment. *See also* Student employees; Student financial aid
   application form, 61-62
   federal aid for, 78, 84-87
   funding sources, 8
   history of, 3-5
Student financial aid
   counseling students, 87-88
   federal programs, 78
      campus-based, 84
      eligibility, 81
         requirements(table), 82
      financial need, 79-81

Student handbook
  in orientation, 92-93
  rules in, 131
Supervision. *See also* Accountability; Leadership;
      Management; Responsibility; Supervisors;
      Time management
  common mistakes, 23
  delegation of tasks, 16
  giving directions, 115
  importance of, 11
  incorrect behavior, 40-41
  negative characteristics, 18
  obtaining cooperation, 116
  potential for, 38
  preparation for, 25-26
  rewards of, 11-12
  skills, 17, 21
    inadequate, 25
  transition to, 20
    stages of, 21
Supervisor qualities
  attitude, 18
  dependability, 18
  energy, 17
  initiative, 18
  knowledge, 18
  leadership, 17, 29-32
  "people" skills, 18
Supervisors. *See also* Management; Supervision;
      Supervisor qualities
  and authority, 108-10
  common concerns of, 182-84
  common mistakes of, 23
  and communications, 113-14
  and counseling, 118-20
  and decision making, 111-13
  definition of, 15-16
  development of, 16
  differences between workers and, 20
  ethics of, 165-68
  expectations for, 22-23
  goals, 20
  guidelines for giving directions, 115-16
  hiring and, 66-75
  incorrect behavior, 40-41
  and job descriptions, 48-49
  job satisfaction, 20
  in library hierarchy, 105-6
  and motivation, 116-18

  negative actions, 24
  and performance appraisals, 139-54
  personal characteristics
    attitude, 18
    dependability, 18
    energy, 17
    initiative, 18
    knowledge of job, 18
    leadership potential, 17
    negative, 18, 23-24
    "people" skills, 18, 41
  perspective, 20
  preparation to become, 25-26
  principles of, 120
  problems of, 21-22
  promotion of, 19, 38-39
  reasons for failure, 25
  relationships, 21
    with student employees, 10
  responsibilities of, 20
  and responsibility, 110
  role in training student employees, 95-97
  roles of, 10-11, 15
  selection of, 17
  skills, 21
    inadequate, 25
  and student employee problems, 126-36
  and student financial aid, 88-89
  training checklist, 102
Supplemental Educational Opportunity Grants, 78
  family contribution, 79, 84
Supplemental Loans to Students Program, 78, 83

Tauber, Maurice F., 4
Team management. *See* Management—team
Technical competence, 18
Technical services
  bibliographic searching, 3
  bindery preparation, 3
  catalog maintenance, 3
  clerical, 3
  receiving, 3
Termination. *See also* Discharge; Discipline
  documentation related to, 177-78
  generally, 172
  legal rights regarding, 157-60
  psychological impact of, 180
  reasons for, 174-76
  types of, 173

Time management, 35
  guidelines, 36-37
  timewasters, 35-36
Training
  coaching in, 117-18
  developmental, 100-101
    methods, 101-2
  errors in, 98
  extending, 98
  for higher-level work, 101
  implementing program, 100
  to improve performance, 101
  improving, 98-99
  orientation, 91-94
  role of supervisor in, 95
  steps in, 96-97
  supervisor's checklist, 102
  types of, 95
  versus development, 94
Transition to supervision, 20
  stages, 21

Unions, 161-62
University of New Mexico
  college work-study program eligibility notification,
    60

student employment application form,
    61-62
University of New Mexico General Library
  Humanistic Management by Teamwork, 106-7
  pay system at, 56-57
  sample job descriptions, 51-52, 54-55
  Student Employment Advisory Committee, 50
U.S. Department of Education
  loan counseling suggestions, 88
  Office of Student Financial Assistance, 78
    financial need, 79, 81
U.S. Department of Labor, 157
Utley, G. B., 3

Vietnam Era Veterans' Readjustment Assistance Act
  of 1974, 72, 158

White, Emilie C., 5
Wilson, Louis R., 4
Work
  as formal activity, 9
  motivation to, 8-9
Work study. *See* College Work-Study Program